CULTURES OF DOING GOOD

NGOgraphies: Ethnographic Reflections on NGOs

The NGOgraphies book series explores the roles, identities, and social representations of nongovernmental organizations (NGOs) through ethnographic monographs and edited volumes. The series offers detailed accounts of NGO practices, challenges the normative assumptions of existing research, and critically interrogates the ideological frameworks that underpin the policy worlds where NGOs operate.

CULTURES OF DOING GOOD

Anthropologists and NGOs

Edited by
Amanda Lashaw,
Christian Vannier,
and Steven Sampson

The University of Alabama Press
Tuscaloosa

The University of Alabama Press
Tuscaloosa, Alabama 35487-0380
uapress.ua.edu

Typeface: Bembo and Futura

Cover design: David Nees

Cataloging-in-Publication data is available from the Library of Congress.
ISBN: 978-0-8173-1968-7
E-ISBN: 978-0-8173-9153-9

Contents

Introduction: Engagements and Entanglements in the Anthropology of NGOs
  Steven Sampson   1

PART I. CHANGING LANDSCAPES OF POWER

Introduction to Part I: Dilemmas of Dual Roles, Studying NGOs, and
  Donor-Driven "Democracy"
  Mark Schuller   21

1. Anthropologists' Encounters with NGOs: Critique, Collaboration,
   and Conflict
   David Lewis   26

2. NGO Fever and Donor Regimes: Tanzanian Feminist Activism within
   Landscapes of Contradictions
   Victoria Bernal   37

3. Habits of the Heart: Grassroots "Revitalization" and State Transformation
   in Serbia
   Theodora Vetta   56

4. Reformists and Revolutionists: Social Work NGOs and Activist Struggles in
   the Czech Republic
   Hana Synková   75

5. Leveraging Supranational Civil Society: Critiquing Czech Gender Equality
   Policy through Academic-NGO Collaboration
   Karen Kapusta-Pofahl   94

PART II. DOING GOOD WORK

Introduction to Part II: Life in NGOs
  Inderpal Grewal   113

6. Faith Development beyond Religion: The NGO as Site of Islamic Reform
   Nermeen Mouftah   122

7. Interdependent Industries and Ethical Dilemmas: NGOs and Volunteer
   Tourism in Cusco, Peru
   Aviva Sinervo   142

8. Rebuilding Justice: Jewish Philanthropy and the Politics of Representation
   in Post-Katrina New Orleans
   Moshe Kornfeld   163

PART III: METHODOLOGICAL CHALLENGES
OF NGO ANTHROPOLOGY

Introduction to Part III: How to Study NGOs Ethically
   Erica Bornstein   183

9. The Ethics and Politics of NGO-Dependent Anthropology
   Katherine Lemons   194

10. The Anthropologist and the Conservation NGO: Dilemmas of and
    Opportunities for Engagement
    Amanda Woomer   212

Conclusion: A Second Generation of NGO Anthropology
   Christian Vannier and Amanda Lashaw   230

References Cited   237

Contributors   263

Index   267

CULTURES OF DOING GOOD

Introduction

Engagements and Entanglements
in the Anthropology of NGOs

Steven Sampson

In 1992, I took a few weeks leave from my university existence in Copenhagen to work as a European Union (EU) consultant in Romania. I had been invited to join a team of Danish environmental engineers and management specialists, our task being to provide "technical assistance" to Romania's new Ministry of Environment as part of EU aid to Romania. I was the only person in Denmark with any social science knowledge of Romania, having done ethnographic fieldwork there in the 1970s and 1980s, and I had written about Romanian affairs in the Danish press. And I spoke fluent Romanian. My name had come up in the consulting firm's database, and I joined this team of specialists as the "the culture guy," so to speak. It was my job to explain, mediate, and assist in case there were conflicts between the Danish consultants and the Romanian staff in the ministry, most of whom were holdovers from the Ceausescu era's forest and water departments.

Soon after our work began inside the ministry, my boss commented on a very strange situation: upstairs, on the third floor, occupying an office right next to that of the minister, sat the head of the major Romanian environmental nongovernment organization (NGO). Both the NGO leader and the minister were from the same (governing) political party, so we knew there was something political going on. Perhaps it was just a legacy from communist times, when party and state functions were intertwined. My boss was perturbed: "What the hell was this?" he lamented. "NGOs don't belong inside a government ministry. In Denmark, the environmental organizations are not even allowed past the reception area. Steven, this is a ministry, we've got to get this NGO guy out of here. Find out what these environmental protection NGOs are all about."

So began my sojourn into the world of NGOs in postsocialist Eastern Europe. Since this trial by fire, I have participated in a variety of NGO and civil society development projects in Romania, Albania, Kosovo, and Bosnia. I have been an appraisal consultant for donors looking to give money away, I have been asked to "map the NGO sector" in Bosnia so that donors could "find NGOs we can trust." I have reviewed NGO grant requests, monitored NGO projects, trained NGO staff, evaluated NGO programs, helped to set up a government-NGO partnership program in Romania, worked on NGO law in Kosovo, set up NGO foundations in Albania and Kosovo, done SWOT (Strengths, Weaknesses, Opportunities, Threats) analysis with NGOs in Bosnia, trained NGOs in how to deal with donors (read Marcel Mauss and invite them home for dinner), and helped NGOs write slick grant proposals with the latest hot slogans ("good governance," "climate change," "capacity building," "gender mainstreaming"). While working as a consultant for firms, donors, and government aid offices, I have also functioned as a personal sounding board and as a mentor and confidant to ambitious NGO activists and frustrated local staff members, newly stationed consultants, and suspicious government officials. (For the purposes of this book, an NGO activist is an individual or group committed to solving a social issue or problem and is organized or works toward this end in, with, or through NGO organizational structures.) I have participated in hundreds of hours of meetings, consultations, and discussions, and I have observed and probably contributed to intrigues in the NGO scene in the Balkans. At home in Denmark and Sweden, I have advised on various cooperative projects between Scandinavian NGOs searching for the perfect "partner" abroad. While working for donors in Tirana, Prishtina, Bucharest, Mitrovica, and Sarajevo, I have been approached on the street by people seeking funds, had CVs stuffed into my hands, and asked by NGO staff members to help them find a scholarship abroad for them or for their children. With all my good intentions, I have stimulated false hopes of grants, been accused of being part of the notorious "Soros mafia" of NGO project elites, and of wasting money from Brussels by giving it to the wrong people. And as an academic plunged into the world of high-powered consulting, where deadlines are deadlines, I have been suddenly hired, and then just as abruptly let go, by various consulting firms or government donors who did not like the advice I gave them, did not appreciate the reports I submitted, or simply thought that having an anthropologist was a waste of their time and money.

As a result of my immersion into this "social life of projects" (Sampson 1996), some of the NGOs I helped get off the ground continue today, having become well established and professionalized. Others folded long ago, their leaders becoming functionaries in state organs, staff of international NGOs, or starting their own consulting firms. Many former NGO staff members entered academia to gain degrees in law or nonprofit organization at universities abroad and have never returned. Like many of the contributors in this book, I have watched civic energy become "NGO-ized," and I have observed how NGOs develop as organizations and become "more bureaucratic." I have also formed close relationships, even friendships, with individual NGO activists and professionals. My NGO consulting career also peaked as the consulting landscape changed, and back in academia, I have done what I could to understand and teach about "The NGO Sector" as a world worthy of study by anthropologists.

Since entering the NGO world in the early 1990s, the context has changed drastically. What Victoria Bernal in her chapter calls "NGO fever," so prevalent in the 1990s and early 2000s, has evolved into what Katherine Lemons calls "NGO-dependent anthropology." The daily practice of NGO life, what Hilhorst called "NGO-ing" (Hilhorst 2003), has become more routinized. Those NGOs that survived the original surge of NGO expansion and subsequent donor exit are now more established; and NGOs are routinely invited as observers and participants at the highest levels of government or international meetings and contracted by state organs to write policy papers. But this also means that governments have now enacted NGO laws and stringent financial regulations, including surveillance of NGO activity and foreign funding. NGOs are not just a spearhead of social movements. They now participate in "public-private partnerships" or pursue "social entrepreneurship." They market themselves and promote their brand, competing with other NGOs, private firms, and state agencies for lucrative contracts. In the meantime, many of the original donors have left the countries, some suffering "donor fatigue," others moving on to more urgent projects in war zones and fragile states. Former socialist states that were EU aid recipients have now become donors themselves. NGO activists and office staff have now become so professionalized that NGO work is no more a calling or passion. It can now be a career path that includes the master's degree in nonprofit management or "NGOs studies" or a consulting job abroad. For example, while working as an evaluator for a peace-building project in Kosovo, my boss was a Moldavian expat project manager who had earned her degree in international law from Amsterdam and was then attached to a Dutch NGO specializing in social entrepreneurship. The NGO elite itself had taken on cosmopolitan characteristics.

Finally, the role of NGOs in society has changed due to changes in the nature of the state, the labor market, and social services. Under neoliberal restructuring and other kinds of reform, NGOs compete for grants and contracts but are also subjected to new responsibilities for performance and efficiency. "Doing good" is now itself a competitive market, with some NGOs better equipped to do good better than others. With the popular reaction to the recent economic crisis having spawned social movements and the pressing needs of people now segmented by class, race, gender, ethnicity, health, or migration status, NGOs must maneuver between legitimating themselves as authentic participants in social movements seeking justice versus policy advocacy able to present concrete policy options to government decision-makers.

It is in this scene of NGOs trying to do good, in a professional way, while embedded in the policy process, that anthropologists now find themselves. As anthropologists, we do not enter this scene simply as field researchers from academia, trying to describe ways of life and identify social structures and cultural meanings. We are urged to participate as activists, assistants, networkers, and even friendly critics. In terms of ethnographic fieldwork, NGO anthropology has become messier, with the boundaries of inside/ outside, us/them, engagement/detachment increasingly unclear. But in this messiness lies the potential for new insights into the world of NGOs and the people who inhabit this world. For anthropology it also means new ways to conceptualize what engagement and "doing good" mean to their actors. The goal of this book is to flesh out this "messiness" in the relationship between anthropologists and NGOs. We have thus assembled a set of chapters on NGO life, all of them written by anthropologists with an intimate knowledge of and engagement with NGOs in a wide range of national and cultural contexts.

Anthropology and NGOs

Anthropologists are social scientists. Like other social scientists, we study groups of people in particular contexts, and as anthropologists, we try to describe how people form and then experience their world. In this project, anthropologists distinguish themselves from other social scientists in three principal ways. First, we are particularly interested in less powerful or subaltern groups. Understanding the way of life of these groups means going beyond the formal organizations and categories of those elites who describe, treat, or organize them. Hence, anthropologists have traditionally been interested in studying subcultural and social minorities and peoples on the periphery of urban societies, in outlying villages, in mountains or islands, and in small communities.

Second, anthropologists have tended to highlight the importance of the informal, interactional foundations of human behavior in everyday life. Anthropologists go beneath the hierarchal institutions, official statements, formal rules, and idealistic or ideological self-understandings. We describe how people organize their lives by focusing on their routines, their everyday lives. We take nothing for granted. Even as we have begun to study elite groups, financial institutions, and government policies (Ho 2009; Shore and Wright 1997; Shore, Wright, and Però 2011; Wedel 2009), we still look beyond the formalized, official structure trying to discover and explain the informal, oral, secondary network or underground aspects. We dig deeply, emphasizing depth over breadth.

The third feature of anthropological research is our method of study: ethnographic fieldwork or participant observation. Anthropological research, more than the research of other social scientists, involves a personal engagement with the people whom we study. We generally immerse ourselves in "our" communities, villages, networks, or groups, sometimes for years, and we do this with much greater passion (and frustration) than the other social scientists for whom ethnography is but one of several possible social science methods (the others being observation, statistical surveys, questionnaires, interviews, experiments, and textual analysis of documents and archives). This immersion into the lives of our informants gives anthropologists deeper insights into everyday life, although we end up in a smaller, more intense universe of people. It generates personal relationships with informants but also forces anthropologists to constantly reflect on and reevaluate our own role as researchers, academics, and advocates.

These three essential features of modern anthropology—who we study, what we study, and how we study—have been adjusted to the way anthropologists research NGOs. NGOs are certainly not always a subaltern group; they can be part of a cosmopolitan, well-educated elite. NGOs highlight their formal structure but they have an informal organization as well that members or staff may not want to expose. And since an NGO is an organization and workplace, with a family life outside the organization, the NGO may not be amenable to the kind of intense participant observation for which anthropologists are trained. Adapting anthropological perspectives and methods to the study of NGOs has thus been a challenge for researchers. It is these challenges that form the backdrop for the engagements and entanglements that I describe in this introduction and that appear in the subsequent chapters.

NGO Research

As David Lewis points out in chapter 1, the study of NGOs is an outgrowth of anthropologists' involvement in development issues. Development is a moral mission, seeking to improve the quality of life for people in other societies. NGOs, understood here as voluntary nonprofit organizations, were part of this human improvement project, both promoting it through social movements and advocacy and implementing it through development project activities. In this context, it was only natural for anthropologists, who so often study powerless peoples and subaltern groups in the developing world, to become involved with the work of NGOs.

Anthropologists thus became involved with NGOs in quite different contexts. In Latin America, it was through social movements of peasants and indigenous peoples. In Africa and South Asia, it was through new aid initiatives of poverty alleviation, humanitarian aid, and a more democratizing political climate. In the former socialist countries of Eastern Europe, NGOs were intimately involved in projects of Western democracy export, social services, human and minority rights, refugees, Balkan peace building, and EU accession.

NGOs became both the object of anthropological research and a vehicle for studying development projects and actors, what Lewis calls a "portal." For anthropologists, NGOs became a new kind of tribe, identifying with "global civil society," having its own language (project-speak), its unique kind of local and international networks to donors, consultants, and Western NGOs, and the various rituals and practices of obtaining "funding," "finding donors," conducting "trainings," and "building capacity." Following the events of 1989, anthropologists became enamored of "civil society" (Hann and Dunn 1996; Comaroff and Comaroff 1999) and produced this initial NGO research as a research of discovery. But with this discovery of a new NGO tribe came new kinds of engagements and entanglements—with project organizations, with donors, with consultants, with state bureaucrats, with other NGOs, and not least with the frustrated "target groups," who were the ostensible beneficiaries. Anthropologists, as they latched on to their NGOs, became entangled as well. And we still are.

Through the mid-1990s, NGOs expanded as donors sought partners for implementing development projects, democracy transformation, humanitarian aid, or human rights initiatives. Donors often viewed NGOs as more reliable partners than the state and more amenable than local voluntary associations or religious groups, who might have their own agendas. Aid agencies, donors, consultants, and now anthropologists all buzzed around those articulate, English-speaking NGO activists who had learned to write project proposals and who could carry out training, capacity building, and awareness raising. An "assemblage" (Ong and Collier 2005) was born, and anthropologists were present at the creation. We were there not only as researchers but also as advocates and later on as evaluators and consultants. Bernal calls this "NGO fever," and many of us caught it.

In this golden era of NGO emergence and development, anthropologists took advantage of these opportunities to study NGOs while helping NGOs to identify viable target groups, write projects, and improve their organizational skills. I was part of this wave in southeastern Europe, but several contributors in this book record similar accounts, with the resulting roller-coaster of exhilaration, frustration, and tension. Development aid experts also highlighted both the benefits and drawbacks of working with NGOs, and they were criticized as "development diplomats" (Tvedt 1998) or for being drawn into questionable aid projects (Wedel 2001).

The rise of the NGO sector and global civil society did not go unnoticed in academia and policy circles. Conferences on civil society—globally and in specific regions—brought together anthropologists with other social scientists to discuss developments in the so-called third sector. Within development studies, international studies, and political sociology, an interest in social movements and transnational activist networks (Keck and Sikkink 1998) highlighted the successes of global human rights campaigns, essentially joining together the study of global assemblages, "soft power," and civil society movements. Anthropologists participated in these gatherings, but as so often happens in interdisciplinary forums, our qualitative case studies were drowned out by the larger data sets and grand theories of political science and sociology, as well as by the policy focus of third-sector studies led by the Johns Hopkins Center for Civil Society Studies and the University College London's Center for Civil Society.

Anthropologists needed to develop their own understanding of what NGOs were and what they did. In 2001, Julie Hemment and I organized the first panel specifically on NGOs at the American Anthropological Association meetings. We had twelve papers detailing various kinds of anthropological engagement with NGOs and a full conference room of sixty engaged participants, many of them doctoral students embarking on fieldwork with NGOs. As this initial group has matured, dozens of other anthropologists joined in to study NGOs, development, social movements, and social policy. NGOs have become an object of theoretical speculation and a practical entry point into the societies we study. We now have monographs and articles on all aspects of NGO life, and the way NGOs interact with donors, partners, state officials, and target groups, as well as with each other. Moreover, we have studies of large-scale social processes of state formation, political economy, and neoliberalization in which NGOs are part of the drama and where they do not always play the progressive or benign role they themselves promote (Bernal and Grewal 2014b). NGOs can be agents of social change, but they can also be instruments of neoliberalization and state retreat. Moreover, numerous studies have criticized the appropriation of social movements by the NGO form, the dreaded "NGO-ization" (e.g., Alvarez 1999; Choudry and Kapoor 2013; Lang 2014; Hodžić 2014). The excitement about the rise of the NGO sector two decades ago has given way to a more sanguine view of the benefits and drawbacks of NGO-ization. In sum, the nature of anthropologists' involvement with NGOs has also become more complex, pushing us to become more reflexive about what it is we are doing when we hang out with NGOs.

Finally, in 2013, a group of NGO-interested anthropologists, including Mark Schuller who procured funding from Northern Illinois University, organized the first conference on NGO anthropology in Chicago. The 120 participants at the conference, with over a dozen panels, ranged the full gamut of NGO anthropology. Most of the chapters in this book originate from presentations at this initial conference. Subsequently, we had a follow-up conference two years later in Denver and a 2017 conference in Washington, DC. In addition, with the establishment of an NGO and Nonprofits Interest Group within the American Anthropological Association, an active NGO anthropology listserv, a series of volumes examining NGOs published by the University of Alabama Press (under the editorship of David Lewis and Mark Schuller), and a major review of "Anthropology of NGOs" in *Oxford Bibliographies* also by Schuller and Lewis, NGO anthropology scholarship has come of age. For anthropological researchers undertaking field studies, it is now standard practice to make contact with the local NGOs even before departure, and to use their reports, hire them as field assistants, and depend on them for information and relaxation. NGOs are collaborators . . . and gatekeepers to the field. Anthropologists and NGOs have discovered that they have common ground.

The World of NGOs

Common ground, however, does not mean identical projects or points of view. And it is precisely in our engagement with NGOs that the entanglements reveal themselves in their full complexity. It is this kind of complexity and reflection that the anthropologists in this volume take on. In the process, we discover not only what NGOs are and what they do, but also why and how they do what they do. We have not only sites of NGO practice, "NGO-ing," and portals for understanding broader social processes (as David Lewis describes in chapter 1), but a full-fledged anthropology of the NGO assemblage, with its political, symbolic, and emotional universe. With the anthropology of NGOs, we have the study of political action, organizational practice, and emotional engagement.

What kind of world is the world of NGOs? It is a world of "doing good." The "good" involves a moral claim, and the "doing" involves moralized practice. NGOs are thus a world of *engagement*. To study NGOs is to study organized engagement. NGO people are good people with a good project; they are supposed to be good and good at doing good.

It is this world of engagement that is the subject of this collection. NGOs have become a world unto themselves and for some even a way of life. And if anthropologists are supposed to do anything, it is to reveal what it means to be part of such an engaged world. This does not mean that NGO worlds are somehow more engaged than others. Moral projects are also embedded in forms as diverse as political parties, social movements, missionary groups, pagan cults, or fundamentalist groups. Rather, we might say that the performance of NGO engagement has its own parameters. The morally based character of NGO engagement, the "doing good," is revealed in various forms: in the projects of NGO activists, the way they try to help or support their target populations or causes, the way they interact with state authorities, with donors, and with competing NGOs, all are platforms for a specific performance of engagement. Even when they are compelled to act under the strictest regulations of professionalism and government audit, NGOs must perform as moral actors. NGOs may be professional and even entrepreneurial to varying degrees. They may need to have strong administrative and fund-raising skills. But it is in the moral sphere, of "doing good," of helping "vulnerable groups" through advocacy, mobilization, or channeling resources, that they sustain their moral claim. Convincing moral interventions require some kind of performance of engagement with the world and, preferably, some kind of genuine emotional involvement. Hence, NGOs are marked by a kind of emotional engagement, which many anthropologists find attractive and, in some cases, seductive.

This engagement has a price, which I call "entanglement." And the words "entangled" or "entanglement" appear in several of the chapters to follow. In their struggle for resources and to sustain their moral legitimacy, NGOs are entangled with other actors and institutions: with the state apparatuses under which they operate, with the international or local donors who fund them, with the consultants and evaluators who train and monitor them, with the market for their services and the competing NGOs, all fighting for donors' funds or a lucrative state contract, with social movements and civil society, who consider NGOs less authentic or less representative, with the target group whom they are supporting, and with the individual, career projects of NGO members and staff. These entanglements are not simply the "context" in which NGOs operate. As the chapters that follow show, these entanglements profoundly impact NGOs. They can facilitate, alter, or even undermine NGOs' own projects. When we study "NGO-ing," we study how various actors in the NGO scene pursue their own interests even as they themselves are pushed and prodded. This is what entanglements are all about.

The chapters in this book, introduced by senior NGO scholars, describe various matrices of engagement and entanglement. They describe what happens when moral interventions enter a world of other, competing projects, each with their own moral, material, and political resources. The chapters elucidate these worlds of NGOs in two ways. First, they give us a panorama of NGO scenes and practices, from Roma organizations in the Czech Republic to conservation groups in Tanzania, to women's groups in Delhi, to youth democracy in Serbia, to Jewish philanthropy in post-Katrina New Orleans. Second, they show how an explicitly anthropological approach to NGOs and NGO life can reveal the engagement/entanglement processes that might be overlooked by other social scientists, journalists, evaluators, or even by the most sympathetic social activists.

The anthropological approach to NGOs, with its emphasis on the subaltern, the informal, and the engaged researcher, has its own challenges and contradictions. As anthropologists, we do not simply look on NGOs' engagement as dispassionate outsiders. We ourselves must deal with our own passions and doubts about our engagement and entanglements with the NGOs we study. Personal engagements and social entanglements thus intersect at several levels, both in the NGO scene being described, and in the relationship between ourselves and those we study. The initial NGO studies focused on the NGOs and their projects. It was engaged and supportive, and for most anthropologists, NGOs were a portal for understanding societies whose institutions were under rapid change, rebuilding after collapse, war, or disaster. NGOs were a kind of safe haven for anthropologists. We could meet people whose mission overlapped with our own, and who spoke a language that we could relate to, if not understand.

More deeply theorized NGO research, what Christian Vannier and Amanda Lashaw, in their conclusion to this volume, call "first-generation" NGO research, sought more critical distance from NGO missions. William Fisher reviews the burgeoning anthropological literature on NGOs in his 1997 article titled "Doing Good? The Politics and Anti-Politics of NGO Practices," describing the early strategies of critique. What we call here "second-generation" NGO research acknowledges the inevitable entanglements and even embraces them. It focuses on how NGO practices may perpetuate international or state neoliberal projects and may even stifle social movements that do not precisely resemble the vaunted "NGO form" (Bernal and Grewal 2014a). This second-generation research has also dovetailed with trends within anthropological fieldwork, where the lone academic fieldworker can no longer simply drop in and hang out for a while and then retreat back into academia. Second-generation NGO fieldwork is not just multisited. It is inherently messy, and several of the chapters here elaborate on the various roles that anthropological fieldworkers play while gathering data and the inherent tensions of discovering that NGOs, for all their moral commitment, are also afflicted with much the same kind of organizational intrigues, pathologies, and power games that we find in other organizations and bureaucracies. NGO-ography has thus become more complicated. The gap between "in the field" and "back home" has disappeared. The dissolving of that gap is not simply a result of new communications technologies that make distance obsolete. It is also because NGO projects have global appeal and connections, as well as "frictions" that bring in universal projects and push ethnographers into a more multisited, if not messy sited, mode of research (Tsing 2005). These frictions are illustrated in the chapters that follow.

Here I would like to flesh out the nature of "NGO worlds" both in terms of their engagement and entanglement. All the contributors to this book are interested in a specific anthropological approach to the "NGO form" with its corresponding engagement/entanglement issues.

What is this NGO form? The NGOs described in these chapters are all groups of people with a moral intervention project. They want to do good. Moreover, these groups, while they may be based on informal networks of kin groups, friendship, political alliance, or social movements, also have an additional feature: they are organized as juridical persons. This means they can assert juridical claims, can administer and manage funds, and can be compelled to reveal certain financial or personnel data; they can be sued in court or dissolved. Recent laws in countries as diverse as Russia and Israel, requiring NGOs to reveal any sources of foreign funding and declare themselves "foreign agents," are indicative of this special status of NGOs as juridical entities. Moreover, NGOs have charismatic leaders (see Sinervo's, Mouftah's, and Synková's chapters, for example), who combine their charisma with organization. Still other social groups tend to appropriate the NGO form for tactical reasons, while in some cases they deny being NGOs even as they act like NGOs anyway (Sinervo's and Mouftah's chapters). The NGOs described in this book are corporate in the legal sense and therefore conform to the now hegemonic cookbook definition of NGOs: as voluntary, not for profit, autonomous from government, and juridically corporate. These characteristics are relevant for NGOs' practical status (they can make contracts with donors or with the state).

There is an intimate relationship between NGOs' juridical status and their moral legitimacy, since juridical status allows NGOs to procure and use funds or mobilize political allies. The moral capital that lies at the core of NGOs is both a resource and a burden. Hence, the worst accusations that can be hurled at an NGO is that it is a front for the state or a political party or that it is a disguise for someone's profit-making firm. The moral mission, whether it involves helping a vulnerable group, solving a social problem, raising awareness about a pressing issue, or providing a needed service, forms the charter of any and all NGOs. Hence, NGOs use much of their social and symbolic energy to demonstrate that their charter fits well with the needs of those they want to help; in this way they specify who their potential partners are. The issue of who needs what, or whether the right kinds of needs are being fulfilled, pervades several of the chapters in this book: Synková on the Roma, Kapusta-Pofahl on gender equality in the Czech Republic, the needs of Muslim women in Delhi as they pursue justice (Lemons's chapter), or the strategy and tactics of conservation groups in Tanzania as discussed by Woomer.

The combination of moral mission and organizational form creates the challenge for anthropologists' engagement and the way in which we describe NGOs' entanglement. NGOs like to describe themselves as a "movement." Who wouldn't like to have such a label? But NGOs are also organizations. Like other organizations, NGOs have a rationality, a hierarchical structure, a division of tasks, and a budget. They hold meetings, they have officers, they have everyday routines, and they must perform in a manner that looks competent, if not also "professional." Dorothea Hilhorst summarizes these characteristics by observing that NGOs must be "good at doing good" (2003). NGO-ing, as several of these chapters underscore, is the practice of balancing the moral and the professional in a way that convinces others. It is these others who create and maintain the entanglements described in this book.

The Nature of NGO Entanglements

NGOs operate in a wider social, political, and economic context. Yet the word "context" needs to be understood in a more powerful way, and therefore I use the word "entanglements." Let me describe four of these entanglements here. The first source of entanglement for most NGOs is the state. In the West, states often act as donors by giving grants and contracts, but states now also monitor NGOs to ensure they do not abuse their nonprofit status. In developing countries, donors often require the recipient country to involve their national NGO sector in development work or demand that NGOs provide certain social services. Such partnerships between states and NGOs may appear voluntary, but they are also imposed from outside under the rubric of "conditionality." As outlined in most of the chapters in this book, states fulfill a variety of roles for NGOs: they are contractors with NGOs, they allow or even encourage NGOs to fill gaps in services, they push NGOs to implement neoliberalization, and at times states sabotage NGO work out of envy or suspicion of NGOs' resources or allegiances. The state/NGO boundary is in fact fluid. Hence, in Peru, Sinervo describes how a state agency to assist children masquerades as an NGO in order to obtain additional moral capital, while at the same time, a local activist NGO insists on denying its NGO status for the same reason. NGOs thus do not have a prior claim to moral projects. In Serbia, Vetta describes how the local residents find themselves more comfortable with a state-organized administration than with the NGO initiatives funded by the United States Agency for International Development (USAID). Here the NGO activity is an instrument for a neoliberalization of social services, and this made the residents suspicious. Good intentions aside, NGO-ing always has unintended consequences. Several of the chapters here describe this clash between the good intentions and the more harmful consequences of NGO-ing.

A second entanglement for NGOs is with the donors. Without the money, support, training, and networks provided by donors, who are mostly foreign, many of the NGOs described in this book would not exist. Donors speak the language of "partnership," but it is clear that the partnership is unequal. Donors have resources that NGOs do not have. Donors give away money, offer expertise, and help expand local and international networks. Yet donors also constrain. As pointed out by Lemons, Kornfeld, Bernal, and Vetta, and by many informants in the following chapters, much NGO-ing is not much more than performing for donors, holding the requisite trainings, attending the seminars, writing the reports, composing the budgets, and tabulating the success statistics. Donors need not be far-off foundations or aid agencies. In Peru, some of the donors are foreign tourists who mobilize their families back home as donors. And in Egypt, Mouftah describes how people donate not money but their time and energy as part of an Islamic "duty." If donating is ultimately giving, donations are more than just project grants. Many things are given under the label of "donor."

The third source of entanglement is the competing NGOs and other social activist movements. NGOs never exist alone. Synková describes conflicts in the Czech Republic between an ethnically based Roma NGO and the more academically inclined social service groups. She finds that the Roma NGOs' resistance to professionalization, while it adds to their authenticity, also deprives them of obtaining funds. Kapusta-Pofahl describes a similar conflict between engagement and professionalism in her chapter, where she delineates the tensions between academics, feminist activists, and state gender equality officers. Kornfeld describes conflicts within Jewish philanthropy between established Jewish groups and more activist ones as they competed over how best to give aid to post-Katrina New Orleans.

The fourth and most difficult entanglement for NGOs is with their ostensible target group, the people they are supposed to help. Several of the chapters describe how NGOs may be so preoccupied with legitimating themselves to their competitors, the state, or their donors (the so-called stakeholders) that they end up overlooking their target groups. In other cases, the NGOs may construct the target group as simplistic categories ("poor children," "those uninformed about conservation") in need of NGOs' aid or enlightenment. This entanglement of NGOs with their target group affects the anthropological fieldworker, who may share the NGOs' general objective but is hesitant to critique the NGOs' methods. Our fieldwork agenda among the target group may cause the NGO to become suspicious of our loyalties.

Discoveries and Issues

Anthropologists have long been preoccupied with reflecting on how their presence affects the people we study, or whether our project is only to dialogue with informants or to translate their experience to others. This has created tensions and doubts about what anthropologists are doing when they study NGOs. There is a tendency to forget that anthropologists do fieldwork in order to learn things, to actually discover how social groups operate. So what is it exactly that anthropologists have discovered about the NGO world? First, we have found that while NGOs have certainly become professionalized and even bureaucratized, there is still a lot of engagement out there. NGO activists and volunteers, in various settings, some of them life-threatening, are trying to solve pressing problems, sacrificing to help others, and looking for relevant solutions. As the chapters in this book show, NGOs are operating as agents of change and helping people to become aware of their own positions in larger hierarchies. Women's groups in the Czech Republic, environmental groups in Tanzania, democratic youth in Serbia, Islamic youth in Egypt, and Jewish philanthropy activists in New Orleans, just to take some examples from the chapters here, are constantly endeavoring to help target groups find creative solutions to their problems. Some of these solutions involve expanding the original target group into a more inclusive one (as in post-Katrina New Orleans). Other solutions involve forming alliances between activists and academics or even with the state authorities (Kapusta-Pofahl in the Czech Republic and Vetta's description in Serbia). Still others involve an effort to redefine the nature of religious obligations (Mouftah's chapter on Egypt). The engagement identified by the anthropologists is not only organizational but also intensely personal. NGO activists, staff, and volunteers each have their personal stories. NGOs have a history, but the activists have a biography. They have personal projects that coalesce with their efforts to aid their target group. NGO work, the contributors show, involves *emotions*. And in some ways this emotional involvement is reflected in the way anthropologists become involved with their NGOs. As several chapters show, there is a bond between the researcher and the research population that is simply absent in sociological or policy studies of the NGO sector.

A second discovery by the contributors is the way NGOs and NGO activists are constantly manipulating their activist and professional identities. This oscillation varies according to time and place and belies the simple distinction between genuine activists versus the professionalized NGO career staff. Activism, the emotional engagement in one's project that overlaps with the organizational goal, can take place at specified moments. At other moments, the activist becomes an ice-cold professional. We are not simply talking about "strategic" practice here. Rather it is the ability—perhaps a talent—of NGO activists, staff, and members to switch registers depending on context. It is this talent among activists to flex between the emotional and professional that distinguishes the NGOs that survive from those that disappear from the scene. The flexibility is demonstrated in virtually all the chapters of this book, and several of the contributors come to realize that their interlocutors are more complex than they originally thought.

The third discovery in these studies is that the NGO form is in fact more varied and changeable than imagined. In the chapters on Peru, Egypt, and Serbia, for example, we find civil society activity being carried out under rubrics other that the typical NGO-project form. The children's aid organization in Peru mobilizes foreign tourists as volunteers. In Egypt, the appeal to Islamic "duty" to carry out social work supplants NGO-style volunteering; and in Serbia, the local administration fulfills certain kinds of social needs that were supposed to be met by the American-supported NGO project officers. The "classic" NGO form described in the earlier "first-generation" studies competes with more loosely structured activist networks, as in the Czech movement for Roma housing and in the Tanzanian conservation movements described by Woomer. Social activism is taking place without the formal rubric of NGOs.

The fourth discovery brought out by these the chapters is the crucial issue of representation. NGOs are shown to be in a constant struggle to demonstrate that they speak for some group or constituency other than themselves. What does this performative representation look like? How is it formed, maintained, or changed over time? What happens when NGOs experience a crisis of representation because citizens ignore them, the state restricts them, the donors abandon them, or other movements supersede them? The chapters show how the NGO form is contingent on its ability to perform representation. More important, they show that NGOs must be considered historically, in a life cycle that is more than simply "the rise of NGOs." The demise and disappearance of NGOs' co-optation, repression, alteration, and fragmentation also require a larger view of what happens to the NGO fever that Bernal describes. What happens when NGO-ization comes into conflict with alternative forms of social mobilization (see also Hodžić 2014) or when NGOs simply become irrelevant?

A fifth issue that pervades several of the chapters is that of "the political." "We do civil society, not politics," insisted one of the NGOs in Vetta's study of community building and "fuzzy accountability" in Serbia. Nevertheless, Vetta describes a very political project. In all the chapters, the NGOs are shown to cultivate a discourse of neutrality. Synková shows how some are accused of being too activist and others of not being activist enough. Kapusta-Pofahl describes how others are trying to place themselves somewhere between scholarship and advocacy. But as Kornfeld notes in his study of Jewish philanthropy, highlighting one's neutrality over partisan activism is itself a political stance. Just as anthropologists have begun to take up "secularism" along with religion, we need to examine "neutrality" alongside "politics." The chapters show that we need to view the performance of "neutrality" as a practice embedded in the world of NGOs.

A sixth issue revealed here, often either assumed or overlooked in the earlier studies of NGOs, is that of affect. What does it *feel* like to be engaged? The emotional aspects of engagement, and how various entanglements affect emotions, are the stuff of ethnographic description. In Mouftah's description of Life Makers in Egypt, in Synková's description of the Roma group trying to solve problems, and notably in Sinervo's description of foreign volunteers in Peru seeking out that authentic experience as aid workers, we see how ethnographic descriptions bring out what NGO-ing is all about. The urge to do good and the practice of doing good are tied to an affective dimension, a *regime of affect*. In the NGO world, practice has to have an emotional component. The emotions are there not only when performing "doing good" but also in the kind of guilt that NGO activists or staff often feel about not having done enough or anxieties about having become too professional or too bureaucratized.

Seventh, we anthropologists need constantly to deal with the issue of our engagement with those we study. Lemons describes this as an issue of "alignment," while Woomer unequivocally argues that "deep engagement" can serve the purposes of anthropology and help the people we study better than trying to remain detached. This issue is clearly problematic because anthropologists study NGOs for quite different reasons. Some of us study NGOs as organizations, but for others NGOs are the portal for understanding larger issues, such as the nature of development or neoliberal restructuring. Bernal's description of NGO fever and Lemons's emphasis on our research in an NGO-saturated world require a continuing reflection on how anthropologists can or should relate to these organizations. What, then, is engagement for anthropologists? How should we engage with those for whom engagement is part of their practice? For Woomer and others, researcher engagement is a means of creating dialogue and critique. Erica Bornstein reminds us of the pitfalls involved when a critique of the organization risks degenerating into a mere assessment of outputs and our research critique becomes a policy evaluation. Critique must therefore be distinguished from sheer criticism, especially because NGO activists, staff, or target group informants, with their immediate concerns, may not fully understand the anthropologist's broader mission (or we may have not made our mission clear). NGOs are not necessarily our ally, even if they might have the same overall goal of helping a vulnerable group gain more control over their lives. As several chapters point out, as well as numerous other studies (e.g., Bernal and Grewal 2014b), our sharing of perspectives and sympathies with NGOs and our sympathy with the "grassroots" exist in a context of NGOs' own agendas. NGO activists will try to influence our views of the vulnerable groups and the nature of the issues at stake. We use them, but they can also use us. NGOs have their own interests, and it is clear that they want anthropologists to see the world the way they do. Katherine Lemons warns us about such NGO-dependent anthropology: our alignment with NGO projects and our sharing of a common moral mission may blind us to the fact that there are relevant stakeholders aside from those NGO activists with whom we often feel so comfortable. As Woomer emphasizes, a deeper engagement may be a better tactic than a retreat into academic neutrality: more engagement, not with the NGO as such but with the cause they are advocating, may truly help the people we want to help, the target group, and it may also give us more nuanced ethnography. More engagement may also help build the kinds of theories we need to understand the NGO form and how it operates. More engagement may give us a better understanding of why the word "grassroots" makes us all feel so good. But more engagement may also make the NGOs angry with us. This is the dilemma of engagement.

The chapters in this book all seek to elucidate the relationships between engagement and entanglement. The matrix of engagement/entanglement is simultaneously personal, organizational, and structural. It thus requires both face-to-face ethnography and theoretical reflection. NGOs are engaged and entangled, and so are the anthropologists who study them.

About This Book

In part I, "Changing Landscapes of Power," our journey into the world of NGOs continues with Mark Schuller's introduction to the part, where the emphasis is on deciphering the NGO form. NGOs are revealed as part of larger landscapes of power, immersed in donor priorities, global development discourses, and state power. In chapter 1 David Lewis outlines the relationship between development work and the study of NGOs. With a point of departure in his own work in Bangladesh, Lewis shows how NGOs have served not only as objects of study for anthropologists interested in development but also as portals for understanding larger process of neoliberalism and state restructuring and as sites of anthropological reflection. Part I also offers studies of NGO fever and feminist activism in Tanzania by Victoria Bernal, community development in Serbia by Theodora Vetta, Roma activism in the Czech Republic by Hana Synková, and the role of academics and NGOs in gender equality policy, again in the Czech Republic, by Karen Kapusta-Pofahl.

The internal life of NGOs is introduced in part II, "Doing Good Work," with "Life in NGOs" by Inderpal Grewal. Grewal underscores how each NGO has its own conception and practice of what it means to "do good," and that these practices need to be closely analyzed. The chapters take us to a faith-based NGO in Egypt (Nermeen Mouftah), volunteer tourism in Peru (Aviva Sinervo), and Jewish philanthropy in post-Katrina New Orleans (Moshe Kornfeld).

Part III, "Methodological Challenges of NGO Anthropology," offers three contributions on the methodological challenges to pursuing an NGO anthropology. Erica Bornstein discusses how we should ethically study NGOs, suggesting how we negotiate the gray zone between gaining trust and providing critique. Katherine Lemons and Amanda Woomer then provide further examples of the stakes of engagement, and they offer contrasting visions of what it means to create "good" ethnography. Finally, Christian Vannier and Amanda Lashaw conclude the book by describing possibilities immanent in the "second-generation" of NGO research, which incorporates the engagements, entanglements, and complexity of modern anthropological research.

PART I
Changing Landscapes
of Power

Introduction to Part I

Dilemmas of Dual Roles, Studying NGOs, and Donor-Driven "Democracy"

Mark Schuller

The five chapters in part I offer ethnographically rich understandings of the dilemmas faced by anthropologists and other social scientists studying what Bernal and Grewal (2014a) call the "NGO form." The five chapters all discuss a multiplicity of state forms and postcolonial histories. Given this diversity, the appearance and relative empowerment of NGOs in what Vetta calls the "associational revolution" and Bernal dubs "NGO fever" have distinct and contradictory meanings within the different contexts. This ambivalence is woven into the following chapters, from the liberally quoted interlocutors to the contributors' concluding remarks: Are NGOs part of the solution in promoting democracy or part of the problem in implanting foreign donor directives? Put another way, adopting language from their fieldsites, the five chapters ask: Are "NGOers" reformist or revolutionary? Following some soul searching the texts implicitly answer: both.

As these chapters argue, "NGOs" are elusive objects of study, often defined by "what-they-are-not" (see Bernal and Grewal 2014a; Fisher 1997, for examples of this discussion), which triggers what Amanda Lashaw terms an "impasse" (Lashaw 2013). These chapters employ spatial metaphors to deconstruct ideologically constructed boundaries between NGOs and states on the one hand and social movements on the other. As these chapters indicate, they are not quite nongovernmental, as they are often intertwined with states. Kapusta-Pofahl discusses the intimate interconnections between European Union agencies and NGOs, and Bernal points out that governments, both foreign and national, are primary funders of NGOs. NGOs are also a part of the global order (Schuller 2009), connecting what Bernal calls an "international donor regime" to local communities. Moral judgments are often sought and sometimes made between "good" and "bad" NGOs, which have led to a wide array of classificatory schemes. Lumped together by this single criterion of being nongovernmental, NGOs are a diverse set indeed.

In part this ambivalence results from what the texts identify as a "revolving door" between scholar and practitioner, bringing up core challenges—not only of access but also of the ethics of studying NGOs. James Ferguson (2005) calls development the "evil twin" of anthropology pointing out the similarity of experiences: development agencies, including NGOs, often go to the field uninvited and set up hierarchical, uneven relationships with local communities, just as researchers often do. Kapusta-Pofahl points out the pitfalls of this dual role, with expectations for an NGO often at odds with those for a scholar. All of these chapters reflexively interrogate the disquieting similarities and therefore expectations upon the anthropologist as researcher. These roles are often blurred: some NGOs offer employment opportunities for a budding scholar, which is particularly important as academic employment continues to grow scarce. These chapters offer an honest and necessary, if unflattering, look into our praxis. One particular dilemma posed in the field regards whether to document the nitty-gritty "behind the scenes" information, knowing that the picture may indeed be unflattering, even when such a portrayal might well jeopardize NGOs' abilities to secure donor funding. The belief that NGOs can be vehicles for social justice, particularly for marginalized groups such as Roma or women, animates decisions of self-censorship within NGOs and questions of trust in the ethnographer, who employs an admittedly invasive methodology. Insofar as scholars' praxis is similar to that of NGOs, the ethnographer is also confronted with choices of what narratives to highlight, whose voices to amplify. These dilemmas pose a related question: Who is the audience in the scholarship on NGOs? Kapusta-Pofahl's discussion of the *Shadow Report* highlights the difficulties of "pitching" knowledge production for various publics. More than the issue of, like Goldilocks, getting the language and level of complexity "just right," questions of audience also shape what is brought up and what is suppressed.

Structuring this fraught set of negotiations, of course, are the inherently hierarchical relationships between NGOs and donor agencies. As an interlocutor in Vetta's chapter wryly notes about the USAID website, NGOs also have to perform "success" in an inherently and increasingly mediatized sphere. This tendency to play to the "photo op" transcends NGOs working in aid—across the humanitarian-development continuum—as advocacy, activism, and human rights organizations must also be visible and in the public eye. This demand to be seen is a central trait among NGOs. NGOs' staffs, particularly those engaged in public relations or fund-raising, are acutely aware that their organizations survive because of media coverage. Some staff members grumble about their roles as "PR tools" when they know better. "Remember how your salaries are being paid," one person sardonically replied when I asked why she did things she knew to be ineffective, inefficient, or inappropriate. She left this agency a month after our interview. The five chapters all share similar stories of the need for visibility and thus the need for NGOs to play to the photo op. Decisions about particular courses of action on the ground are often guided at least in part by spectacle. A direct outcome of this need for visibility is competition between NGOs, as Synková demonstrates.

Donor funding configures this competition. Donors play a powerful backstage role in NGOs as the "man behind the curtain," and these chapters are exemplars of critically engaged ethnography. These chapters all attempt to understand what sociologist Millie Thayer, quoted in Bernal's chapter, terms "shadow commodity chains." Inspired by George Marcus's 1995 call for theorizing the world system, ethnographies of NGOs have been multisited and have attempted to theorize the nexus of power wielded by donors (e.g., Davis 2003; Baaz 2005; Kamat 2002). Official donor aid changes NGOs. Metaphors of being on a "treadmill" or a "gravy train" are often used to describe this need to constantly be in fund-raising mode, making and documenting great effort but with little forward motion being accomplished. Donors require ever-greater accountability from recipient NGOs; since the turn of the twenty-first century, "results-" or "performance-"based management has been increasingly en vogue (Schuller 2012). The need for accountability puts pressure on NGOs to produce numbers, which in turn grants greater authority to the so-called expert. The hierarchical relationship forces the production of documents (Riles 2004) and evaluation reports to justify receipt of aid funds, especially continuing funds; in some cases the need to produce documentation shapes official decisions, one aspect of "audit culture" (e.g., Shore and Wright 2000; Strathern 2000; Vannier 2010). Through these documentation requirements, donors also reinforce a certain language, what Bernal terms "NGO-speak," which is bureaucratic and full of insider jargon. In addition, no matter the local language, NGO activists and staff members are required to speak English or some hybrid like "kishwahenglish" (people in Haiti call it Krenglish) in order to access donor funds and write performance reports. The process of legal registration can also serve to discipline NGOs (e.g., Alvaré 2010; Kamat 2002; Sangtin Writers and Nagar 2006; Sharma 2008), causing groups like People in Need in Synková's chapter to bristle, rename themselves, or attempt to bend the rules.

Cyndi Lauper's 1984 song "Money Changes Everything" is unfortunately an apt warning (Lauper 1984). As these chapters demonstrate, donor aid can shift what NGOs do in addition to how they document it and the language they speak. For example, Kapusta-Pofahl discusses how European Union agencies shape the discourse and the issues for NGOs to work on, and in so doing produce a particular type of professionalized feminist analysis and praxis. Donors also set priorities: Vetta describes how donors attempt to instill new "habits of the heart." In such a regime, innovation and local initiative, which could arise from true, "bottom-up" participation (e.g., Hickey and Mohan 2004; Parpart 1999), are actively discouraged. One of Vetta's interlocutors argues as much when she laments that NGO projects are cut-and-paste. In the same vein, Bernal discusses policy templates used by donors and NGOs. Another one of Vetta's research participants invokes the "Yellow Bible"—the policy manual, from donors—that not only sets priorities themselves but also prescribes particular strategies for accomplishing said goals. Donor aid also transforms independent activists into professional staff, what Bernal calls the "monetization of activism." This can be a source of tension and even conflict if funds and employment are not shared equally. When the funding stops, often so does the activism. People in Haiti call this the "yellow T-shirt phenomenon" because independent volunteer civic activity all but stopped when cash-for-work programs (wherein people were identified by their matching yellow shirts) ceased. Bernal also notes this tendency of donor funding to dry up volunteerism. These tendencies are specific examples of projectization, wherein the logic of projects permeates NGO activity (Sampson 1996). Projects tend to be short-term, discrete, and measurable—in other words products to be sold to donors, embodied by the quote in Synková's chapter, "the money that I wrote." A related tendency within the project and market logic is depoliticization (e.g., Edelman 2005; Ferguson 1994; INCITE! Women of Color against Violence 2007). Sonia Alvarez (1999) discusses how donor mandates flatten the "hybridity" of women's NGOs, turning NGOs away from activism and toward direct service, a risk identified in all five chapters, notably in the context of the drift within People in Need that Synková shares.

Shorn of moral or political cover, NGOs can become a means to an end. The questions are: for whom, from whom, and to what ends? It has been long established that the 1990s saw an "NGO Boom," and soon thereafter anthropologists took the lead in posing critical questions. Donors as well as the political scientists and economists hired by them promoted the idea that NGOs were, in Vetta's term, "islands of democracy." From this view, NGOs represent "civil society," a concept revived under Cold War auspices to valorize the "West" as well as to continue colonialist hierarchies within "development" (Comaroff and Comaroff 1999; Hann and Dunn 1996). However, as the five chapters document, activists gravitate to the NGO form to fulfill their own ends. Bernal argues that the primary appeal of organizing as an NGO in Tanzania is that it allows for the receipt of donor funding. NGOs can be spaces for women's activism, as Vetta, Kapusta-Pofahl, and Bernal demonstrate, as well as tools for community advancement and the development of marginalized populations, as Synková argues. Moreover, as Bernal notes, citing a local activist, "donors need us too," and another, speaking back to donor demands, insists that NGOs' participation in a meeting is not a "begging bowl."

Moving beyond NGOs as a static category and demonstrating the complex negotiations of diverse actors, these analyses highlight the multiple and varied relationships surrounding NGOs. These relationships are dynamic, given that actors as well as political context can change. These chapters all outline the importance of certain relationships and explore how these relationships shape NGOs' and NGOers' destinies. All NGOs engage in, produce, support, and engender relationships, and it is through these relationships that NGO-ing is done. A reading of the five chapters together, in a way that tries to make sense of complex human relationships, suggests that rather than focus on the NGO form, it might be useful to think through NGOs as a verb. Examining NGO practices (and relationships), rather than the category itself, may be a more useful way forward. A common critique after Haiti's earthquake was that there was way too much NGO-ing, by which the speaker usually meant adopting a bureaucratic structure or adopting a project logic, justifying the use of foreign funding. "NGO-ing" (either "do-gooding" or "activisting") might make more sense as a signifier than "NGO" as a noun (Hilhorst 2003). NGOs all "act," and these actions serve as justifications for their existence and use of funds. Posed this way, asking what NGOs *do* as opposed to what NGOs *are* can lead to a productive set of conversations exploring similarities between entities across sectors and organizational types. The chapters allow for such a rich and fruitful dialogue.

1

Anthropologists' Encounters with NGOs

Critique, Collaboration, and Conflict

David Lewis

The abbreviation "NGO" is a by-product of the creation of the United Nations system as a club of governments in 1945 and was originally intended to designate nongovernmental observers of UN processes. However, the term NGO was not commonly used until the 1980s when NGOs, as well as the *idea* of the NGO, suddenly rose to prominence. This ascendancy took place within the broad reshaping of Western economic and social policies along lines that were informed by neoliberal ideology and more narrowly within the formalized world of the international development industry. It was here that the so-called good governance agenda emerged, generated by agencies such as the World Bank, within which NGOs were elevated as flexible agents of both democratization and service delivery. A dominant strand within neoliberalism's privatization agenda came to emphasize an ideology of "nongovernmentalism" that increasingly favored secular, professionalized NGOs as private market-based actors in development and wider public policy implementation in both "developing" and "developed" country contexts (Lewis 2005).

Important too was the rediscovery of political ideas about "civil society" toward the end of the Cold War period, particularly among anti-authoritarian activists in Eastern Europe and Latin America (Hann and Dunn 1996; Comaroff and Comaroff 1999). During this period, new generations of activists became drawn to a Gramscian view of civil society as a site of anti-hegemonic resistance. While this rethinking of activist spaces was broader than the original organizational category implied by the NGO term, the growing prominence of NGOs was often mixed in with the discourses of social movements and civil society. In this confusion, NGOs were sometimes taken as proxies for civil society itself. It was not uncommon for development experts to assess the extent of civil society by simply counting up the number of registered NGOs. This conflation of terms meant that as new policy agendas were being advanced such as use of private or NGO contractors to deliver social services, these policies were at the same time being challenged by other NGOs with a more activist focus (Lewis 2005).

In this fluid situation, anthropologists began to step in as researchers, consultants, and activists. These long-standing encounters have taken on various shapes at different times and have been informed by a range of theoretical perspectives. Three different sets of implications are explored in this chapter with a view to provoking further debate and discussion. Such engagements have an elusive quality, partly because the terminology around NGOs is diverse and contested: confusingly, "nongovernmental organization" is often used interchangeably with related overlapping terms such as "voluntary organization," "nonprofit organization," "third-sector organization," and "community-based organization." Each term possesses a distinctive origin and history, often embedded within different geographical and cultural contexts. As Gellner suggests, there is a "definitional instability" here that implies fertile ground for further research. Social theorists might call it an "empty" or "floating signifier" (2010, 5). An additional level of complexity is generated because this plays out both within the formal ethnographic writings of anthropologists and within the less formal interactions that take place between anthropologists and NGOs as both go about their activities in "the field," such as designating their respective "target group," "building rapport," and defining their position with the group.

In this chapter, I focus on three types of anthropological interaction with NGOs: (1) direct anthropological interest in NGOs as social and political actors, (2) the utility of studying NGOs as useful "portals" to other issues, and (3) the methodological issues generated by the ways in which anthropologists become involved with "their" NGOs in the field.

The Anthropological Study of NGOs

The earliest examples of anthropological interests in the broad field that we now call NGO studies had three elements. The first was ethnographic work in the 1960s on "voluntary" and "common interest" associations that emerged in societies undergoing modernization, urbanization, and industrialization. These associations were understood by anthropologists particularly in the context of African societies as adaptive mechanisms to change, as territorial and kinship forms of organization came under pressure (Kerri 1976). These self-help membership organizations were seen as providing members with mutual aid, protection, companionship, and opportunities for social mobility and as vehicles to build cooperation with other groups.

For example, in his 1965 book, *West African Urbanization*, Kenneth Little describes how urban migrants' kinship and territory-based institutions were replaced or supplemented by new organizational forms such as tribal unions, friendly societies, and occupational and recreational associations. Such accounts were heavily functionalist and dualist, viewing associations as assisting in recent migrants' transition from "ascribed" to "achieved" status. Nevertheless, these accounts are echoed in today's world of citizen organizing in pursuit of identities and rights.

Also forming part of this early scholarship was the study of missionary organizations, which can be seen as forerunners of the modern NGO. As Erica Bornstein describes in *The Spirit of Development*, the church in the colonial era provided "what would today be termed 'development' for Africans" (2003, 11) through activities undertaken by charitable missions that worked in conjunction with the state to provide education and agricultural training. The normative universalizing agenda of missionaries was an uncomfortable one for many anthropologists. Like the relationships in the field between missionaries and "natives," relationships between missionaries and anthropologists were similarly complex and ambiguous, often fraught with difficulty and tensions. There are parallels with relationships that arise today around the critical positions taken by some anthropologists in relation to NGOs, particularly (an issue I will discuss later in this chapter).[1]

Applied anthropology was a third area of early engagement between anthropologists and NGOs. The work of "applied" anthropologists engaged in community development brought contact with NGOs, as the latter became more prominent actors in the development field from the 1960s onward. Some applied anthropologists recognized that "private voluntary organizations" were important players in local development processes. NGOs, community organizations, and local associations could serve as useful connectors for anthropologists pursuing applied agendas. As Ward Goodenough puts it, anthropologists could help activists and practitioners engaged in community development to build on local organizational practices and structures through provision of a solid anthropological understanding of "cultural, social and psychological processes" (1963, 378). This was certainly the forerunner to the NGOs' mantra of "obtaining local knowledge" before starting a project. Activist forms of applied anthropology also aimed to influence outcomes, with anthropologists campaigning in favor of marginalized communities and groups (such as the engaged anthropology of Sol Tax [Stapp 2012]).

Each of these arenas of scholarly and practical engagement were focused at the community level and were primarily concerned with understanding *what NGOs do*, rather with than *what NGOs are* or *what NGOs mean*. Despite the long-standing interactions, anthropologists were surprisingly slow to take up these latter agendas. This began to shift in the 1990s, first in the context of the new critical anthropology of development that emerged with the works of Arturo Escobar (1995) and James Ferguson (1994). There had always been anthropological critiques of colonialism and modernization, of course, as well as narratives of project failure and the negative impact of "development" initiatives on local populations. But the anthropology of development had fallen from favor during the 1980s in the face of postmodern reflection and the relegation of "applied" anthropology to second-class status in many university departments. In addition, many applied anthropologists had become full-time development consultants. Back in academia, drawing on a Foucauldian conception of power, the aim of both authors was to reveal more of development's contradictions than those of structural inequalities, not only through the analysis of agency and structure but also through a deconstruction of the power of representation and discourse. Though neither Escobar's nor Ferguson's studies were concerned with the wider workings of development policies and projects driven by governments and donors instead of NGOs per se, these books nonetheless created a foundation for new critical anthropological work on NGOs (see, for example, Hilhorst 2003; Karim 2011).

The rise of the "postdevelopment perspective" also influenced this first generation of anthropological work on NGOs, which were now beginning to be viewed not as progressive actors but as inextricably linked with imperial projects of power. NGOs as incarnations of civil society gave way to a stronger interest in new social movements as sites of resistance. Postdevelopment theorists emphasized the idea of development as reductionist economism, as the imposition of science as power, as cultural Westernization, and as environmental destruction. For Dominique Temple, NGOs are "Trojan Horses" that smuggle a Western economic logic based on the production of exchange value into indigenous economies based on norms of reciprocity (aided in his analysis by the anthropologists who characterize a separate realm of knowledge about indigenous culture) (Temple 1997, 202). But as Jan Nederveen Pieterse argues, the postdevelopment critique offered little in the way of practical politics beyond the romantic assertion of the self-organizing power of the poor. Indeed, postdevelopment showed "no regard for the progressive potential and dialectics of modernity—for democratization, soft-power technologies, reflexivity" (2000, 187).

Finally, studies of NGOs and "civil society" within post-Soviet settings also formed an important part of this body of critical scholarship. For example, work by anthropologists in post-Soviet settings on the promotion of "civil society"—an idea that was prioritized by Western policy makers during the 1990s provided another important foundation for NGO research. For example, David Abramson (1999) reveals civil society in Uzbekistan to be an imposed and locally instrumentalized construct that served to dissemble relations of power between interest groups. In Armenia, the creation of professionalized NGOs through externally funded civil society initiatives formed part of the push toward the construction of a flexible state within the "good governance" paradigm, as Armine Ishkanian describes in her 2008 book (25).

By the 2000s, anthropologists of development had made what David Mosse calls a "shift toward ethnographic treatment of development as a category of practice" (Mosse 2013, 228). This helped to provide a foundation for what can be seen as a second generation of NGO work by anthropologists, in which earlier polarizations between distanced critique and forms of anthropological engagement became less pronounced. The anthropological study of NGOs became part of what came to be known as "aidnography," which included the organizational practices and life-worlds of those who worked in NGOs as well as the structures and processes of the neoliberal architecture of the aid system. Finally taking on board the advice to "study up," aidnography implied a shift away from simply focusing on those being "developed" (by organizations such as NGOs) toward recognition of the value of research on the "developers" themselves. Anne-Meike Fechter and Heather Hindman (2011) argue that anthropologists can contribute to the creation of a literature "that goes beyond accusation and blame" and make a convincing case for the need to make people who work in the aid industry, and the work that they do, more visible. Drawing on Bruno Latour (2005), they also highlight the distinctiveness of aid labor as a form of intermediary work, in which the life histories and motivations of individuals shape, rather than merely implement, aid processes. Amanda Lashaw has also examined such NGO labor in the United States. She characterizes the distinctive cultural labor of middle-class NGO-based reformers in the education sector, whose "passion lends credence to otherwise implausible claims" (Lashaw 2013, 519). Within these various perspectives, NGOs are seen as playing new roles as "brokers and translators" within both community-level and wider institutional configurations (Lewis and Mosse 2006).

After the critical Foucauldian analysis of the 1990s, the anthropological study of development in the 2000s was also reinvigorated by engagement with classical gift theory, which opened up new space for thinking about exchange and morality (Gardner and Lewis 2015). Moving away from understandings of development as unequal power relations, there was now a new interest in ethics and beliefs that in part reflected the growing profile of NGOs, philanthropy, and social enterprise in the world of development aid.

Anthropological understandings of "the gift" influenced by Marcel Mauss emphasized gift relationships as invested in social meanings as well as characterized by unequal power (Stirrat and Henkel 1997). This opened up ways forward for analyses of aid and charity that went beyond either notions of benevolent giving on the one hand or the will to control on the other. As the development gift travels from charitable giving through international NGOs to local organizations and communities, differences are demarcated and hierarchies reinforced. NGOs, being agents of donors, become gift givers, gift mobilizers, and gift accountants.

Seeing through NGOs: NGOs as Portals

William Fisher's 1997 review article titled "Doing Good?" recognizes the wider importance of NGOs and civil society as global political actors that offer connections to far wider issues. This early key anthropological text offers a wide-ranging overview of NGOs' roles and positioning within the neoliberal restructuring of governance relationships that was taking place during the 1980s and 1990s. Drawing on both Gramsci and Foucault, Fisher shows how states have increasingly viewed NGOs as flexible tools for maintaining or extending their power. Ferguson and Gupta explore in more detail the outsourcing of state functions to NGOs that was also part of "an emerging system of transnational governmentality" (2002, 990). Within ethnographies of globalization, NGOs began to be portrayed as both vehicles for and responses to the impacts of globalization on national and local processes. For example, Anna Tsing's ethnography (2005) describes how an emerging environmental justice movement in Indonesia contributed to a countercultural alternative to the authoritarian state, provided in part by a dynamic national NGO sector supported by transnational donors and able to mobilize global environmentalist discourses. At the same time, anthropological work explored and revealed increasingly blurred boundaries existing between NGOs and states (see, for example, Lewis 2011).

NGOs are also implicated in the operation of global markets and the forms taken by international capital. In the course of Dina Rajak's ethnography of Anglo American mining operations in South Africa, she describes how corporate social responsibility (CSR) increasingly underpins corporate power, drawing local NGOs into its activities in the context of the collapse of donor funding for NGOs in the postapartheid state. This rendered social entrepreneurship "an economic imperative for NGOs, as much as an ideological or spiritual aspiration" (2011, 187). The consequence of this shift is that CSR has taken the place of, rather than strengthened, civil society. Gift theory informs Rajak's discussion of company funding in terms of the coercive power created by conditionality and asymmetric power, "veiled by the elevation of the partnership paradigm" (189). The relationship between company and NGO has become a transaction between customer and vendor, who must provide a value for money service that yields the returns that are demanded. The company becomes different from the impartial market model of contractor within so-called new public management because the gift reciprocity expectation transforms the company "from client to patron" (192).

Studying NGOs also lead to broader themes within global restructuring that draw on ideas of "moral economy," a fertile theme of NGO work. Researchers may debate at length among themselves what is and what is not an NGO, but Dorothea Hilhorst's analysis of NGO-ing, which is highlighted by Steven Sampson in the introduction to this volume, focuses on NGO as a "claim-bearing label" (2003, 6). She asks, when an organization or group presents itself as an NGO, what should we make of the implied claim to be "doing good" and of the right of certain groups to deserve access to public or private donor funds and representation of a vulnerable target group. There is a need to problematize our assumptions about what Philip Fountain terms "the goodness of NGOs" (2011, 85), which has been a recurring theme, from William Fisher's article "Doing Good?" (1997) to Didier Fassin's work on the practice of humanitarian reason (2012). A reconfigured concept of "new moral economy" is central to Fassin's framing of a shift away from responses of solidarity to conflict, poverty, and oppression to responses based on humanitarian assistance and advocacy. What, he asks, are the social and political implications "when we use the terms of suffering to speak of inequality, when we evoke trauma rather than recognizing violence, . . . [and] when we mobilize compassion rather than justice" (2012, 8)? An anthropological engagement with NGOs therefore remains a particularly fertile site for the further investigation of issues of "goodness" and moral economy.

Finally, research on or with NGOs is about better understanding contemporary landscapes of change. Henry Delcore (2003) shows that studying local NGOs in Thailand tells about more than just "development" but also about modernity and changing cultural identities. NGOs can be viewed as "creative reactions to global integration" (61), where community leaders find their power threatened by state-led interventions and by market intrusion. NGOs and NGO-ing become vehicles for reimagining the past and remembering and reconstituting identities. Thomas Yarrow (2008) also uses the study of NGOs as a route into wider issues of history and identity, showing how NGO leaders in Ghana are embedded in historical and political contexts. These leaders identify with wider national-level change through a set of distinctive ideological beliefs about commitment, sacrifice, and activism.

Fisher argues that ethnographies of local activism and their transnational networks can help us to understand "the relationships among local lives, local social movements, and global processes" (2010, 251).

NGOs as Sites for Anthropological Reflection

NGOs play important roles as navigational tools during fieldwork, as I learned as a graduate student in Bangladesh in the late 1980s. I did not set out to engage with NGOs when I embarked on my doctoral research, which was to study changing agrarian relations at the village level under the expansion of new agricultural technologies as the country's "green revolution" was taking hold. Before leaving the UK, I had been given some local NGO contacts by my supervisor, who had long-standing ties with alternative development activists within one of the country's radical organizations. Following up on this particular contact led me to its headquarters in the capital Dhaka, and their friendly offices quickly became a valuable meeting place and hangout place for general information gathering, local gossip, and for ideas about identifying a village fieldwork site.

The NGO turned out to be incredibly useful to know. Junior staff members were usually foreigner friendly, eager to discuss development ideologies, and curious about what I was doing in their country. NGO leaders were also approachable and keen to argue politics and policy and were influential in my understanding of Bangladesh's turbulent recent history. They were also open to exchanges, where I could occasionally get introductions to useful contacts, access to desk space, and help with transport in exchange for proofreading documents or giving advice on overseas postgraduate training opportunities. There were also many international NGOs working in the country and in the relatively small expatriate community of the capital. At language training classes and later on in the field, I would encounter their staff members regularly. Outside Dhaka, NGO signboards dotted the rural landscape as I traveled around the country looking for a suitable fieldsite. These signboards frequently indicated the locations of NGO offices. I made a habit of stopping off at these offices and chatting with the occupants to gain very valuable local knowledge.

Within a relatively short period of time I became embedded in NGO worlds. These contacts helped me orient and structure my research and influenced my access to and understanding of the research environment in which I found myself. My experience of engaging anthropologically with NGOs in the field at this time was not to view NGOs as objects of my research (though later in my research career they would become such). Rather, they had been part of the wider landscape that I had to cover as a researcher.

The facilitating roles played by NGOs during my field research has shown me how NGOs may operate as connectors during ethnography, as partners for engagement, and as helpful "mirrors" of the potentials and contradictions of anthropological work.

My contacts with local NGOs were on the whole productive and comfortable for me during this period. This was not simply because they were helpers in my research rather than "other" but also because NGOs were not my research object. Anthropologists seeking to maintain such relationships while also doing "NGO-graphies" face more difficult challenges. For example, Amanda Lashaw brings out the contradictions strongly in her account of fieldwork with middle-class activist groups in the US small schools movement. She reflects on distinctive dilemmas that emerge from the relationship between ethnographers and NGO staff members when the task is to both engage with and critically examine the moral sentiments of "progressive" actors. It is unreasonable to expect that these sentiments will always be shared, leading to friction and to the ethnographer sometimes "adopting a discomforting, possibly duplicitous position" (2013, 518). Such friction could easily lead to a breakdown of the relationship between the researcher and the practitioners, as I found when studying issues of government/NGO "partnership" within a fisheries project (Lewis 1998).

NGO activists share social worlds, artifacts, and bureaucratic practices with anthropologists. This proximity has its difficulties and helps to generate the "entanglements" that Steven Sampson sets out in the introduction to this book. Annalise Riles suggests that nongovernmental networks and organizations are difficult to study because they themselves are already likely to be producing critical representations and perspectives on their work. Like academic researchers, they try to reach out to their constituents using a set of techniques that resemble the approach of the ethnographer, placing a high level of importance to being among them and being part of their communities. Such insights pose a "challenge to the distance between data and method in the ethnographic imagination of information" (2001, 191) and provide rich opportunities for reflexive critical engagement. Temple's post-development perspective on the parallels between anthropologist and NGO roles is harsher: "They share out the community, or the ethnic group, one the body, the other the soul" (1997, 203).

The field of NGOs therefore offers anthropologists a terrain upon which the boundaries between applied and pure work can continue to be questioned. Feminist scholarship has long explored such tensions, as some of the arguments within Bernal and Grewal's *Theorizing NGOs* collection suggests (2014b). For example, in Saida Hodžić's work with NGOs and women's rights activists in Ghana the collaboration that takes place between ethnographer and activist has elements that are both shared and contested and may eventually fracture or bifurcate. Hodžić concludes that "NGO activists from northern Ghana may agree with my analysis, but they 'make do' and move on. As they consider explicit and public critique of power and inequality neither gracious nor pragmatic, I take responsibility for its dangers and implications" (2014b, 245).

Others seek to renew the idea of an applied approach as "anthropology in use"; Rylko-Bauer, Singer, and Van Willegen write about the need to assert the relevance of anthropology through "strong scholarship and defensible professional ethics, and guided by concrete strategies for social engagement" (2006, 187). In a related vein, Hale makes a persuasive argument in favor of closer links between two different kinds of politically aligned anthropology: activist research, with organized activists engaged in struggle, and cultural critique, which is radical yet distanced from action and which may be explored further in the context of anthropological work with or alongside NGOs (2008). Yet we must also be careful to ensure that we continue to protect the idea that good anthropological work requires first and foremost an analytical distance that needs to be achieved prior to the anthropologist's engagement with people and communities—and cannot simply be reduced to NGO-based activism with some ethnography added.

Conclusion

Critique, collaboration, and conflict have characterized the encounter between anthropologists and NGOs. The idea of the NGO (along with the idea of civil society, the third-sector idea, and all the rest) as progressive, or as an authentic voice, remains contentious. Some scholars view the NGO as a policy instrument for undesirable forms of neoliberal restructuring, while others see it as a potential or actual site of resistance. Within first-generation studies by anthropologists, NGOs were primarily seen as but an instrument of development policy and practice, and there was a pronounced tendency for anthropologists to engage more readily with social movements as representatives of subaltern groups.

Anthropologists have continued to engage with NGOs across at least three interrelated parts of a complex landscape. NGOs have been approached as a subject in their own right, as portals into wider social processes, or as analogues that reflect back to the anthropologist a set of theoretical, practical, and methodological issues that have the potential both to discomfort and illuminate. Engagement has shifted and evolved as NGOs have grown increasingly important as social and political actors. Earlier functionalist approaches shifted toward a period of sustained distanced critique, which have in their turn evolved into the contemporary focus on "NGO-ing" as a category of practice that serves as the foundation for the second-generation studies that we have identified. Regardless of which perspective one takes, it is clear that NGOs constitute a rich area for continuing anthropological work. The engagements between anthropologists and NGOs that have taken place in the field, with all their entanglements, may offer potentially useful space and opportunity not only for methodological reflection but also for the reframing of anthropology as an engaged, relevant discipline.

Note

1. Missionary anthropology nevertheless provides a tradition of work that remains useful for researchers interested in what are now sometimes termed "faith-based organizations" within the modern NGO sector.

2
NGO Fever and Donor Regimes

Tanzanian Feminist Activism within Landscapes of Contradictions

Victoria Bernal

NGOs have opened new spaces for women's activism and created new local and transnational linkages while presenting new configurations of power and terrains of struggle. In particular, I argue that donors have come to constitute another regime with which activists must contend due to the ongoing necessity of appealing to donor priorities and complying with donor funding requirements. Such conditions create a landscape of contradictions, where the boundaries between state and nonstate, grassroots and global, altruism and self-interest, and Western and postcolonial feminisms are at times shifting and contested and at other times erased. The incongruities produced by these relationships, I argue, help to explain the ambiguous results achieved by so much NGO activity and millions of dollars of funding.

Neither the view of local organizations as representing an authentic civil society or grassroots operating independently of global power structures and finances nor the view of such organizations as merely agents of external interests or self-interested profiteers will allow us to understand the dynamics of postcolonial political activism by and for women. This chapter draws on a year of research on NGOs and donors in Dar es Salaam, Tanzania, during a period characterized by what I call "NGO fever" to reveal the contradictory forces that have both encouraged and constrained NGO efforts.

Recent scholarship has focused on the NGO sector as an essential part of the global order. But there is little consensus among scholars about how to conceptualize the role of NGOs, and the category of NGO itself lacks clear definition (Bernal and Grewal 2014a). Inderpal Grewal and I argue that this lack of definition actually contributes to the power of the category since "the NGO form" is globally legible yet serves as a capacious umbrella under which a diverse range of projects, politics, and organizational structures can exist. NGOs, moreover, are inherently ambiguous. Despite their "nongovernmental" designation, they are deeply entwined with states. They are sometimes seen as parallel states, as the glue of globalization, as translators and as intermediaries that create and sustain translocal and transnational circuits, as civil society, democratizers, and social movements, and as elites that reproduce inequality, among other things (Schuller 2009; Bornstein 2003; Appadurai 2002; Richard 2009; Thayer 2010). While initially hailed as a solution to the problems of bureaucracy and the entrenched power of the state, NGOs are increasingly viewed as part of the problems they ostensibly address, reproducing unequal relations locally and globally (Costa 2014; Hearn 2007; Velloso Santistiban 2005; Shivji 2007). The variation in scholarly positions on NGOs may be due as much to the diversity of NGOs and the resulting differences in researchers' data as to the shifting paradigms described in the introduction to this volume. However fraught the operations and achievements of these organizations may be, the appeal of the NGO form remains strong as a way for people to organize and to attract funding. Despite their ubiquity, or perhaps as a result of how quickly they have spread to many contexts in various shapes and sizes, NGOs remain elusive, problematic objects of study (Lashaw 2013; Hilhorst 2003; Sharma 2014).

NGOs are nothing if not varied, and some are clearly better than others when judged according to criteria such as egalitarian organization, efficient use of resources, and/or public impact. However, research focused on distinguishing good NGOs from bad NGOs, evaluating project outcomes, or identifying "best practices" may obscure some of the fundamental contradictions that underlie NGO activity. This approach has long characterized much of the interdisciplinary literature on NGOs that is gradually being supplanted by anthropological scholarship that refuses to start from normative assumptions. In this chapter, my approach stands in contrast to the rigorous studies that assess NGOs, projects, and related policies on various functional criteria; what I foreground is the messiness, inconsistency, and creativity that characterized the NGO scene in Dar es Salaam at the turn of the millennium. By calling it "NGO fever," I shift the focus of attention from the bureaucracy, projects, and technocratic rationalities that have dominated NGO literature to the ambiguous social relations, intense energy, and ambitious imaginaries that galvanize people around NGOs. I broaden the focus from "the NGO form" to a wider scope perhaps better described as "the NGO scene" that one might think of almost like a force field or gravitational energy that connects and animates diverse groups and individuals around NGOs including many who are not part of an NGO, among them donors, government officials, consultants, and aspiring NGOers.

I argue that NGOs are the product of, and contribute to, complex landscapes of power in ways that allow them to be simultaneously one thing and its opposite. NGOs are at once nongovernmental and governmental, deeply local and inherently foreign, an expression of the global South and an instrument of the global North, grassroots and elitist, expanding possibilities for women's activism and yet also limiting those possibilities. NGOs' relationships with donors are a particular source of contradictions and my primary focus in this chapter. I argue that, taken together, the practices of international donors have regime-like effects, governing the NGO landscape in ways that stimulate and constrain NGO activity. I start the discussion by situating my research in the context of Dar es Salaam in the grip of "NGO fever" alongside reflections on NGOs and knowledge production. In the sections that follow I analyze the conditions that give rise to NGO fever, investigate what I call the international donor regime, and explore the quandaries generated by donor money. Donor money can have its insidious aspects, one of which I have dubbed "the monetization of activism"—which, through practices like paying people to attend workshops, distorts the conditions of possibility for activist work.

Research Dilemmas

Conducting research on NGOs is a sensitive and frustrating process. Obstacles and setbacks in my research felt like personal failures or a lack of hospitality on the part of Tanzanians. Reflecting back on the experience, however, I am now able to see how problems arose from the nature of NGOs themselves. There were three main dilemmas I encountered in the field. First, it is often difficult to observe how NGOs operate. If the NGO has an office, it may be staffed by a few people working on computers, but there is little to see there. Grant proposals are being drafted, reports written, and events are being planned perhaps, but this is not easily subject to observation in office visits. Some NGOs do not even have offices. Events such as workshops, conferences, and public outreach activities provide one way of seeing NGOs in action. Interviews with individuals across a range of positions within the NGO field and sitting in on meetings provide other ways.

The second dilemma I encountered is that the dependence on donor funding creates the need for NGOs to constantly maintain a good public image and cordial relations with donors. NGOs in Tanzania were wary of exposing their behind-the-scenes operations, wishing to guard against anything that might detract from their public profile, and people were similarly wary of voicing critical views that might be construed as bad-mouthing by donors. Thus, conducting candid interviews and gaining access behind the scenes were delicate matters. In the end I suppose the magic of participant observation is that if you come around often enough, you eventually become familiar to people, and the barriers begin to erode, and stray remarks and chance events gradually begin to connect and coalesce around common themes.

The third dilemma arose from the fact that NGOs were already spending time and effort actively engaging with foreign donors who wanted meetings with them and information from them as part of the process of applying for funding. Tanzanian NGOs were thus subjected to scrutiny and site visits, the purpose of which was to assess how any funding received was being used. As a researcher, I was a foreigner from the global North who appeared to want similar things from NGOs that donors wanted, while having nothing to offer in return. In other circumstances people may welcome a foreign researcher as an international connection. In my case, many of the people involved in NGOs were already enmeshed in international networks that provided them with a wide range of resources and opportunities. Donor-funded travel to workshops and training in other countries was a common perk that also facilitated further networking in NGO and donor circuits. Even as the people I met pursued opportunities with donors, they experienced their own form of donor fatigue and complained of feeling inundated by foreigners.

All of these factors make NGOs an elusive object of study. They are everywhere and nowhere at the same time. NGO fever was raging like a contagion that affected everything but at the same time had no clear form or boundaries. I had arrived intending to focus my research on women's political activism through NGOs, but my interest soon shifted to the nexus of relationships that animated the NGO scene, specifically those between NGOs and donors. In Dar es Salaam I interviewed donors and Tanzanian NGOers and would-be NGOers. I conducted participant observation at various public events and in informal settings. I visited offices, centers, agencies, and embassies. I attended seminars, workshops, and meetings and compiled a media archive of press coverage of the NGO scene. On a few occasions I was able to sit in on meetings between NGO leaders and donors and was thus able to observe these women interacting and negotiating (both the European and North American donors and the Tanzanian activists working on gender issues were predominantly women). I was very aware of the ways NGOers were actively engaged in knowledge production and analysis of their own NGOs, the field of NGO activity, and donors. My research efforts were not unique but intersected with and built upon the expertise of the people I encountered in the field. This research was conducted in a particular place, Dar es Salaam, during a particular time, 1999, that allowed me to observe an NGO boom in full swing. NGO fever may happen or has happened in different ways at other places and times, but the conundrums and contradictions of donor funding and NGO proliferation I uncovered are significant because they are not unique to the time and place of my observations but point to challenges that are widespread.

NGO Fever in Millennial Dar es Salaam

The rapid proliferation of NGOs was striking when I arrived in Tanzania's capital city in 1999 to study women's political activism. According to a US Embassy employee working with NGOs in Tanzania at the time, 80 percent of NGOs were women's organizations. One of my first field note entries observes that "the internationalization of Tanzania is very evident in Dar. The newspaper headlines every day report on some new aid from abroad, while at the same time running articles on local officials saying dependency should be reduced. Everywhere around the city there are signs for the offices of international agencies, NGOs, and so forth." I was struck by the way abbreviations and acronyms pervaded everyone's speech; "alphabet soup," as some people called it, was the order of the day. In addition to terms for organizational forms—NGOs, CBOs, and CSOs—people spoke of TANGO, TAMWA, TAWLA, TGNP, WRDP, WLAC, and WILDAF, among others. (In these actual names of organizations, the Ts stand for "Tanzanian" and the Ws stand for "women.") Elsewhere in this chapter I avoid naming individuals and organizations because my goal is not to separate good and bad NGOs or donors but to examine the spectrum of compromise, struggle, and competition arising out of the complex relationships operating in the NGO field.

From the start of my fieldwork I was impressed by the high visibility of women and gender issues in public life. An early field note observes that "the press covers gender issues virtually on a daily basis. There are pieces written by women journalists, reportage on the activities of women's organizations, and on significant women. Women leaders of organizations are quoted on various matters and women appear in photos." NGOs were regularly in the news. An article in Tanzania's *Daily News*, for example, reported on First Lady Mama Mkapa's visit to the United States, where she "attended a dinner hosted by non-governmental organizations operating projects in Tanzania." The article went on to mention that "Mama Mkapa who is also the chairperson of the Equal Opportunities for all Trust Fund [NGO] . . . received text books worth one million dollars" (*Daily News* 1999). Just the day before, a front-page article in the same paper with the headline "Dar Vows to Cut Down Dependence" paraphrased President Mkapa as saying that his government had "managed to restore donor's confidence by enforcing financial discipline and the donors were now ready to assist in various sectors" (Kitururu 1999). The headline of another *Daily News* article announced, "Sida [Swedish International Development Agency] to Give Women NGO 25m [25 million Tanzanian shillings]" (Mtema 1999), while an article in the Tanzanian newspaper the *Guardian*, a top news provider, was headlined "Canada to Provide 7.2m for Human Rights Training" (*Guardian* 1999). This article explained that the funds would come from the Canadian International Development Agency (CIDA) to support two Tanzanians from different NGOs to take a three-week course in Montreal.

A typical article is this one from the *Guardian*: under the headline "Swedish Aid Helps Tanzanians Combat Poverty, Improve Lives," the article reported on "Sweden's growing partnership with Tanzania," mentioning sums in the millions and billions of shillings, and asserted that "judging from the Swedish-supported programs, there is no doubt that eradicating poverty and social sector development are given high priority, with particular emphasis on gender equality" (Liganga 1999). There were many articles reporting on workshops, like an article in the *Guardian* describing a "women empowerment project" held at a luxury beachfront hotel organized by the British Council and two Tanzanian women's NGOs (Lyimo 1999). Another article, describing a "gender training workshop" sponsored by the United States Agency for International Development (USAID), quoted a USAID official at length but hardly mentioned the leading women's NGO that was involved, describing them as "participants" when it did so, thus giving most of the publicity and credit for the event to the donor (Kilivata 1999). Stories and headlines created the sense that money was flowing in from donors and that NGOs were proliferating. "Arusha Hosts Capacity Building Workshop" reads one headline, while another says "New NGO Determined to Keep City Clean" and another announces that "Moshi NGO Spreads Service to Rural Areas." Newspapers also featured notices placed by donors soliciting funding proposals.

The late 1990s was a key era in the development of NGO culture and practice, not only in Tanzania but in many regions of the world due to the rise of neoliberal policies that saw decreased aid going to states and more international funding channeled to nongovernmental organizations (see, for example, Thayer [2010] on Brazil and Schuller [2012] on Haiti). The 1995 UN Fourth World Conference on Women in Beijing had drawn global attention to NGOs, in particular, as vehicles for women's empowerment (Bernal and Grewal 2014a). While a number of Tanzanian women's NGOs were formed in the 1980s, women's rights activists explained that the real boom in Tanzania took off in the mid-1990s, as Tanzanian women organized in preparation for the 1995 UN Conference on Women in Beijing. National preliminary meetings brought government, NGOs, and citizens together around gender issues (Bouvard 1996). After the conference, Tanzania's NGO sector continued to gain momentum as more women and more donors got involved. These resources and activities produced workshops, seminars, trainings, and outreach efforts to different populations and constituencies, as well as generating documentation, research, and policy recommendations on gender issues. They were also producing new challenges.

Tanzania was experiencing a watershed moment. Donor funding was flowing into the country, and NGOs were not only growing but being formed in response to new opportunities. Everyone seemed to be or to want to be part of the NGO scene in some way or other. This included Mama Mkapa, the then-president's wife, who had launched an organization focused on women's empowerment called Equal Opportunity for All Trust Fund, EOTF. It has since broadened its focus. According to its website, its mission is "to facilitate and support all segments of society in all works of life economically, socially, educationally and legally." However "women's empowerment" is a major theme listed below the organization's name. This example illustrates some of the ambiguity surrounding the nongovernmental nature of NGOs in that an organization headed by the wife of the president clearly has ties to government and will be perceived that way even if the ties are informal rather than official. This example also reflects how strategic considerations related to funding shape NGOs. The shifting trends and varied priorities among donors are the most likely rationale behind EOTF's attempt to simultaneously be about empowering women and to be for everybody in all walks of life. EOTF is certainly not the only NGO claiming to address an increasing range of issues. Claiming a broad scope of possible activities and concerns provides flexibility, making it possible to seek diverse sources of funding since money is often earmarked by donors for specific issues.

The frantic energy of the NGO sector, NGO fever, did not take hold simply because women yearned for empowerment; nor was it driven by other very real and pressing needs of many Tanzanians. What animated so much activity around and through NGOs was the lure and potential of donor funding that opened up a range of possibilities and generated new circuits through which resources, jobs, and other benefits were distributed. Not only was information about all kinds of donor funding and related NGO initiatives reported in the media every day, it was also littered around the cityscape, where banners, billboards, and signs announcing workshops and other initiatives were visible along public roads.

One reason for the dynamism stimulated by donors is that the funding of NGOs is unlike the funding of most development projects or infrastructure initiatives, which is channeled through governments or corporations. While such efforts may ultimately benefit ordinary people with better living conditions, improved roads, or electric power, the projects offer little chance for citizens to access resources directly, obtain a salary, or partici-pate fully. In contrast, NGO funding was scattered and piecemeal, involving small amounts as well as large ones; it was almost personal in that money seemed to flow to and from individuals rather than along established chan-nels between institutions. NGO funding initiatives offered the prospect of being accessible to a wide range of people, spawning a multitude of dreams of personal and societal transformation through donor funding.

When I asked two women their views on a particular NGO and whether they were involved in any organization, one immediately remarked to the other, "This makes me think we ought to start an organization." Starting an NGO was akin to being self-employed; there was no barrier to entry into the field. At one NGO event I attended, each person present introduced herself by name and organizational affiliation or occupation. When one Tanzanian woman, after giving her name, was asked where she was coming from, she replied, "I am not doing much," prompting the facilitator to quip, "freelance activist" and everybody laughed. The impact of donors might have been particularly profound in millennial Tanzania because other avenues of eco-nomic advancement or even day-to-day survival were so few.

One result of these circumstances is that Tanzanian NGOs were being produced and animated as much by foreign funds, initiatives, and dis-courses as by anything or anyone Tanzanian. Many Tanzanian NGOers I met were fluent speakers of the international language of democracy, hu-man rights, gender issues, and development. Indeed, I noticed that when speaking the national language Kiswahili, people often struggled awkwardly for ad hoc translations of key terms such as "gender mainstreaming" or else simply adopted them in their English form (a way of expressing things that people sometimes called "kiswahenglish"). Tanzanian women's rights activ-ists needed to master certain ways of talking about issues in order to com-municate with donors. This had mixed effects, since any jargon can easily become a set of superficial catchphrases. At the same time, however, hav-ing an international language for naming and addressing gender issues also can be a powerful tool for feminist organizing across cultural boundaries.

While, on the surface, the role of foreign donor funds was to support the efforts of Tanzanian NGOs working on particular problems, NGOs were instead popping up or shifting focus in response to potential funding. This created a proliferation of NGOs that existed on the ground to varying de-grees, from the proverbial "briefcase NGO" (a single individual claiming to be the head of an NGO) to well-established NGOs that had offices and paid staff members. No one knows for sure how many Tanzanian NGOs ex-isted at the end of the 1990s and the answer would, moreover, depend on what one counts as an NGO. Today, some NGOs exist, at least on paper, simply because they are officially registered; others may be active but unregistered. In 2012, according to the Tanzanian Association of NGOs (TANGO) there were nine thousand registered NGOs in Tanzania, which gives some sense of the scale of the phenomenon. What I observed in 1999 was a fertile spawning ground where many NGOs were being born or incubating, some to never really see the light of day (or donor funding), others to have a short-lived existence struggling with limited success for resources to sustain themselves, while still others had already established a record of activity and relationships with donors. The most successful NGOs managed to keep funding streams coming in, giving them a more permanent existence beyond any particular project or donor of the moment.

"NGO fever" captures the free-for-all energy, enthusiasm, and seemingly wild proliferation of NGOs I observed in Dar es Salaam. No one knew what all of these NGOs were doing, who they represented, where their funding came from, or even whether they were who and what they said they were. Many people I met were connected to an NGO in some way, whether as an activist or a community constituent, or they aspired to be. NGOs, moreover, often operate more like networks than bounded organizations, bringing people together in connection with projects or events when funding was available and shrinking when funding dried up. In this dynamic field, moreover, people moved from working in local NGOs to working for embassies and international agencies and vice versa. Many academics at the University of Dar es Salaam also had sideline careers as consultants to foreign donors or had launched their own NGOs. There was a revolving door between donors' gender issues desks (units or focal points working on gender issues) and NGO personnel so that, for example, Tanzanian women hired by foreign aid offices to provide local expertise on gender issues would move on to become leaders of NGOs while NGO activists left for jobs with foreign foundations or embassies. Individuals maintained ties to a range of organizations, thus maximizing their networks and their chances of getting paid work or other benefits if funding came through for any of them. NGOs remained in flux, receiving various and changing sources of funds and engaging in the varied institutional relationships associated with them. Shifting personnel, networks, and revolving doors across local and foreign governmental and nongovernmental organizations characterized the complex, globalized terrains of Tanzanian NGO work.

The leader of one NGO told me proudly that their "trainers eventually become full-fledged consultants who are sought out all over, so we have to recruit new ones." She herself had started off working for a European embassy before moving into full-time NGO work. In another conversation, a woman told me about one former leader of an NGO: "She proved herself. She proved that she was good. She has a good job now with UNESCO." As she then reflected on that NGO's prospects for the future, she remarked, "But what constituency is there? I don't think there is one. Without her there is nothing." As the focus of our conversation shifted to a different NGO, she commented, "They are closing down because the funding has disappeared." (In fact, the organization has managed to survive up to now.) She then speculated about another, well-known NGO, saying, "I also wonder about [that NGO]. They moved into so many areas. They thought the funding would never stop, but I don't know if they can keep it up." The same NGO came up in a conversation I had with a USAID official who said, "[That NGO] is essentially Zakia Mohammed [the organization's leader]. Without her, there is not much."

Some of these remarks may be cynical or pessimistic in their take on the situation. But they also reflect the vitality, instability, and ambiguity of the NGO scene in Dar at the time. People were coming and going from NGO leadership and donor employment, funding was coming for and then disappearing from particular issues and particular organizations. Donor priorities and personnel changed, and it was often hard to tell what, if anything, stood behind or beyond the public face of any given NGO. I explore these issues further in the following section, where I analyze the consequences of donor funding practices.

I was surprised to find that the funding pipeline flowing from donors into Tanzania was often allocated based on little information or research. For example, in 1999 the US Embassy put out a call for proposals from NGOs and selected a number of organizations for funding. When it tried to notify the successful NGOs of their grants, some of them could not even be found. Apparently they existed only on paper and were unable even to sustain a working mobile phone number or address for the length of time the funding process took. In the course of fieldwork, I became familiar with numerous NGOs and women working on gender issues, so I was puzzled by a newspaper story about a huge sum being given by a European donor to a woman of whom I had never heard, heading an organization of which I had never heard. According to the article, the funds would support work on eradicating female genital cutting. When I asked around among the women NGOers I knew, they had never heard of this woman or her organization either. These kinds of funding decisions on the part of donors helped fuel NGO fever by contributing to the sense that anything might be possible with an NGO, that anyone might get lucky with funding. For activists as well as donors, this sense of randomness drove a speculative market in NGO activity.

Yet, when I asked one of the women's rights activists about the case of the woman who had received funds for her project to prevent female genital cutting, she commented, "Well, maybe she will do some good." Her optimistic comment should be considered seriously because the actors on the scene in Dar, whether donors or Tanzanian citizens, were not necessarily only pursuing self-interested agendas, nor can their activities be understood solely from the perspective of the corrupting influence of money and the power donors exercise through it. Such a cynical view fits comfortably into simplistic stereotypes about corruption in Africa that ultimately have little explanatory value and obscure the role of the global North in creating conditions conducive to corruption (Smith 2010). Corruption, moreover, fails to account for the fact that so many of the participants and aspirants I encountered in the field were ardent in their commitment to issues and their desire for change. Donor funding appeared to offer the possibility of bringing about change and that prospect was part of the excitement motivating people. Some of the expatriate women working in the donor field were also feminists seriously committed to ideals of gender equality. Through the work of NGOs, gender issues were being raised in many contexts. Activists were networking with each other and with various communities as well as lobbying government and forging connections with activists in other countries. Women were gaining knowledge and experience as leaders, speakers, and as authorities on gender issues. Their visibility and status in NGOs gave them access to media coverage and to government officials they would not otherwise have had. Yet NGO fever also had some disturbing symptoms and many of them were tied up with money.

The Donor Regime: Governing the Nongovernmental

Donor funding enables much NGO activity and this certainly was what was most obvious during my fieldwork in Dar es Salaam. But in less visible ways, donor funding also constrains NGO activity. Tanzanian women's NGOs were not simply struggling in relation to the Tanzanian state and various local authorities; they were also struggling with what I came to think of as an international donor regime. Relations between donors and activists in the NGO field are shot through with questions of power, about who gets to decide what, about who takes credit for what, and, at the most fundamental level, about the degree to which funding creates a certain kind of chain of command. The donor landscape like that of NGOs is quite diverse, but there was considerable convergence in donors' focus of interest on women due to global trends. Donors also shared a bureaucratic culture and even notions of what constitutes a "good NGO." The "success" of an NGO in the eyes of donors was generally tied to their record of fiscal management and accountability rather than to the impact of the NGO's activity. But while supposedly objective measures of accountability like budgets and reports purport to be reflections of internal NGO management skills and practices, there was a significant subjective aspect to donors' assessments. In practice evaluations had a lot to do with how an NGO managed their relations with donors and packaged themselves for donor consumption. In order to be successful, NGOs had to develop skills in donor relations, navigate intangible emotions of trust and respect, and attend to image management and reputation.

Conversations with donors in Dar revealed shared discourses and opinions. What varied most was that some of the people working for or with the donors clearly knew something about Tanzanian society, while others possessed mainly the stock set of ideas, described in donor terms as "not country-specific." In an article on civil society and development, Mercer and Green (2013, 107) argue that there is a "policy template [that] is to be realized on the ground in Tanzania, as elsewhere, through targeted donor funding. It is a template because it provides a standard set of replicable tools for assembling a national civil society sector with a specific set of roles. It is globalized because it can, in theory, be replicated wherever donors choose to do so." The content of such templates may shift in accordance with new trends and paradigms, but at any given time, they constitute an accepted set of assumptions and practices that guide donors and create homogeneity.

In Dar, the donors, in addition to relying to some extent on standard templates, undertook efforts to communicate among themselves and in a loose way coordinate their activities. One donor, for example, was disturbed to learn that a proposal they had funded was simultaneously funded by someone else, going so far as to try to get their money back from the NGO. A major European donor state organized a large meeting of donors to discuss funding priorities and tactics that I attended along with some representatives of Tanzanian government ministries. No NGOs or representatives of Tanzanian civil society were invited. While donors were far from monolithic, the degree of commonality, convergence, and coordination I observed had regime-like qualities.

The international donor regime exerts its control in the NGO field in several ways. Donors set priorities about the issues to be addressed and the kinds of activities through which to address them. They demand certain kinds of accountability, with particular emphasis on financial reporting. They establish timetables and deadlines, require that particular types of reports are produced and submitted, and so on. This process may reflect global trends in neoliberal ideologies and audit culture, but its significance extends far beyond mere bureaucratization or the professionalization of NGOs. What is at stake are the kinds of political, social, and economic issues that are addressed or neglected (conditions that depend on whether or not they match donor interest and receive sustained support) and the forms and avenues of citizens' activism.

Much of the international funding comes from donor governments, and the nongovernmental sector in places like Tanzania is largely sustained by government funding, just not that of their own government. Key donors contributing to NGO fever in Dar included government agencies such as Sida (Swedish International Development Agency), CIDA (Canadian International Development Agency), USAID (United States Agency for International Development), the British Council, foreign embassies such as the Netherlands Embassy, the Royal Danish Embassy, and the Irish Embassy, international agencies such as UNFPA (United Nations Population Fund) and UNICEF (United Nations Children's Fund), along with private foundations including the Konrad Adenauer Fund and the Friedrich-Ebert-Stiftung.

NGO activity, even where it is regulated by the state, is largely governed in practice by this donor regime that sets the conditions under which NGOs sustain their activities or fail. NGOs are most directly held accountable to their funders. This accountability is tied to actual accounting, to financial transparency, and represented in the reports and documentation required to show that money allocated by donors for particular purposes was used for those purposes. But the sway donors hold over recipients and potential recipients is much broader than that, as NGO fever makes clear.

Furthermore, despite the purported value donors place on fiscal accountability and transparency, donor money and the power relations associated with it are largely hidden in the NGO field. When an NGO holds an event, publishes a newsletter, or does a radio show, what comes across to most observers is the name of the NGO or its representative and the issue being raised. Sometimes the donor sponsoring an activity gets publicity, sometimes not. What is never visible is the process whereby this particular NGO was funded rather than another one, why this particular issue was selected as the focus, and why it is being addressed in this particular way. Donors play a huge, yet often hidden, role in all of these processes in Tanzania. There is no public accounting, oversight, reporting, or review of the entire scope and process of donor funding or of NGO activities. Various amounts of money change hands and actions are mobilized in this vast field that, while highly visible, still remains very murky behind the public facades of donor and NGO offices.

Ultimately, donors possess power since money gives them great leverage. NGOs, however, have developed various strategies to assert autonomy despite their dependence on donor funding. The underlying tensions between

NGOs and donors raise questions about what is at stake politically as activism gets channeled into NGOs that are funded not by their own members or even fellow citizens but by foreign sources. Even where goals (such as getting more female candidates to run for office) were shared and agreed upon, tensions arose because NGO leaders did not want to simply implement other people's projects but had their own ideas. Some NGOers spoke of this in terms of their efforts "to educate donors," and some strategically cultivated relationships with particular donors they viewed as less controlling and more receptive. The inequality of donor-beneficiary dynamics was experienced as institutionally limiting, and sometimes as personally grating. One NGO leader, describing her meeting with a major donor, told me, "I said to her, 'I came here because you invited me to a meeting. I did not come here with a begging bowl.'" The image of the begging bowl conveys the uncomfortable feeling of being treated as a supplicant. It also reminds us of the poverty in Tanzania that makes it difficult for NGOs to obtain local resources for their work.

One problem with dependence on foreign support is that donor agendas and priorities tend to be short-term and result-oriented. Activists complained, for example, that seen from the donors' perspective, democracy means electoral politics, defined in terms of voting and running for office. Activists, in contrast, approached democracy as a way of life in which decisions are made with popular participation and there are mechanisms for holding public officials accountable to their constituencies. Thus, the very process of democratization being promoted by international agencies was being stymied by the way they exercised control over local NGOs, prioritized issues, and made only very narrow, conservative goals worth proposing for funding. This results in a process of depoliticizing politics, breaking it down into small technical steps that can be carried out by different organizations and on a project-to-project basis. In 1994, Ferguson called development aid the "anti-politics machine." A similar logic operates in the NGO field of civil society organizations. Donors focusing on democracy promote activities that are largely about form rather than content. For example, donors focused on elections and on getting more women to run for political office but without much recognition or engagement with the actual political issues at stake in Tanzania. As Bernal and Grewal (2014a, 10) point out, moreover, however progressive an NGO's goals might be, "the NGO is not radical in its form." The scattered and piecemeal approach to democratization, women's empowerment, and other issues that northern donors support through NGOs may create conditions that make it harder for powerful social movements to develop in the global South.

An interview I conducted with two USAID staff members (both of them women—one American and one Tanzanian) working in the democracy and governance section is telling. The Tanzanian staff member said, "You have to realize this is just starting in Tanzania. Most of the NGOs are new and they are very small. There is usually just one person who is doing everything and they don't have resources so even that person has another job. They may have some help in the office, but if the main person is not there, there is no one for you to talk to in the office. They don't have much capacity." I then asked how USAID formed relationships with NGOs and oversaw the funding. The American staff member explained: "Up to now it has been very small amounts for very specific tasks like workshops or reproducing materials, $5,000 to $10,000. We look at them first to make sure they have the capacity to carry out the task and administer the funds, but since it is very specific, there hasn't been much need to assess the organizations. We run an ad in the newspaper asking for proposals and that's how we select them." She added, "We are interested in capacity building. We plan to offer training in proposal writing, development, and management." In effect, USAID will spend money to teach Tanzanian NGOs how to be better recipients of aid. As one Tanzanian activist put it: "The donors need us, too. They have to spend their money."

The Wages of Activism

The influx of donor funds gave rise to what I call "the monetization of activism." Donors were not simply providing funds to help NGOs achieve things, they were causing NGOs to come into being. Furthermore, through earmarking funds for certain issues and activities, donors determined the kinds of NGOs that could emerge, survive, and/or become significant actors, and donors helped set NGO agendas. From a perspective of empowerment, civil society, and democracy this is disturbing indeed.

Thayer argues, based on research in Brazil, that the relations connecting southern activists and NGOs to donors and agencies in the global North can be understood as "shadow commodity chains" through which material resources from the North are exchanged for symbolic resources from the South (Thayer n.d.). Here, however, I am not so much concerned with symbolic value as with the fundamental material foundation of these relations— money. In Dar, it seemed that everything had a price. For example, it was established practice to pay participants for attending workshops. Ostensibly this started as a way to compensate people for taking time off of work and to reimburse them for transportation costs. But, the effects of these incentives were insidious. The relative value of various activities was influenced by funding or potential opportunities for funding.

This process increased the power of donors since, if everything is monetized, those with the money dominate. Midway through my research in 1999 the Tanzanian government banned workshops on the grounds that they were taking so many civil servants away from their work. Donors and NGOs then began to call such gatherings "consultative meetings," and the practice continued. The way in which the monetization of activism enhances donors' power is illustrated in what one woman told me about her experiences: "I was invited, this was funded by the Friedrich-Ebert-Stiftung. We came for one hour, there was no time to really discuss, and then they gave us each thirty thousand shillings [approximately forty dollars at the time] for participating and they say we were consulted. I was upset about this, because what if I don't want to be associated with what is in the document and they will say, 'You were consulted.' Then I thought if not me, someone else will take the thirty thousand shillings anyway." An expatriate working with the Institute of Finance Management lamented that "academics here are used to being paid for everything they do by NGOs, so there is no independent motivation. If you come with a purely academic interest, no one can be bothered. . . . We wanted people to write and submit proposals, but no one took initiative. We had to pay just to get people to even submit proposals to us." Professors, he said, earned the equivalent of about one hundred dollars per month at the university, while they receive that much per day consulting for NGOs. An NGO leader had this to say about the problem of paid consultancies: "How do we get academicians to be activist? Look at gender activists at the university, even gender activists. We have so few coming out, out of their little boxes. They never leave their little boxes to help us. They can reflect on a process once it's out there, but what about participating in the process? They're busy with their consultancies." If money is generating so much activity, then without money it becomes more difficult to motivate people to carry out the work that needs to be done for an NGO to operate. Donors set such a high standard of remuneration that unpaid involvement in NGO activities and even salaried government employment pale in comparison. In this way funding is not simply enabling but also disabling because it fosters a culture of activism for pay. NGOs and issues that do not attract donor funding are then marginalized.

It is difficult to follow the money and the decision-making processes surrounding donor and NGO relationships with regard to money. Neither donors nor local NGOs are transparent about funding. NGOs do not want to encourage competition for funds on the part of other organizers, and neither do they want to be seen as creatures of the Netherlands Embassy, USAID, UNDP, or any other funder. On the website of one established Tanzanian

NGO that I looked at while writing this chapter, I found a link about their "foreign partners" ("partners" being a widely used term that covers up a lot of inequality), but when I clicked on it I only got a page that said "coming soon." As the preceding discussion indicates, the problem of donor money is not as simple as quid pro quo or donors imposing an agenda on NGOs. Rather, it involves a process of influence and shifting priorities in ways that alter the context of NGO activities.

Even though people are not simply "in it for the money," money matters, and the ebbs and flows of resources have a significant impact. The conundrums of donor largesse were something about which NGOers themselves expressed concern. NGOers were not only engaged in managing relationships with specific donors but also grappling with the general form of these relationships and developing strategies to advance their own various agendas, while reflecting on these conditions and processes.

At a seminar held by an NGO I was struck by a presentation given by an activist who was also a lecturer at the University of Dar es Salaam. This was remarkable because those who gathered at such events were mainly Tanzanians involved in NGOs or hoping to become involved. Indeed, part of the motivation for attending these kinds of events was the opportunity to network. I used this myself as a research strategy. The speaker explained that "foreign/international NGOs have their own agenda and their own priorities. If you go for funding, they say, 'We don't have money for that, why don't you apply for this?' Sometimes they look for organizations that can do *their* work. I say, '*Their work.*' They say, 'We have money for governance, civic education. We don't have money for land [rights].'" His mention of land rights relates to the fact that many NGOs had just been involved in a successful nationwide movement to reform land tenure laws in ways that would expand women's land rights in particular. Therefore, the idea of donors refusing to fund land reform was a powerful example of how donor priorities can diverge from local interests.

The speaker also told the attendees: "Sometimes NGOs have to comply with terms and conditions. If an NGO wants to survive, you need to be seen doing something. If you fail to get money for what you want to do, you're compelled to get money for something else to keep you busy for the next few months." As his analysis shows, not only do donor funds come with "terms and conditions," they render certain things possible while at the same time constraining other possibilities. His advice that "you need to be seen doing something" highlights the subtle, yet pervasive influence of donors as the arbiters of NGO survival and as a prime audience for whom appearances must be kept up even when they are not funding you.

Conclusion

While the global circulation of universalist discourses such as human rights and gender equality has been the subject of much debate, less attention has been accorded to the transformations of public cultures and politics within national arenas as these have been globalized through diverse linkages that connect local activists and organizations to foreign regimes and resources. Analyses of women's struggles, NGOs, and democratization are inadequate if they fail to capture the complex interpenetrations of local and global governmentalities. Civil society and "local" NGOs have been seen as local alternatives to states within states; yet their resources, priorities, discourses, and practices often depend on support from foreign governments. This creates ambiguity in the distinctions between governments and so-called nongovernmental organizations. It gives rise to contradictions in the relations of accountability that are supposed to connect government, civil society, and wider constituencies within the nation.

My point is not that there is a need to purge local activism of donor involvement, which would be impossible in any case. It is rather that we can only understand the real struggles around issues of democratization, the empowerment of women, and civil society by seeing these global relationships and processes as an integral part of the conditions of activism and organizing. A new picture of NGO work emerges when we include all the efforts surrounding relations with donors from courting and proposal writing to reporting and handling site visits. Much of the quotidian work of NGOs involves raising funds and managing and maintaining relationships with donors rather than working on issues, mobilizing constituents, lobbying government, or in other ways pursuing their goals. Hence, much of the struggle in which Tanzanian NGOs were engaged, thus, was over the conditions governing the existence and workings of NGOs themselves and how to develop strategies to counter the constraints of the donor regime. To this end, some NGOs were working in coalitions, banding together, and dividing the labor as they did in the land reform struggle. NGOs also had established an umbrella organization, TANGO, which is an association of Tanzanian NGOs, and others had created FemAct, a coalition of NGOs working on gender issues. One NGO sought to reduce the work of managing multiple donor relationships through adopting the practice of "basket funding," where donors agree to contribute to a master budget and to receive a common report and accounting.

The wider context for developments in Tanzania includes the way that civil society has been constructed as a solution to political problems in Africa. Donors have bypassed what have been seen as inefficient and/or corrupt states and channeled resources to local NGOs instead. But the implications for power relations are profound. Donors can act much more directly through the Tanzanian NGOs that they fund (and in some cases virtually create) than they are able to do with government institutions. The flourishing of NGO civil society, which can be taken as a hallmark of an active citizenry, may thus mask fissures in the political arena, where local NGOs are primarily held accountable to governments or foreign donor organizations. The globalization of civil society through NGOs, moreover, is occurring at multiple levels so that local organizations are as imbricated in global circuits as in local ones, nationalist and parochial interests operate transnationally at global levels, and political spheres, publics, and constituencies are reconfigured and renegotiated.

Maybe what I observed in Dar es Salaam is indicative of another stage of North-South power configurations on the global level—from colonial rule, to neocolonial domination by trade and investment relations, to a new kind of political order where "human rights," "gender equality," "the rule of law," "transparency," and the like serve the global North as a means of exercising surveillance and intervention across national boundaries. However, this view must be tempered by a recognition of the women and other activists who are doing important work of various kinds and whose work is sustained by the support they recieve from international sources. Despite the fact that the activities of Tanzanian NGOs are made possible largely through funding from non-Tanzanian sources, whether from foreign (northern) governments, northern NGOs, or international agencies, it would be a mistake to dismiss these organizations as inauthentic and to search for some pure form of indigenous or grassroots feminism. Tanzanian women's activism in NGOs illustrates the complex and contradictory power relations at work where it is no longer possible to draw clear boundaries separating governmental and nongovernmental, local and foreign, grassroots initiatives and international agendas.

Acknowledgment

Research in Tanzania was supported by a grant from the Wenner-Gren Foundation for Anthropological Research and a Fulbright fellowship.

3
Habits of the Heart

Grassroots "Revitalization" and State Transformation in Serbia

Theodora Vetta

During the turbulent 1990s and particularly after the overthrow of President Slobodan Milošević in 2000, Serbia experienced its own version of the so-called associational revolution, that is, a spectacular proliferation of NGOs. Like other cases of the postcommunist world, "civil society" as a political slogan, with NGOs as its main carriers, acquired an axiomatic status (Hann and Dunn 1996). The Western international community treated local NGOs as key symbolic operators of a distinct ideological field. Within a hegemonic analytical framework of "dictatorship versus democracy," NGOs acquired political and moral significance. In the case of Serbia, local NGOs were not only celebrated for their activist past against Serbian institutional nationalism but were also considered, after 2000, as the "watchdogs" of European integration. This distinction was not simply discursive, nor did it have solely symbolic connotations. As I argue elsewhere (Vetta 2017) many of the more established Belgrade NGOs had endorsed a sort of *practical cosmopolitanism*, a symbolic capital of identity distinction that played a constitutive role in their consolidation as a new social actor—courtiers or brokers (Bierschenk and Olivier de Sardan 1993; Blundo 1995; Lewis and Mosse 2006)—in the emerging political scene since 2000.

As NGOs were self-proclaimed and recognized by their donors as the "cultural infrastructure of society," they assumed an additional moral duty to transmit the new democratic culture to unreformed "others." These others consisted of the civil servants, stigmatized for their assumed communist mentality of dependency (Vetta 2012), or those who supported nationalist political options. In this chapter, I focus on such a democracy-promotion project, the USAID-funded Community Revitalization through Democratic Action (CRDA). CRDA started its operations in the summer of 2001, that is, just a few months after the so-called bulldozer revolution and Milošević's overthrow in 2000. Implemented by four US NGOs, its main goal was to foster local democratic activism by ultimately creating local NGOs outside the usual metropolitan spaces. Thus, NGOs were both the means and the target goal of this intervention.

I collected my data in two phases: first, during the last year of the program in 2007, and second in 2008, after CRDA officially terminated its actions and informants were not under any contract obligation. My primary intention here is not on strictly depicting the project's success and "lessons learned" but on approaching it as a window for understanding the NGO phenomenon: What do democratization/NGOs actually do? How are this particular narrative structure (embodied in Western imaginary) and the material/symbolic resources it mobilizes subscribed in their very sociopolitical consequences? How do such NGOs create new social realities and reconfigure existing structures of power relations (see also Elyachar 2005; Heemeryck 2010; Hilhorst 2003; Kamat 2002; Sampson 2003; Schuller 2009; Tvedt 1998; Wedel 2001)? My aim is to go beyond some ahistorical or locally confined understanding of embeddedness, by situating NGO formations and aid within wider global processes of structural transformations: namely within the political project of neoliberalism (Wacquant 2012). As I demonstrate, NGOs acquired a very important role in postsocialist settings (and beyond) not so much in building some independent civil society but in contributing to a particular state restructuring at the grassroots level. Against a totalizing and acontextual discourse of the "neoliberal dismantling of state" (Clarke 2008; Peck and Tickell 2002), my goal is to carry out a grounded analysis of the project's claims and practices in order to grasp the sociohistorical complexities that frame this intervention. I begin by describing and contextualizing the CRDA project within the democracy aid realm, followed by an analysis of the conflicts that emerged among various actors, to show the underlying logics that sustain and inhibit certain practices regarding the public sector.

The Democratic Kickoff

Local nongovernmental organizations in Serbia, as elsewhere, were heavily supported by the international aid industry in the form of development project grants, the intention of which was to promote so-called democratic reforms and values. Of course, NGO engagement within the aid field is far from a novelty. In fact, already by the mid-1970s NGOs had emerged as major implementing organizations at a time when development aid, following the crisis of "big push" theory and Keynesianism, was taking a distance from large state-led programs (infrastructure or industrial ones). The shift to microprojects, destined to cover "primary needs" (such as education, housing, and nutrition), spotlighted NGOs as the best-suited grassroots implementers of aid, enjoying particular comparative advantages such as flexibility and cost-efficiency (Rist 1996). By the late 1980s/early 1990s, democratization studies had taken the lead from modernization development theories, bringing a renewed focus on political transitions of the developing world (Guilhot 2005; Ottaway and Carothers 2000): economic development and democratization were now perceived as parallel processes. Most important, after the first poor results of introducing democratic institutions (parliament, judiciary, elections, etc.), development interventions focused on local political actors: political elites/parties and, of course, the ultimate symbol of institutionalized civil society, NGOs. Local NGOs incarnating active citizenship were both the ideal subject of liberal democracy and the ideal organizational model to achieve it. More NGOs came to signify more democracy. NGOs became, thus, a development project in themselves. Civil society had to be "built."

The CRDA project offers an important window to analyzing the aforementioned understandings. Following the internal restructuring of USAID in the mid-1990s along cost-effectiveness lines (Brown 2006, 6), the CRDA project was outsourced to five highly professional US NGOs, the so-called implementing partners, who received $200 million to conceptualize and realize a five-year "revitalization" plan covering the whole territory of Serbia except Kosovo and metropolitan Belgrade. The municipalities of Vojvodina, where I collected my data in 2007–8, Kikinda, and Subotica, were under the "responsibility" of the America's Development Foundation (ADF), one of the five US subcontractors. ADF is a large US nonprofit with headquarters in Virginia. It was established in 1980 and, until today, has been repeatedly supported financially by US government contracts (either through the USAID or other US government programs such as the National Endowment for Democracy). Initially engaged mostly in food aid and agricultural-production programs, ADF shifted its focus in the late 1980s toward technical assistance in "free-elections" and voter education, realizing projects in Central America and the Philippines among others. For the past decade, it has specialized in democracy projects and community mobilization in post-conflict situations around the world, in places as different as Angola, Bosnia-Herzegovina, Haiti, Iraq, and Egypt.

CRDA was "designed to focus on heavy community participation and rapid results. It is a citizen-driven program wherein local communities organize themselves and decide on priority development projects that they wish to implement" (USAID 2005). CRDA was branded as an innovative and think-out-of-the-box solution. But to what problem was it a solution?

Like any other development project, the CRDA was based on a prior "needs assessment" that had examined the local context of intervention in order to propose relevant solutions. This might appear contradictory to the idea of already-existent package solutions that travel around the globe and respond in the same way to extremely different sociohistorical contexts. CRDA was itself one of these ready-made postconflict remedies, since it was previously implemented on a smaller scale in Lebanon and afterward found its way to Iraq. Although, some "general solutions," such as free elections, are not in principle contested (since democracy is indeed a hegemonic political project), standardization seems less viable when the "local problem" is understood in cultural terms. In fact, the definition of Serbia as a democracy-needing target depended on a particular regime of representation (Escobar 1995). Serbia, according to mainstream political science categorizations, was identified as a "fragile state" with a ruined economy and a "weak civil society" (Milivojević 2006; NGO Policy Group 2001). Within a postcommunist context, it was generally believed that an overgrown public sphere of almost fifty years of Yugoslav-style socialism had practically suppressed the needed private space for civic initiatives. USAID points out that "the historical legacy of centralized power has created a *culture* where people are not accustomed to taking local action" (USAID, Czajkowska et al. 2005, 18, my emphasis). All the numerous associations linked directly or indirectly with the socialist political project (e.g., women's groups, self-management structures, war-veteran clubs, professional groups, and youth associations) were selectively overlooked or discredited on the grounds of lack of autonomy (Stubbs 2001). In other words, it was thought that Serbian people were suffering from some kind of "learned helplessness." The stated goal of CRDA was the creation of a new political subjectivity: a modern and democratic citizen with rich associational life, "the development of a culture characterized by self-help initiatives" (USAID, Czajkowska et al. 2005, 18).

Civic apathy is indeed one of the problems that democracy projects are supposed to solve; trying to cultivate what de Tocqueville called the "habits of the heart" (USAID 1994, 31). The assumed "culture of dependency" was considered even more deeply rooted in the countryside, away from the urban "islands of democracy," as the Belgrade NGOs were called at the time. However, Vojvodina was perceived by the local ADF staff as the "easiest" Serbian region for development work: First, because it was thought to have comparatively fewer economic problems and, second, because its people (according to popular emic assumptions) supposedly had a more "modern" mentality. Indeed, Vojvodina spreads over 21,500 square kilometers of flat land in the northern part of Serbia and 84 percent of its territory is arable fertile land, producing cereals, fruits, and various industrial herbs. However, its economy is mixed rather than purely agricultural, since there are a few urban centers (including Kikinda and Subotica) that were highly industrialized following Tito's modernization plans. Since 2000, these urban centers have been undergoing major socioeconomic transformations. The national economic policy projected a shift of interest toward agriculture-for-export production and tourism, while privatization processes of publically owned firms and factories occurred along with widespread economic deprivation, massive layoffs, and withdrawal of social security entitlements. Economic deprivation was even deeper in other regions that were said to lack not only prospects for economic recovery but also the very base of democratic political culture. Following popular narratives of nesting orientalisms (Bakić-Hayden 1995), Vojvodina was considered more "civilized" and prodemocratic, since prior to its integration into the kingdom of Yugoslavia in 1918, it had been part of the Austro-Hungarian Empire and not the presumed culturally backward Ottoman Empire. Leaving culturalist stereotypes aside, since 1974, with the exception of Milošević's highly centralized rule, Vojvodina has enjoyed extensive rights of self-rule deriving from its political status as an autonomous province within the Republic of Serbia. Thus, it has had a more decentralized administration, its own separate budget, and its own regional parliament.

In 2001, ADF identified and started working within 120 local communities in 14 different Voivodina municipalities.[1] ADF gave responsibility for mobilization and outreach to a team of 25 people called "community mobilization specialists" (hereafter to be called "mobilizers"). Apart from one of the two unit directors, all of these mobilizers were native Serb citizens and had either origins or strong connections with various regions in Vojvodina. Aged between 35 and 50, these community-development experts had previous professional experience within the aid world, whether by working in international NGOs in the former Yugoslav region (or having founded their own NGO) or through delivering training courses and doing freelance consultancy work for various clients. The majority of them had also worked at some point in public companies and municipalities in Vojvodina as lawyers, managers, or reform experts, while others were running private firms.

ADF's mobilizers convened "open citizen meetings" in all communities in order to present the project, define the community's priorities, and help the citizens to elect a council with their representatives, called Groupa za Razvoj (development group). These open town meetings, apart from a method to solicit participation, were sorts of "democracy courses" in themselves. So-called alternative methods for decision-making and group meetings were introduced through standardized facilitation and decision-making models (such as Owen's "Open Space Technology" and "Dot-mocracy," a technique of prioritizing issues through cumulative voting) (USAID 2005). As one of the mobilizers commented, "you don't debate much but it's very effective; direct democracy. In two minutes you have priorities." The new councils usually comprised around ten to fifteen volunteers who would decide and prioritize the needs of their community. Those needs would then be formulated under a project model that would be submitted for funding by USAID. The councils were also responsible for contributing 25 percent matching funds, confirming in that way "that the community was really committed to the project and took ownership of it" (USAID 2005). The ultimate goal of ADF was to transform these informal councils into officially registered NGOs. As civic actions were channeled into NGO project-work, sustainability was measured by the ability to procure external funding. To improve their fundraising skills, these councils received various trainings, ranging from theoretical seminars on civil society, tolerance, and democratic values to more technical training in project proposal writing, project management, strategic planning, fund-raising, advocacy, and communication skills. Overall, by using the "carrot" of funds for the satisfaction of some basic needs, ADF designed an alternative way of delivering aid, while aspiring to simultaneously create an ideal type of grassroots civic activism: new local NGOs. It was precisely because of these newly established local councils that CRDA was branded by USAID as "a civil society program and not simply a community development activity" (USAID 2005).

"An Elephant in the Greenhouse": The Conflicts around Mesna Zajednica

By the end of CRDA's program in 2007, ADF was reporting to USAID its success: 1,035 projects had been developed and implemented; 1,382,282 people in 26 municipalities had been beneficiaries; 248,273 people directly participated in CRDA activities; 128,975 months of employment were created; 1,500 citizens participated in local economic development strategy planning processes; capacity building had been provided to 175 citizens' community and cluster committees with 4,396 members; a network of Community Development Associations (the previously informal community councils) had been established with an official membership of 1,500 citizens; 39 health centers and clinics, 5 hospitals, 85 schools, and 32 kindergartens had been renovated or equipped; 400 citizens' meetings had been held, where more than 37,000 people had participated in decision-making processes (USAID 2007).

From ADF's final report, it is clearly evident that numbers count. Results have to be tangible and quantified according to predefined indicators so as to be presented in long reports justifying to the donor the proper and effective use of the allocated money. When the CRDA project was completed in 2007, it was archived as a successful democracy program and continued its journey to other to-be-revitalized places. As one of the mobilizers sarcastically told me, "you can find a lot of success stories in the USAID website, so, if you want to see smiling faces saying thanks to the American people, check that." Obviously, there is usually a big difference between how a project is officially presented and how various groups experience and interpret what happened.

As one could expect, the new councils, the main mechanisms of the program, were not introduced in a virgin field. Even though CRDA claimed that it had introduced local communities to new ways of thinking, since local people were purportedly "not accustomed to taking local action" (USAID, Czajkowska et al. 2005, 18), elements other than a collective citizen identity organized social life. These elements were ethnic affiliation, kinship ties, religion, political party affiliation, and farmers' cooperatives. Despite such solidarity patterns, socialist Yugoslavia, and particularly Vojvodina, also had a strong tradition of decentralization and participation patterns. One of its aspects was the *mesna zajednica* system (MZ). MZ stands for a community organ at the lowest level of local self-governance, a territorial and administrative subunit of the municipality. Usually there is one MZ representing every village and one for every neighborhood in the cities. Elections at the MZ level are held every four years, when the residents elect the *sekretar* (secretary) and the MZ board through proportional representation. Except for the secretary, who usually receives a salary from the municipality, the rest of the MZ members are volunteers. MZs should represent the collective interests of their residents and deal with community problems. During the wars of the 1990s, apart from administrative roles, they were also responsible for distributing humanitarian aid and for organizing civil and military defense. Every MZ develops its five-year plan (mainly containing communal infrastructure tasks) and, in order to realize it, establishes a collective fund financed by a monthly local tax (*samodoprinos*), usually 1 to 3 percent of the MZ residents' salaries.

When CRDA started operating in the region, a question arose: What kind of position should be taken toward the MZs? According to ADF's mobilizers, the MZs did not meet the criteria of CRDA's civic engagement because they were considered to be communist and old-fashioned structures and completely dependent on the municipal administration. Indeed the MZs today are surely "nonfunctional," but the causes are rather historical and socioeconomic. Serbia is a postconflict country, where ten years of war and ethnic conflict, economic embargo, inflation, migration and refugee flows, NATO bombing, and an authoritarian state have weakened community life alongside civic and political participation. Most importantly, MZs lost much of their power after 1990 following the recentralization policies of Milošević's socialist party. At the national level, Vojvodina and Kosovo lost the levels of autonomy that made them autonomous provinces according to the decentralized constitution of 1974. At the local level, the political power and even the local voluntary taxes that constituted MZs' budgets were transferred under the auspices of the municipal administrations. Despite the "democratic changes" of 2000, the MZs never reacquired their former status and entitlements.

Against this historical background, ADF decided to "finish with the past" and instead of including MZs in the project, they sidelined them. ADF equally undermined (initially) the few existing local NGOs, considered, ironically, "too modern" and "somewhat extraordinary." The CRDA project was aggressively and urgently challenging the balances of local networks, an intention that could not be understood by people engaged in local NGOs or MZs. Zivko, an ex–local NGO activist, described it as being, "like an elephant entering a glass greenhouse. Whatever was here worthy, they [USAID] took it and broke it." The new councils assumed the economic capital and decision-making roles over responsibilities that had previously been managed by the MZs, and this generated an unprecedented conflict between them. Several ADF staff members understood the conflict around MZs as a mark of competition around USAID's financial resources or as a sign of some culturally prescribed "love for leadership" (*ljubav za vodstvo*).

However, a closer look reveals that the conflict had much deeper origins and implications, since it erupted from the very restructuring of local political power and of the ways that livelihoods were organized for accessing resources. On the one hand, in people's perceptions, MZs still represented a legitimate structure of power. Questions of accountability and legitimacy often arose when the MZ, as locally and formally elected organs, claimed to be the only legitimate actor to express the common interest and represent the local community. Many people within MZs felt dispossessed, not so much by their loss of decision-making power, which was already extremely limited, but because they felt patronized and symbolically isolated. They insisted that "Yugoslavia was not Africa" but still "Americans wanted to start from zero." On the other hand, people felt they had to "defend" (*da brane*) the MZs because of the very entanglement of official state structures with local (and often unequal) relations of mutuality and obligation. Indeed, everyday life in an MZ revealed that bureaucratic work and personal (often clientelistic) networks were interwoven into a social ensemble of meaningful relationships that blurred the boundaries between public and private

spheres. Just by spending some time at the MZs premises, one could capture the ambiguous and overlapping roles of MZ members, who, apart from
being local officials of various kinds, are also somebody's cousin or in-law,
members of a political party and of an ethnic community, somebody's neighbor or client. People pass by the MZ office in order to complain about the
sewage or a hole in the asphalt in their street, to sort out a dispute with their
neighbor, to ask information or obtain some administrative documents, to
register for heating benefits, or simply very often to have a coffee and gossip.
People maintain paradoxical engagements with such institutions that may
at times demand discipline and control while providing a realm for entitlements, rights, and appeals (Jansen 2009).

The resolution of this MZ-CRDA conflict depended on the local dynamics of each community. We could generally observe two scenarios. In more
urban communities, where the proximity to the municipality had disem-
powered the MZs, there was ultimately a fusion of CRDA councils and MZ
structures. In the town of Kikinda, for example, the conflict was resolved
when the mobilizers finally accepted MZ members into the new councils.
In various rural settlements, however, CRDA reconfigured the established
power relations—but still using the existing structures (that is, the MZs).
In the case of some villages in Subotica, the new councils turned out to be
leading local organizations, visible in the public sphere and thus recognized
by the residents as more important than MZs. Many of them, capitalizing
on the success of the CRDA-funded projects, developed political ambitions
and started to seek political power. Those councils, after the first year of
CRDA, were transformed into political parties under the label "Citizens'
Movement" (*Pokret Građana*) and started their own political campaign, and
indeed most of them won the leading role within their MZs at the upcoming local elections.

Through the agitation around such conflicts, CRDA managed to enhance
some local engagement in the commons. However, local ADF staff members judged this participation as too politicized to be characterized as civic.
These developments were in fact nowhere to be found in official reports because losing the normative label of "civic actions" would mean losing the eligibility to be funded by CRDA. To make matters worse, after the end of the
CRDA program, very few of these new councils remained active as newly
established NGOs. In the towns of Kikinda and Subotica, the civic legacy of
CRDA continued, but in a quite dormant state, without ongoing activities,
and sometimes run by people who had been engaged in project work prior
to CRDA. In most of the rural communities, not only did I not find any of
the newly established NGOs after the end of CRDA, but the political parties' "Citizens' Movements" (the transformed CRDA councils) had also dis-

solved. Overall, very few councils remained active as NGOs (although some in other communities were admittedly very successful). Most became part of municipal bodies and others remained as "one-man-show" NGOs for attracting (together with the municipality) projects that demanded private/public partnerships. Why was there an apparent failure of sustainability?

Too Much Carrot, Too Little Stick?

Among virtually all the ADF mobilizers, there was a profound feeling of disappointment regarding the failure to achieve their primary goal of enhancement of a democratic culture. Two main explanations by informants were often given for such a failure: first, the constraints of project work with its administrative requirements; and second, the perceived incapacity of local communities to understand the real mission of CRDA.

Although an internal audit report explicitly expressed some serious reservations about CRDA's implementation by observing that "CRDA has developed an overriding emphasis on projects over process," whereas "the projects are only supposed to be a means towards that end" (USAID, Czajkowska et al. 2005, 4–5, 20–21), the mobilizers stressed instead that such a "mistaken" focus lay at the very heart of CRDA's design. To begin with, CRDA included a "quick start-up" phase: this period was described as a frenetic rally of ninety days during which ADF's mobilizers had to do research on communities, identify where they would work, hold open town meetings, establish local councils, help people define their priorities, train the councils' members, design at least one project, procure the logistical requirements and implement it—and this simultaneously in sixty communities! CRDA was supposed to be a kind of political shock therapy. On the one hand the speed required was intended to prevent an operational or bureaucratic slowdown; on the other hand it would prevent the floundering of the democratic movement after 2000, whereas by rapidly alleviating suffering, it would "buy some time for implementation of major policy reforms at the national level" (USAID 2005).

In practice though, rapid start timeframes proved counterproductive, first because mobilizers had so little time to familiarize themselves with the communities of their intervention and second because it created competition and a sense of urgency among communities that started to fear that they could be left out if they did not manage to meet the deadlines. As a result, everyone had to cut corners in order to meet the extremely short-term goals and actually spent much time later on in correcting their mistakes. As many of them told me, "if you need results you make results," or "in order to have quick start you had to squeeze the idea, it's always like that. In the sector there is a rule, copy something and you'll be fine. In the third sector, that's the rule, copy everything, paste, not invent! Use whatever is already available." This rule, born from hasty decisions and pressured time demands, also explains the passive acceptance of the mergers of MZs and councils or the partisan politicization of certain councils. After all, a major goal for all people involved was to deliver, that is, to spend the money. In the development industry, there is no bigger failure and embarrassment than for a grantee to send the money back to its donor. Such an event would entail a direct loss of credibility and indicate a lack of professionalism.

Problems stretched beyond this initial operational phase, as conflicts arose between administrative levels and between groups with different responsibilities. Tensions were evident among the mobilizers as well, particularly between people using a more managerial approach and others with more activist aspirations. The first group included supporters of the mainstream development tool of Logical Framework Analysis (LFA). These mobilizers had a firm belief that there are systematic causal "logical" linkages among various social elements that enable the project maker to make predictions and plan the outcomes of his actions by using game theory and risk management tools.[2] "If you were to follow the Yellow Bible," as some mobilizers were saying (a book with a yellow cover, including action plans, guidelines, and expected results), you knew that all would work properly. For others, though, this very Yellow Bible was the source of their alienation. Their concerns were linked to the very pathology of project-oriented methods: the focus on fast and tangible results and the quantification of participation. Sonja, a forty-year-old ADF mobilizer, shared with me her frustrations:

There were a lot of people who were really enthusiastic. Such an enthusiasm! For the first time this was a possibility to achieve your ideas. So it was a good powerful engine in the beginning. It was a good idea. I say idea because unfortunately I'm not so happy with the results. The CM [community mobilization] component was a bit lost because it's not so tangible. USAID, like other donors, didn't have the right hands to catch it. They want tangible results. They want boxes, to tick them. Because engineers and economic development staff, they are not so sensitive or sensible about relations. It's really technical, aha you'll give us [US$] 20,000, or you will dig this hole. With societal changes, it cannot go so fast; it's not so obvious. It was easier for them when they were monitoring to focus [on] counting councils . . . the "trees" [not the "forest"]. USAID is not the only case; it's always like that with donors. And I want to understand it, because they have to justify the money the American people gave here. We were really working on changes from the root; we educated people in new ways of thinking. It takes time and you cannot measure the results after one year of education. It takes 5 years, 10; and this program was great in idea but too much immediate result focused. Tangible results, it's difficult, you will most likely lose focus on things that are not so visible. Maybe it was a good experience for me too, because I was far away very idealistic before!

Sonja and some of her colleagues thought that they had failed as mobilizers because—trapped between deadlines, budgets, and innumerous reports—they missed their primary target, the focus on people. Such accounts, while openly pointing to project-based alienation, also contained seeds of self-critique. For example, as the mobilizers often said, "we were holding too much of a carrot and too little stick," a phrase quite indicative of the internal hierarchies of project making (since one has to hold the stick while the other has to chase a carrot). "Why the need of a carrot?" one might ask. For many mobilizers, the patronizing answer to this question was also part of the explanation of the CRDA's failure. The vast majority of mobilizers seemed convinced that the locals never understood the real mission of CRDA (and thus their own needs?). The ADF mobilizers provided several explanations for the failure of the CRDA program: the "stagnant and depressive mentality" of Vojvodinians (a geocultural ascription invoking the topographical flatness of the Vojvodina plain), the Balkan inclination toward laziness and cheating (which is often popularly referred to as just the "Balkan business"), the "mentalities that belonged to the old socialist structure," or some generic human inclination toward power/leadership and money. The locals were said to be interested only in the financial "carrot," whereas, as the mobilizers' argument goes, locals could not realize that, for better or for worse, CRDA was not a straightforward development project and the locals were thus not "mature" enough to understand the virtues of civic participation and NGO-ing. As one mobilizer said, "CRDA was a college lesson of democracy. And here we are in kindergarten."

The Quest for Sustainability

The mobilizers' laments about people's expectations were correct. People's material needs were at the core of the "beneficiaries'" expectations from CRDA, and in fact, the failure of this task was what created the local disappointment. For the residents of Subotica and Kikinda, the more positive aspects of CRDA were tied to the American funding for basic equipment and reconstruction of community infrastructure such as schools, roads, clinics, and ambulance centers. These, along with the support of local production structures, came after 2003, when USAID (probably for reasons linked to both local grievances and to parallel municipal reforms on economic decentralization) decided to emphasize more "local economic development." Many citizens could not see any point in training sessions and tutorials about democracy, civil society, strategic planning, and PR techniques. As Darko, a fifty-five-year-old council member from Kikinda, explained, "it is their [mobilizers'] job to train. They love it. But for us . . . is it necessary for you to have training in swimming if you are living in the desert? We had to do it." In a situation of economic dispossession and widespread pauperization, minor infrastructure projects made little sense to the inhabitants because they offered no real solution to their economic and employment problems. Marko, a forty-five-year-old new farmer and former cook in a bankrupt social enterprise near Subotica, explained: "When ADF came here, we told them, 'Why don't you finance economic programs? Because if we have strong companies people will have work and then [the companies] will in their turn fix the roads and streets and schools and everything.' It was like that always. But the program was conceived in another way: the Americans would fix what they had destroyed [through bombing] and like that, they would compensate the state by fixing roads, streets, and schools."

Of course, Marko, based on his own lived experience of Yugoslav market socialism, had a very particular idea about what a company is and should do, namely care about the general well-being of communities. Nevertheless, and far from some communist-driven apathy, most Vojvodinians were puzzled because their own "priorities" focused on more material and subsistence issues, such as unemployment and everyday survival. Abstract civic engagement was not part of people's immediate concerns. Nevertheless, members of these new local councils proved to be quite pragmatic, managing to co-opt USAID's discourse and mechanisms. "Participation" was just a quantifiable frame of negotiation for ticking eligibility boxes; as they said, "we made sure that there were always *enough* people." However, when participation concerns became more grounded in organizational structures (e.g., new councils) and started marginalizing the MZs, the situation, as we saw, became far more complex and strained. Far from pointing to big egos or lust for power, the informal mergers between MZs and councils or the occasional politicization of the latter was a means by which local people gained access to various resources or a strategy to guarantee their provision in the future as well. Zarko, a member of both MZ and CRDA council in Kikinda, explained that the ADF "couldn't have avoided people from MZs because those are the people who are active here. Where will we find completely new people now? Out in the streets? And those that are already here, to tell them that they have to leave? These people have been here from before because they are interested in their community and its development. And they *are going to stay* here after CRDA leaves" (my emphasis).

In rural settlements, MZs were even more important since they were the only administrative structure in the community. Marko—the MZ secretary of a village in Subotica and former member of the local Prokret Gradana party (Citizens' Movement)—explained to me why their CRDA council decided to transform itself into a political party: "If you want to accept some responsibilities, this means you need some [political] power from the beginning, we knew CRDA would leave. Then what? Being in authority is more useful than in an NGO." However this Pokret-experiment did not last long. After CRDA shut down its operations in 2007, most of those new parties ceased to exist. Marko elaborated on the trajectories of this group:

> Pokret doesn't exist anymore because after CRDA left . . . I don't know why . . . we all divided into different political parties, but in some sense, we didn't split. The people from Pokret are still present at the leadership of the MZ, but are part of different parties, like the Democratic Union of Croats in Vojvodina, the Democratic Party, the G17. . . . You know, you cannot find resources when you don't have a specific influence on some parties. NGOs have the smallest influence. We could remain an NGO, but how could we find resources? Maybe because of that, unconsciously, we split. If you don't know people from the local administration, you can search for resources for months, they will listen to you, oh, those people always listen to everything, but when it comes to material support. . . . So if I want to do something, I have to be theirs.

The former CRDA council was indeed "absorbed" by different political parties. Most of the time, party affiliation had nothing to do with concrete political and ideological programs but was determined along ethnic lines (minority parties) and in relation to the political constellation at the municipal and government levels. Political parties and their local representatives functioned as a kind of local brokers. Most of the time, they do not directly control resources but provide access to those who control them (Boissevain 1974). They provide contacts and *veze* (links) for fulfilling both individual and collective agendas. When a communal problem arises, all MZ members, regardless of party affiliation, try to pull strings within their political networks in order to find a solution. These clientelistic networks are considered by their members to be mutually beneficial even if they are built among actors occupying very asymmetrically stratified positions, whereas engagement in patronage relations of this kind may not be a matter of choice. Political parties are not just a channel of resource allocation or of access to or control over information. Even when there is no actual exchange taking place, political parties can offer an effective safety net: "You know that you cannot do anything if you are not a member of an existing party. Because they watch each other's backs, they take care of each other, all of them, the radicals, the democrats, in all levels; from the local to the highest. . . . If you want change, you need to be part of it. That's the price."

The conflicts and "solutions" around MZs were not mentioned in any official report. Even if they appeared quite normal for the local people in the communities, they actually made most of the ADF staff members feel quite uncomfortable. First, because the new councils should serve as apolitical springboards to civic engagement, and second, because so-called *partitokratija* (partitocracy) was perceived by the mobilizers as a sign of a lack of democracy and even a lack of "modernization." In fact, it was quite impressive to see the double standards that USAID had regarding understandings of "politicization."

Officially, the enmeshment of CRDA structures into local political life was not acceptable, and USAID always insisted on its impartiality and distance from partisan politics. Invoking what he said was USAID's motto, an ADF mobilizer explained to me, "We do civil society, not politics."[3] While it is true that USAID wanted to establish a clear-cut separation from its former more overtly politicized missions (e.g., the Office of Transition Initiatives), which had directed funds to anti-Milošević forces (Cook and Spalatin 2002), in reality, there remained a political color to the CRDA program. In the post-Milošević period, following the rise of the nationalist Radical Party in numerous municipalities, USAID unofficially forbid involving the Radical Party with the CRDA program. This decision obviously impeded the ADF's job, since, in most cases, the 25 percent of cofinancing that was conditional for the funded projects was to be raised from the municipal budget. The mobilizers had to be "creative" and find alternative paths for the money to reach their communities: the municipality would fund the MZs for some virtual activity, and the MZs would in turn use the grant to provide the cofinancing for CRDA.

Despite USAID's ambiguities around the meanings of political intervention, many ADF local mobilizers had their own political agendas. When CRDA started in 2001, ADF hired as a consulting group the Belgrade NGO G17. Back then, G17 was a promising neoliberal think tank that turned into a political party of "experts" in 2002 and held key governmental positions regarding financial and economic policy until 2014. The result was that many people in ADF were engaged in party politics and were planning to embark on political careers, most often at the municipal level. A small group of mobilizers had even more radical political projects. For them, CRDA had nothing to do with building civil society. They believed that USAID's "hidden" or "unwritten" goal was to destroy the remnant Milošević's structures at the grassroots level by "cleansing" the MZs, a structure that in the past had provided a public realm for citizen participation *and* an entry point for political advancement through the channels of the Communist Party (Simmie and Hale 1978). For these mobilizers, the CRDA was their tool for destroying the MZs. The conflict that erupted in the local communities between MZs and new councils was not a side effect of CRDA. It was the mobilizers' own intentional strategy, even if it had some uncontrollable outcomes. For many of the ADF's staff members, the problem was that CRDA was not political enough. For them, the municipal electoral results in 2003 and the rise in local power of the nationalist Radical Party of Vojislav Šešelj (at that time, on trial for war crimes in The Hague) represented ten steps backward for the route of Serbia's European integration and "return to normality."[4] They thought that a change in "people's mentality" had not taken place during the implementation of CRDA and that part of the responsibility was theirs. Their mistake was clear to them. As an ADF explained to me, "We were playing democracy instead of going clear with our [political] message."

Conclusion

A simple reflection on the concrete operations of CRDA reveals how even the best-intentioned people were often caught in a paradox of trying to build bottom-up civic engagement through a standardized top-down method. For the local communities, CRDA was always perceived to be an outsider initiative. As Zarko concluded, "why should we [local residents] be happy? You [USAID] came to us; you asked us if we want money, we answered, 'Yes.' It's up to you. It is clear. Why to be so happy? It's your project. You wrote the project for us, instead of us. So what happened? OK we have a new school, heating . . . but why should we be so excited because you want to spend your money? It's your job." CRDA was indeed a ready-made template for solving "problems" of perceived democratic deficit by cultivating the "habits of the heart." The standardization and global circulation of package solutions (such as CRDA) and the technocratization/depoliticization of neoliberal state restructuring have also prompted a sort of universalization in the understanding of local problems, that is, their culturalization (in the sense that the problem is always perceived to be local culture). The diagnosis of democratic deficit was based on a definition of Serbian civil society as weak. As the argument goes, NGOs were not numerous and influential (outside metropolitan Belgrade) because of a so-called civic apathy, induced to people's habitus through a so-called communist legacy of state-dependency. CRDA was therefore conceived as a mechanism to boost participation, even if it used the "carrot" of aid funds for local projects. But, if CRDA *was* indeed responding to "local needs" for participation, why the need for a "carrot and stick" to begin with? "Participation" remained mainly a concern external to the local communities. Nevertheless, all the actors involved in the CRDA project—ADF's mobilizers, MZs, Grupe za Rozvoj (development groups), and others—operated with "participation" as their main category for measuring their achievement of goals and negotiating with each other.

"Playing democracy," though, even when framed with the most technocratic terms, was still a political strategy of considerable weight. As shown here, the CRDA's main political function in the first post-Milošević years was nothing less than a restructuring of the state. To build a strong civil society meant to disperse and decentralize state power so that certain functions could devolve to the private NGO sector. In the process, the stigmatizing of the MZs as an out-of-date, dysfunctional institution was intended to challenge a system of social organization ideally built around public structures of power. The conflicts that arose around questions of legitimacy and representation, around different understandings of what and who is the state, were treated and stigmatized as cultural pathologies (e.g., "Balkan culture"), not as different political options. The epithet "communist" did not refer to a political societal project but to a culture of dependency. At the same time, the axiom of neoliberal autonomy and "freedom" was never questioned or problematized.

Unpacking such essentialisms means grasping people's paradoxical engagements with state institutions even in "phantom limb" situations where state security and welfare functions have all but dissolved. MZs persist and maintain their legitimacy, but this is not due to some Yugo-nostalgia or state cutback. On the contrary, people were blaming "the state" all the time for the current dispossession, but this criticism referred to the governments/political elites and it articulated a demand for transparency, better organization, and intervention. These citizens who viewed state structures through the prism of entitlements and rights and those who refused to dismantle or sideline these entitlements and rights in favor of future (and always volatile) NGO projects were not apathetic or culturally resistant to change. MZs were "defended" not because people were irrational but because they provided an intimate public sphere where the state is personalized and is expected to care for its citizens, transforming their everyday personal problems into public interests. As Stef Jansen argues about the post-Yugoslav context, "oppressed, normalized and disciplined by state practices, people may also desire the state, appeal to it—and in that way, continually call it into existence. . . . The most interesting line of analysis, perhaps, lies in the very contradictions that run through such experiences: cynicism and hope, detachment and investment, rejection and appeal" (Jansen 2009, 58–59).

To be sure, I do not claim that the aid industry has some kind of anti-state mission, and I firmly believe that producing analytical dichotomies such as NGOs/state inhibits rather than reveals the complexity of social realities (Vetta 2012). Furthermore, and parallel to civil society programs, hundreds of development aid projects are targeting state institutions, and this with a considerably bigger budget than the one destined to NGOs. Yet, such efforts aimed at "reforming" state bodies are never politically neutral. The state is never a neutral player among many others (namely the market and civil society) but a site of political struggle over socioeconomic regulation and entitlements among social actors who are structurally positioned unequally. The whole conception of CRDA and the exaltation of self-help NGO initiatives thus revealed a *particular* political positioning vis-à-vis the role that the state should acquire in the newly established democracy. We can then reinterpret CRDA as essentially a project of neoliberal statecraft, targeting the creation of an "enabling" rather than a providing state (Gilbert 2005), a state that is outsourcing policy making (or the creation of feasible policy options) to expert networks or international bodies and service provision downward to "responsibilized" communities (Mosse 2007; Vetta 2012). With fuzzy responsibility comes fuzzy accountability, and in such cases, democracy promotion becomes a hollow democracy. Unfortunately and sometimes unwillingly, NGOs, instead of becoming the solution, become part of the problem.

Acknowledgments

I would like to extend my sincere thanks to all the people in Belgrade and Vojvodina who shared their insights and helped me gather the material for this research; to Jonathan Friedman and the reviewers for their very useful comments and inspiration; and to Jaime Palomera for his help editing this chapter. Fieldwork was supported by the Marie Curie SOCANTH Program Promoting Anthropology in Central and Eastern Europe (FP6-MOBILITY, Project reference: 20702).

Notes

1. ADF's use of "community" did not carry moral/symbolic connotations (Joseph 2002; Taylor 2010) and was simply equated spatially with the lowest-level administrative unit of Mesne Zajednice (local community authority).

2. The Logical Framework Analysis (LFA) has its origins in US military planning and has become a mainstream tool for development project planning, monitoring, and evaluation. For a critique of LFA, see Gasper (1997).

3. For a critique of the depoliticizing claims of development operations see Ferguson (1994).

4. The rise of the Radical Party was very superficially associated with a rise of nationalism, isolationism, and collectivism. Elsewhere I have argued that the support for the Radical Party had more to do with the material and symbolic dispossession that accompanied privatization schemas that had been backed by the so-called democratic parties, rather than with political manipulation or identity dilemmas (Vetta 2011).

4
Reformists and Revolutionists

Social Work NGOs and Activist Struggles in the Czech Republic

Hana Synková

In the Czech Republic, two types of organizations provide social services in the areas inhabited mainly by a Romani[1] population: Amaro,[2] which claimed cultural proximity to their clients as the basis of their expertise; and People in Need, which bases their expertise on professionally educated staff. In this chapter I show how, despite some ideological differences, these two social work organizations gradually came to resemble each other, to the extent that they could be criticized by activists of being the same thing. I show why identity-based organizations, compared to mainstream NGOs, have problems in attracting the support of academics, who serve as legitimators of organizational ideologies, and how both types of NGOs have experienced limited potential for their political action. The advocacy network Platform for Social Housing, the third type of organization described here, instead proposes grassrootness as the main value that should contribute to the solution of social exclusion. Finally, I discuss the roles played by activists and NGOs in advocacy networks and the difficult task of maintaining the network composed of very diverse actors with different concepts of change (revolutionary versus reformist). I identify which kinds of NGOs tend to join these networks and what the barriers are for joining. Overall, this chapter presents a case study of the professionalization of NGOs and possibilities and risks of coexistence of these NGOs with more activist actors.

NGO Competition around Expertise

NGOs take pride in their capabilities to help. They promote their own expertise, which contributes to their credibility, and denounce the lack of it with other organizations. A construction of expertise based on professionalism and neutrality toward the clients seems to be more successful than the expertise built on the cultural proximity to the clients. This thesis is illustrated in the following example of two competing organizations.

The organization Amaro, with which I volunteered,[3] was located in a small office, the base from which their members left to carry out their counseling activities at several sites. The first site was an asylum house and its surroundings, where families from a dilapidated brick factory had moved. A second site was a regional prison and a third a traditional working-class quarter, where Amaro organized mainly free leisure-time activities for local Romani children who could not afford to pay for activities. Some clients, such as released prisoners, occasionally also came directly to their office. An energetic Romani woman, Anna (the founder of the organization) and her oldest son saw them. Anna also employed one part-time non-Romani social worker, the only person with a formal social work education in the organization, and some women volunteered, two of them of partly Romani origin who were students of Romani studies.

The way Amaro functioned did not in any way resemble the ideals of professionalism and transparency promoted by the new ideologues of standardization that gained force at the beginning of the new millennium. Not only was there a "family atmosphere," facilitated by big common breakfasts, which were financed by Anna, but the organization was indeed partly composed of her family through the employment of the first and later the second son. Errands were frequently run in the luxury cars of the sons, the room was nicely equipped, partly with Anna's own furniture. There were family dogs present and Anna's grandchildren waited for her in the office to be taken to ballet classes or other activities. Anna's Roma family had attended secondary school. Despite being an elite among the group, they, too, still struggled to find official employment. Forming an NGO to obtain some kind of salary for staff was therefore quite an accomplishment.

When Anna talked about clients, she spoke about "our children" or Miss/ Mrs. X and about the need to "teach people to catch fish," which was the rhetoric that she developed spontaneously through working with people. Clients were considered as people who could become our friends, and Anna was available to them nonstop on her mobile phone. The working time was rather flexible, and employees did not have to sit in the office if they had done their work. However, if it was needed, virtually all the week could be spent working—the organization often spent the weekends together, usually at the home of the non-Romani social worker, discussing the future of the organization and possibilities to acquire funding. There were few divisions between the clients and the employees. All of them were considered by Anna to be part of the "Amaro family." The legitimation of organizational mission was simple. It was based on the construction of common ethnic and cultural background. Workers at Amaro were mainly Roma, so they presumed that by understanding Roma they could help them better than anyone else. The organization had problems doing paperwork, such as reports from client meetings or grant applications, so Anna redirected a lot of important administrative tasks to the university student volunteers. The organization functioned as an organism, where the tasks shifted and each person contributed with what suited him/her most.[4] Such informality or intimacy of the functioning was precisely targeted by the reformers, representatives of the Ministry of Labor and Social Affairs, and mainstream organizations working on the standards of quality, who needed recognizable signs of quality of organizational work such as perfect paperwork, job descriptions, and accounting.

Amaro's more organic character could be contrasted with many non-Romani NGOs, which build their reputations based on professional expertise, mastery of office routine, and project management skills. These organizations functioned and presented themselves rather differently from Amaro. They displayed inexpensive furniture in their offices, had set working times, divided this time more strictly between work and leisure, and used the expert language of "users of services," which Amaro considered disrespectful. Non-Romani organizations displayed more organizational stability, as they were larger and knew how to diversify their funding sources. The university-educated employees of these organizations generated a lot of written documents, attempting to standardize their work and methods. They criticized organizations that expressed their goals with the lay rhetoric of "fishing." They hoped that planned standardization of social services would improve the quality of social work and drive what they viewed as nonstandard or amateurish organizations out of business. They were active in contacting the Ministry of Labor and Social Affairs and offered to collaborate on the formulation of a methodology of social services. Through creating the methodology or participating in the drafting of the 2006 Social Service Law, several organizations were able to influence the functioning of the whole social service sector.

These characteristics were especially the case for the largest and most powerful non-Romani organization, People in Need.[5] The leader of the field programs[6] called people from Amaro and similar organizations "heartists," people who claim that they can do social work based on their compassion, or on their "little Romani heart," a phrase used by Romani social workers. He also criticized the methods that organizations like Amaro used: being available to the clients twenty-four hours a day is not professional and not educative because in this way the clients could not learn institutional routines. Being friends with clients also threatens professionalism and the concept of "contract"[7] between the client and worker, as the roles become blurred. In this claim, he is supported by the discourse of some English-language textbooks such as the social work classic by Sarah Banks (2006), *Ethics and Values in Social Work*, which warns that certain types of social workers—engaged, radical, and bureaucratic—are a danger to the client. According to Banks, the professional worker is the only appropriate type, since s/he is educated and autonomous enough to keep the relationship with a client at the professional level and does not allow an ideological background to influence the social work. This typology, cited in Janoušková and Nedělníková's 2008 Czech textbook (487), was created for field social work training in the process of the standardization of the social services. The textbook was co-authored and coreviewed by the head of the social work staff for People in Need.

The leader of the People in Need's field program especially criticized any organizations that used ethnicity as legitimation for the quality of their social work. He described the ethnic approach as ineffective because clients are primarily "people who are in a difficult situation." These people need good social workers, whose quality is ensured by their professional education. He denounced ethnic labeling of clients as unnecessary and as stigmatizing all Roma. People in Need themselves renamed their Romani programs "Programs for Social Integration."

The de-ethnicized rhetoric of organizations assisting Roma has now diffused. Since the turn of the millennium, majority (non-Romani) organizations have gradually started to prefer the terms "socially excluded localities" and "socially excluded people," even when all their target groups are Roma. This change of rhetoric had several causes. First, organizations considered it important to point out that the localities are not 100 percent Roma and that non-Roma can also end up in the same kinds of "difficult situations" as the Roma. Second, any terminology that emphasized Roma directly might lead to ethnic discrimination or incite unnecessary racist reactions. NGOs were often refused support from local authorities, if support would be directed only toward Roma. The third reason was that this "nonconflictual" language is part of EU jargon[8] and regularly used and considered appropriate in grant applications.

Together with de-ethnicization, the discourse of social exclusion became very instrumental, explaining what the problem and solution was and indicating the influence of neoliberal cultural tropes of individual responsibility and managerial construction of the self (Wacquant 2010, 213–14). Clients should learn the necessary competencies and skills to solve their problems and function in modern life. Raymond Apthorpe (1997, 43) warns that these instrumental policy languages may fail because they silence alternative discourses. Romani NGOs, Amaro included, accused People in Need and other organizations of making Roma virtually invisible and hiding the fact that the social disadvantage was a frequent result of ethnic discrimination.

Majority organizations created a discourse where alternative strategies of "doing NGOs" (Hilhorst 2003; Fisher 1997) could be effectively delegitimized by the accusation of essentializing or amateurism. The criticism coming from Romani NGOs accusing big non-Romani organizations of monopolizing access to government structures or initiation of standardization mechanisms was interpreted as the envy of the unsuccessful. These problems of "ethnic" NGOs are an example of a more general tendency. NGOs that are too identity based, or composed of members from a single group, who want to mutually share their situated knowledge, have bigger problems in NGO competition. In research of NGOs in Bosnia-Herzegovina, Elissa Helms (2003) shows that donor funding was predominantly given to multiethnic NGOs, who used NGO-speak, the more secular and antinationalist the better, while associations of Bosnian Muslim women were ignored. Economic and political marginalization of identity-based minority organizations seems to occur frequently (see also INCITE! 2007 or the comparative account of Ramakrishnan and Bloemraad 2008). There has been also a critique of essentialism whenever it has been claimed that the members of the group can understand other members better, as in the case of "standpoint feminism," the idea that women researchers understand other women because of their assumed shared experience of oppression (Hesse-Biber and Yaiser 2004, 15).

Social work programs such as People in Need and the profession of social worker are based on the principle of proclaimed neutrality; being "neutral" is valued as more professional. Such a stance is similar to many humanitarian organizations, for which denominational or ethnic allegiance would "contradict the 'neutrality principle' that is the cornerstone of humanitarian intervention and the very condition for ensuring that such intervention remains legitimate" (Fassin 2011, 49).

Co-optation of Amaro

The continuing professionalization pressure, narrowing the possible ways of "doing NGO," and solidification of power structures put Amaro and similar organizations at a distinct disadvantage in the struggle for resources. The push to professionalize and standardize social work coincides with the possibility of financing through the European Social Fund (ESF) money that is channeled through the state ministries. ESF programs, however, are very complex. "European money" presents a possibility of organizational growth and bigger stability, but organizations like Amaro lacked the experience to proceed through the application processes.

When Amaro received three big projects by chance at once, it presented another problem—it needed to hire quickly tens of people and learn to manage them and administer the projects, which were followed by strict controls from the ministry. Administrative requirements of running an NGO, especially the need for documentation of work and spending and report writing, grew immensely. The volunteer organization, originally based on close contact and mutual help with tasks, became a big organization overnight, in roughly two months of 2006, and some people could not cope. Anna's older son, Josef, struggled with writing reports about clients and following more systematic procedures and ended up being demoted to the level of support worker, driving and running errands for the organization. The younger son, Victor, after spending some time at the position of the executive director, left the position to become head of the prison workshop program. Romani employees were replaced by non-Romani university-educated professionals who had the writing and administrative skills. The need for writing project applications to sustain the organization rose, and the staff grew to around 140 employees in its peak (around 2011), working in many regions of the Czech Republic.

Projectization compelled Amaro to adopt the more neutral language of social exclusion, to managerial rhetoric, to partly accommodate its organizational structure to survive the controls of quality and audit visits from the Ministry of Labor. For some time, it looked as if the former leadership would be sidelined altogether, as had happened to other organizations that professionalized, which had Roma working only in lower positions. However, as Anna always kept her position as managing director with decisive power and employees saw Amaro as "her business," she was able to make her son Victor an executive director again.

Skills in project writing became so important that they caused an organizational crisis in 2012. Regional Amaro directors, who were good at obtaining funding, began criticizing the need to support the central office using "their project money" or as one of them said, "the money that I wrote." They wanted to be more independent to the point of almost breaking away with a group of close collaborators. At last, the directors of the regional offices were dismissed from the organization, and Amaro set up a more centralized system where the money would only be "written" centrally by specialized project fund-raisers.

Victor married one of the former volunteers of Romani origin and she, too, became part of Amaro's management team. The well-being of three generations of the family in 2015 depended altogether on the success of Amaro's projects, which was worrying for them. For the two brothers, however, it meant that that they could leave odd, manual, or half-legal jobs behind.

Overregulated social work NGOs, despite their antagonisms, grew to resemble each other structurally and partly also discursively in the competition for projects. Involvement in provision of social services seemed also to temper the ethnic activism of the organizations. Amaro was never a completely activist or human rights organization, but it had some cultural and community activities, which were sidelined by the dominance of social services. The leadership of Amaro had a narrow choice of activities if it wanted to stay employed. Funding for social services (in contrast with funding for organizing cultural activities and doing community work) was the only resource that can sustain a considerable number of full-time employees. Despite the professionalization and reorientation of minority organizations to the social work agenda, their social networks remained limited in comparison with mainstream NGOs, who attracted bigger numbers of university-educated employees and academics. The process of professionalization itself does not have the power to overcome the social split between NGOs.

Barriers to Supporting "Ethnic" NGOs

In the following discussion, I describe why mainstream NGOs were attractive for academics, anthropologists included, which further contributed to the already privileged status of these NGOs. The split between NGOs is caused mainly by a dearth of overlapping social networks, differing levels of social capital, and different approaches toward essentialization.

In the case of postsocialist countries the "antisocialist" young professional generation founded many NGOs in the 1990s. NGOs tried to promote reforms of the ineffective state apparatus and this attracted both progressive social workers and young academics. People in Need was itself founded by one of the student leaders of the 1989 Velvet Revolution. When anthropologists searched for their niche on the Czech social science market and wanted to get employed, many of them turned to Roma as their topic of interest. Anthropologists became involved in NGOs as project managers, creators of legitimization for organizations and applied researchers. NGOs were the starting point in the career of these academics, and some of them continued further to the state administration or back and forth, creating an effective social network of contacts and cooperation. For this group of young professionals NGOs became an effective channel of career mobility. In comparison with mainstream NGOs, "ethnic" NGOs have not attracted such a broad social network.

Evolution of like-minded social network can be explained through the kind of professional habitus or epistemic community (Haas 1991) that was similar for anthropologists and other workers from NGOs. They were in their twenties or thirties, entering the labor market with university degrees and knowledge of English and criticizing previous practice in their professions. Instead of kinship links like Amaro, they were linked by what Bourdieu (1994, 10) describes as nepotism and favoritism of a social group produced by school. They were critical of the familial Romani NGOs and thought of their own organizations as transparent and established their access on the basis of merit that must be proven through strict entrance policies. However, membership in informal friendship networks served a similar purpose as a family environment—it provided the trust, which eased the cooperation. A kind of network that progressively defined what "counts as skill and expertise" (Konrad 2002, 236) had been created, giving value to formalized education.

Anthropologists were encouraged to write practical textbooks or policy-aimed texts. They described mechanisms of social exclusion and a "culture of poverty" among the Czech and Slovak Roma. This old concept introduced by Oscar Lewis (1959) is presented in one of the early collections of texts on Roma by one of my academic colleagues as something that can enhance the understanding of the situation of Roma and that will counter the ethnicized explanations that "Romani culture" is responsible for the situation of Roma. To improve the situation of Roma, social work understood as an acculturation into the middle-class values was needed (Novák 2003). Social scientists thus played the role of experts fighting against ethnicized explanations of the situation. However, these same social scientists introduced theories that were themselves problematic and criticized for not giving enough attention to systemic inequalities, effects of discrimination, and reproducing middle-class views (e.g., Valentine 1968, Wilson 1987). In such situations, the Roma NGOs and their leaders, regardless of their common mission of helping disadvantaged people, were left isolated.

Academics also criticized government programs directed toward identity building as ineffective in improving the situation of Roma (see Jakoubek 2006, Krištof 2006, and Moravec 2006). This critique angered Romani and pro-Romani activists or people from the Romani Studies Department of Charles University. Such a critique, however, is not unique to Czech social scientists: leading anthropologists focusing on Roma have argued that ethnically based and nationalist activism has had little impact on impoverished communities (Gay y Blasco 2002, 173; Stewart 1997, 4).

The reserved approach of anthropologists toward "ethnic" activists with accusations of essentialism is not uncommon in cases of other groups. Anthropologist Natasha Gagné of the University of Ottawa describes similar denunciations by the anthropologists of the essentialization of "indigenous" elites in the case of the Maori of New Zealand (2009). Jonathan Friedman (2008, 40) demonstrates how competition is created between anthropologists and the "natives" for control over their identification process and how it pits them against each other when the "indigenous" try to contest the anthropologist's own power of categorization. Anthropologists' own identification as a part of a cosmopolitan elite contributes to these critical tendencies. Gagné warns that such a critique delegitimizes the potential for political changes and also masks that essentialization is a product of the historical orders of the modern state.

The discussions inside local "anthropologies" that were established in the 1990s and that embraced postmodernism often make it difficult to respect, let alone support, the activities of nationalist, ethnicizing, and romanticizing actors. The same authors who criticized Romani ethnic promotion also criticized traditional Czech ethnology/ethnography. This kind of activity "does not in any way have anything in common and cannot have anything in common" with cultural/social anthropology because its subject—"the folk"—is disappearing in the modern society "in the same way the National Upheaval (or later Marxist) ideology, that backed it up, did" (Nešpor and Jakoubek 2004, 63). Supporting an ethnic group or identity-building project was something that was proper only to ethnographers associated with the old regime and with nationalist thinking. In the same text, the Romani Studies Department is criticized because of the same reasons: "The science is mistaken for 'national agitation,' artificially creating Romani ethnic group, or more precisely a nation" (Nešpor and Jakoubek 2004, 64). Within such a context of denunciation of essentialism, many anthropologists became employees or allies of non-Romani social work organizations and government structures, rather than of Romani and pro-Romani antidiscrimination activists. The intellectual hostility to essentialism understood as unprofessionalism contributed to a social split among "good" and "bad" NGOs.

Challenging the Established Model of NGOs and Bringing the Ethnicity Back

This section introduces new actors on the scene—activists—and the challenge they posed to NGOs. The recent global economic crisis created the need for more flexible modes of organization, yet NGOs came to be increasingly identified with the dysfunctional models of financing and too conservative social action. Economic crisis worsened the NGO legitimacy crisis; the solutions they offered were too slow for activists and, for some politicians, too costly. It is not surprising that provision of housing became the important issue also in the Czech Republic and one of the main focuses of activists. These activists were inspired by leftist theorizing, which got certain publicity after the years of enthusiasm for market reform. NGOs were identified as part of this market reform and delegation of the state responsibilities to other actors.

The power constellation of academics supporting mainstream integration NGOs began to change in 2012–13. These years brought the vocal critique of these NGOs and triggered other types of organizing that later ended in establishment of an organization that, more than a hierarchical structure, resembled a network. Involvement in NGOs was so far the case of elite networks (Romani, non-Romani, and academic), but despite the fact that most of the activists were also from these networks, they for the first time tried to organize together with the people who were the "target group" of NGOs. Activists also challenged the cautious de-ethnicized NGO rhetoric and openly talked about ethnic discrimination.

At first, left-wing non-Romani activists became active in the protests against anti-Roma marches in Czech cities; anti-Nazi activities were their traditional domain. They also became interested in the issues of evictions of Romani families out of the dilapidated houses in several cities in the Czech Republic. When housing owners cut off the water and electricity supply (e.g., in Ostrava and Ústí nad Labem), the activists started house occupations in support of Romani families living there. Being close to the anarchist movement, only some activists established official structures in the form of civic organizations. Rather, they created a kind of network that supported the social movement and criticized the larger, established NGOs. Some political scientists and younger anthropologists (usually doctoral students), inspired, for example, by the events in Chiapas, by Marxism, critiques of development, and postcolonial theorizing, were part of the movement; many of them started writing articles criticizing the approach of People in Need. They called People in Need "the guardians of post-communist good" and reproached it for its selective international development policy.[9] They viewed their policy as based on anticommunism, aligning with state ideology, love of the United States, de-ethnicization, victimization of Roma, individualized social work, and rhetoric of self-development in which Roma should transform themselves into the mainstream middle-class when they would rather have pride, acceptance, and empowerment. For them, People in Need taught people to catch fish while there were no fish in the pond and the pond was being emptied (Slačálek and Rychetský 2013).

The recent chief of the People in Need Social Inclusion Programs replied to this critique by saying they were not idealists and that the critique reflected the political and theoretical persuasions of the authors, not the real practices of People in Need, which also had instituted many successful community projects. According to the chief, People in Need was a pragmatic organization that preferred to reflect on reality first and only later try to change it. It did not think in "the logic of social conflict" as activists did, and their workers did not want to "use poor families with whom they cooperate as a new proletariat in the fight against the system, but they want to make their conditions better through the long-term work" (Člověk v tísni 2013, 28; Černý 2013). There exists a wide tendency for NGOs not being willing to call their negotiations with other political actors, or their competition within NGO networks, as "political." Raúl Acosta (2004) calls this tendency the "halfhearted politics of NGOs." In my research, the "political" discussion that NGOs fear could mean anything connected to a proclaimed ideology (ethnic, socialist) or an activity, which goes beyond a simple project and is overtly activist or militant. Activists, however, do not acknowledge that everyday careful negotiation would be the way forward in tackling social problems. Such conflict is a familiar conflict of "reformists," who want to repair the system, versus "revolutionists," who would rather dismantle it (Acosta 2004, 3).

An excerpt of an activist's interview with the director of inclusion programs, which was published by a rather small intellectual journal together with the previously mentioned critique, illustrates the discussion:

> Activist: Why don't you rise up against the bad functioning of the city [city of Ústí, which ignored the critical situation of houses, where Roma lived] politically?
> Director: We are not a political organization.
> Activist: Yet you are doing other political campaigns with success.
> Director: Yes we do, but not while we negotiate with someone.
> Activist: And don't you think that this cuts the ground from under your feet?
> Director: But it is our choice. We have a custom that one does not do that, because it is mutually exclusive. Either you play practical jokes and do activism, or you negotiate about what should happen. (Černý 2013, 20)

People in Need, Amaro, and similar social service organizations have been working in many cities for years. In order to function (find spaces and finances for counseling and running of children clubs, negotiate clients' issues, etc.), they enter into complex local power relationships. Possibilities to act more critically toward the local authorities are curbed and they can become part of the institutional setting that is unable to significantly improve the situation. Calling their activities "pragmatic" or "practical" thus helps them to survive. Activists are portrayed by these NGOs as people who come and go, bringing the danger of radicalizing the local situation and worsening fragile relationships with the authorities. In Ústí, for example, activists were accused by an NGO of misleading people by informing them that the city is obliged to offer them housing (Poradna pro občanství 2013).

In the case of People in Need, the position toward activists was in some ways similar to the position toward Romani NGOs in the past—it used a rhetoric with moral overtones that condemned activists for being amateurs and being too political. Romani NGOs were criticized because of their ethnicized ideology of special relationships between workers and clients and nationalist agendas. Now the unprofessionalism of activists has been linked also to their ideological backgrounds—accusing them of taking people "hostage" in their own ideological fight of people against the establishment. For example, in the case of Ústí nad Labem, where activists occupied the dilapidated dormitory trying to prevent the forced evacuation of families by police to even worse conditions or complete homelessness, People in Need was angry at the activists for openly criticizing them for not dealing with housing issues, not protesting against privatization of the public housing stock, and repeatedly sending clients to substandard yet expensive housing characteristic of the kind of secondary housing market available for Romani families.[10] Such criticism of People in Need was expressed not only in the media but also in front of clients as part of their awareness raising, such that these clients lost part of their trust in the organization.

Activists formulated their position in the following manner: "The problems of the poor Romani communities would not be solved by university-educated *gadje* [non-Roma in Romani], who try to provide them social services, but by activation of their inner resources and potential of their members" (Brož 2012). The logic of such an argument goes against the professionalized relationship between social service worker and client and supports the idea of participation of equals, self-help, and activation of grassroots. The main cause of the poor situation of Roma is identified as ethnic discrimination, not lack of education or jobs; therefore, talking about ethnicity of the people is the essential part of the activists' strategy.

The activists were indeed quite successful in reaching local Roma. They even radicalized some younger and older Roma from evicted families, who came to Prague to several seminars to speak about the cooperation of evicted families and activists. In two of the meetings I attended, an older woman from Ústí spoke in tears about the fact that for the first time in her life she saw non-Roma defending Roma and suffering with them. Non-Roma activists talked about the difficult search for trust and how transformational "house occupations" were for them. A young Romani man from Ostrava spoke about how the Roma were previously passively waiting for eviction, but now they knew they could fight. He wanted to establish a network of Roma in the whole Czech Republic who would help each other. He started a Facebook page for the network and has been active, speaking at different venues. The activists were able as well to communicate with some so-far uninvolved older Romani activists and bring them to these meetings to speak, including a Romani leader of a political party, and so contributed to the meeting of "Romani elites" and people facing evictions. For the first time a bigger number of non-Romani activists from other anti-inequality movements joined together with Roma activists. This was a sign of a linking strategy that political scientist Peter Vermeersch (2005, 455) recommends to Roma activists, whose identity strategies failed to create cross-cutting alliances. Such events connected different sorts of actors and created a fertile soil for future cooperation in the form of an advocacy network.

From Social Movement toward Advocacy Network

The social movement that challenged the established models of help and institutional forms opened space for novel forms of organizing. Protests thus created possibilities for diverse actors to join in a common effort. Sometimes these efforts became again institutionalized, for example, in the form of an advocacy network. What do social movements and the possibilities created by protests offer NGOs? Which NGOs are more and less likely to get involved and stay in the newly established networks, and what are the challenges for running a functional network?

The upsurge of activity around the anti-Roma protests and house occupations prompted several anthropologists (including the secretly participating members of the government's Agency for Social Inclusion), activists, and NGO workers to start the Platform for Social Housing. The platform was considered "too activist" for organizations like People in Need or Amaro. This network connected very different kinds of actors, from individuals to NGOs to departments of social science. Some of the NGOs, such as the Salvation Army, were traditional actors providing social services to homeless populations; others were smaller participatory groupings of homeless people supported by academics, which were formed only very recently and as a complete novelty inspired from abroad. The young Romani man from Ostrava mentioned earlier, the NGO Romea (the NGO that runs the biggest Romani media server[11]), and the important activist organization Konexe, which unite non-Romani and Romani activists, were also members of the network. Such broad membership reveals the strength of the platform but, as we will see, also its weakness.

Some social work NGOs also joined the network. We can interpret their participation as an effort to establish an alternative and competing model of social work against the most traditional and biggest actors, like People in Need, and the effort to create their own links with policy makers. Thus on the one hand activity in the advocacy network represented a tool to enhance competition in the NGO field, to become a major player and present their own practice as the most ethical and effective. On the other hand joining such networks required NGOs to experiment with and actively transform their own provision of social services. It was an opportunity to push ahead "self-reform."

The platform organized discussions, seminars, and campaigns and communicated with ministries on the wording of the proposed law on social housing. It invited people with the experience of homelessness to take part in the seminars and workshops. Some of its members also supported other forms of social work than just individualized social work promoted by the mainstream—radical social work or community work. The platform presented an innovative approach to collective action that was able to get political attention. Compared to traditional actors, the platform was able to achieve what McAdam, Tarrow, and Tilly define as "transgressive contention"—the platform created uncertainty, made people rethink concepts, created new repertoires of action, aligned previously separate bodies, and "force[d] elites to reconsider their commitments and allegiances" (2001, 9). In contrast to established NGOs, it did not divide people into those who are "solving the problem" (professionals, social workers, etc.) versus those who "have problems" (clients, users of services, etc.) but united them all as people with a common interest.

The alliance of established NGOs, academics, and activists is, however, rather fragile and threatens to lose activists whenever it is considered too "collaborative with the system." The idea of a "state and municipality system" of social housing or solution with the help of social work was difficult to accept for activists who were part of the platform, but oriented toward an antisystemic critique. Grassroots activists themselves are not much involved in organizing conferences or in high-level negotiations with government ministries. It requires too much balancing and compromising. The associated smaller activist organizations or looser networks are most active during the critical moments of public protests. The negotiations are done by "activist academics" or NGOs. Activist academics were able to get some short-term financial support to carry out lobbying and organizing. These activities were indeed partly successful, and the Social Housing Law (the form of which is the subject of constant negotiation) became a government goal. Heightened involvement of "elite" or "less radical" members can, however, lead to deradicalization of the network.

The platform also struggled to keep other actors involved. Traditional NGOs working with homeless people were against giving too much voice to their clients (who were also invited to the conferences to speak), who tended to criticize these organizations. These organizations then threatened to leave the association because the platform was "too activist" for them. For example, the Salvation Army left the coalition. Involving people threatened by homelessness on equal bases was another challenge. Hence, platform coordinators had to manage a very diverse network of actors with different goals and ideas about the system of social housing. Broad diversity of membership has been documented as being potentially destabilizing to social movements and networks (Edelman 2005), while other anthropologists point out that incorporating dissenting voices of members into the position of the network "strengthens networks' political capital when negotiating with policy makers" (Acosta 2012, 25).

Missing in this network completely were numerous NGOs (like People in Need and Amaro) and individuals (e.g., researchers) that proposed getting people into an open housing market or into punitive social work programs, where clients had to learn the competences of living in a standard apartment before moving to it (which frequently never happened as the people remain indebted). In October 2014, the platform organized a conference on access of Roma to housing, hosted by the Office of the Government. International speakers there presented innovative social housing models. The organizers, however, gave space to the opponents as well. I was surprised to hear a dreadlocked social worker of Amaro speak about their housing program that was designed for people who already had enough competencies to live. Amaro was seeking the "relevant partner for the business part" of the housing project, meaning a "user" (a client of social services) who would be able to "manage his/her finances and maintain hygienic norms and [had] communication skills." To succeed in the housing market, Amaro first trained the client in the "summary of obligatory tasks" and supported the "development of his/her character." The NGO provided to a housing estate a "tested/audited tenant," usually with a "secured payment of social benefits" and provided services to an estate agency. It thus offered a certain product with a guarantee.

Despite being a strong critic of People in Need, Amaro definitely has not gone the way of searching for alternatives. Over the years it rather developed in some ways a more conservative discourse and policies than People in Need. In the discussion, the Amaro representative stated that indeed its

Romani clients encounter discrimination, but it was searching for ways that are open to it and did not want its actions to be blocked on the basis of stereotyping of its target group. It had lawyers in case the clients wanted to act but did not necessarily use them against the discriminatory practices of owners of housing. Amaro had thus been blocked in its more activist or human rights agendas by the fact that it wanted to secure cooperation with municipalities and estate agencies. Involvement in activist agendas presented a risk that all the NGOs could not afford to take, especially those that were mostly locally financed and had troubled relationships with local authorities. NGOs that strive for professionalization but have problems securing everyday operations do not necessarily have the capacities to get involved in other activities requiring time and finances. Employing people who could themselves be disadvantaged on the job market can be another reason for maintaining a low profile. Such NGOs then tend to create more conformist and hierarchical models of their service provision. The largest organizations that are successful in the system too do not seem to be eager for big reforms. For these organizational types, stability is the important goal. Social work organizations that are willing to "take risks" seem to be rather mainstream middle-sized actors.

The network is weary of the risks presented by professionalization and participation in grant application processes, which profoundly affected the functioning of social work NGOs. Despite searching for some financial support, the network is trying to keep its focus on the adoption and implementation of the nondiscriminatory law of social housing and sustain the network of a very diverse membership. It is attempting to network also with sympathetic municipalities, connect them with innovative NGOs, and create and research local social housing policies. The network is also threatened by the fact that the actors differ in the perception of the level of acceptable criticism—for traditional provider NGOs, it is "too activist," for activists, "not activist enough." These actors then become less active or leave the network. Activist academics and NGOs trying to challenge the status quo and experimenting with increasing participation of their clients remain the most active.

Conclusions

The lesson learned by an advocacy network created to build a relationship between activism and professionalization is that professionalization can weaken the radicalism of activism, but it does not have to exclude activism completely. Although activists criticized professionalization and bureaucratization of NGOs, when cooperation in advocacy network is concerned, professionalism of certain NGO members is not a complete barrier.

The activists' critique was directed against social work NGOs, such as Amaro or People in Need, who in their eyes failed to meet the needs of communities and promoted the ideology of individualized social services. This presumed failure happened despite the fact that Amaro and People in Need had different levels of social capital, composition of their original trust networks (kinship- vs. friendship-based), and sources of legitimation of their work—more ethnic or more social and professional. By becoming providers of social services, they both became subject to the constraints of the state funding programs, thus becoming closer to both state and to private organizations. This trend is in general described as an increasing hybridity of the organizations, especially those connected to welfare provision (Billis 2010). Project funding and associated professionalization transform NGOs and limit their political agendas to the point that some members of NGOs said to me that they are "not doing politics" at all. Activists however have not condemned NGOs completely and have invited some of them to join the advocacy network. The fact that their issue-based network comprises actors with different agendas and identities (mainstream social work, Christian, activist, or academic) does not block their ability to act.

We can identify here a certain circular process. A protest movement that criticizes state and municipal actors and NGOs transforms into an advocacy network, which tries to influence NGOs not only by direct critique but also by inviting them into the network. Such NGOs can test the new activist approaches with their clients and serve as an example of different practices in social services. NGOs can be thus co-opted both by the administrative projects regimes and also by the networks that seek innovation. By participating in the network with different actors (academics, activists, and clients), the professionalized NGOs can benefit from the informational service of the network, which is sharing research, examples of innovative practices, and day-to-day experiences of people threatened by homelessness. By serving as a testing ground, NGOs can be used by the network as domestic proof of feasibility of some network's ideas. Academics and activists will gladly share NGO examples of best practice during their negotiations with municipalities and the government, contributing to the mutual symbiosis of network members. Academics will also provide research of these innovations to further support the political goal of the network.

The quest of the network for domestic applications of innovations is important because it has a much better chance of influencing local political actors, who tend to dismiss foreign innovations by the claim that such approach cannot be transferred to the special financial, political, and cultural context of their country. Inclusion of local NGOs thus contributes to the nationwide acceptance of the goals of the network, even though some of these NGOs can be much less innovative than foreign actors. The network can choose which members should be activated for which tasks. The associated smaller activist organizations and other revolutionists are already most active during the critical moments of public protests, while the reformist NGOs are more interested in negotiating technicalities of the reform and implementing them into their own practices. Balancing the network on the scale between conformism and revolution, however, needs constant attention. Keeping the diverse network together requires effective mechanisms of communication, while not losing sight of making real change.

This chapter has shown that although the initial legitimation of organizations can differ, the processes of professionalization can cause significant organizational conformity. It is therefore useful to study not only the differing organizational rhetoric but also to look at the extent of professionalization of the organization and how this process progressively influences its rhetoric and practice. It has been shown that especially professionalized NGOs tend to call their activities pragmatic or practical and avoid the connection to politics as a certain survival strategy. Some of them can however engage in networking with activists through the creation of advocacy networks. The chapter has identified some mutually beneficial connections of activists and NGOs—activists can test innovations with NGOs and get the local credibility, while NGOs can benefit from the information service, new insights into the importance of accountability toward "clients," and participate in the creation of advocacy proposals without having to engage in activism in person. Even the more passive NGO members of the network who are afraid of the politicization of their work can provide some background support and share their experiences. Participation in such networks can thus be a partial solution to NGO co-optation of project regimes. It can help to redirect their accountability from the elite networks back to the communities. The network can provide a stimulating context for an organization, which can afford to experiment with its social service provision.

There are also several risks involved: the risk for NGOs lies in the threat to their survival. Activism is not easily accessible for every NGO, and involvement is influenced by the level of social, political, and economic capital. There are only certain types of NGOs that tend to join or can afford to join such networks. The well-established and largest organizations with active links to the political system use other channels than activism to reach their goals. Small professionalizing organizations often do not have the financial and personal capacities to engage and have more localized donors, who can threaten to withdraw their funding. Advocacy networks are joined mainly by NGOs that have more diversified resources and the capacity to devote their time to the cause. The risk for activists is the deradicalization of the network due to its professionalization and also returning from revolution back to reform, because most activities in the network tend to be performed by "not so radical" actors. This leads to a sort of mitigated activism that can, however, still bring some desired changes.

Notes

1. An adjective of Rom (singular) or Roma (plural).

2. A pseudonym meaning "ours" in Romani.

3. This chapter is based on 2005–10 research on the strategies of Czech NGOs working in dilapidated city areas inhabited mainly by Romani populations (Synková 2011) and continuing observation. Apart from volunteering in Amaro, I participated in the Czech academic circles that are involved in the topics concerning Roma and worked in the Agency for Social Inclusion at the Office of the Government, where I coordinated applied research.

4. For deeper analysis of the working of Amaro and kinship and friendship networking, see Synková 2010.

5. For example, the treatment of researchers is indicative of their organizational complexity: to get a few interviews and explore the possibility of going to the field with their social workers (after a longer stay had been ruled out), I had to be approved by several levels of management.

6. Field programs are social work programs not provided in the office but directly in the community, often including visits to their houses. The most frequent target group of their programs were poor Romani populations.

7. An individual agreement between the client and social worker with set goals and topics.

8. Combating social exclusion and promoting social inclusion and cohesion have been the main goals of social policy of the so-called Lisbon agenda (EU strategy for 2000–2010) and continue to be goals of a new Europe 2020 strategy launched in 2010.

9. The original and main focus of People in Need is international development.

10. Analysis of the case from the point of different modes of policy work can be found in Čada and Ptáčková (2014).

11. The website romea.cz is the most vocal voice of Czech Roma; however, Romea does not have any stable financing for its server. It has to finance around ten of its members from other, less visible social and educational projects and cooperate with volunteers.

5
Leveraging Supranational Civil Society

Critiquing Czech Gender Equality Policy through Academic-NGO Collaboration

Karen Kapusta-Pofahl

Distinctions between public and private, foreign and local, and state and NGO are often ambiguous and always contested.
—Victoria Bernal and Inderpal Grewal, "The NGO Form: Feminist Struggles, States, and Neoliberalism"

In 2004 a multisectoral coalition of gender experts from academia and NGOs in the Czech Republic attempted to advocate for improvements in implementing and monitoring gender equality policies in the wake of their entrance into the European Union (EU). In this chapter, I analyze this collaboration that worked to incite what Keck and Sikkink (1998) call a boomerang pattern of influence—appealing to the authority of the EU to pressure the Czech government to improve its efforts at promoting gender equality. Due to the ambiguous and contested relationships among these various actors, however, such collaborations can be fraught with dilemmas. The case of the creation of the *Shadow Report on the Equal Treatment and Equal Opportunities for Women and Men* discussed here highlights these nuances. In working to leverage the opprobrium of the EU in an attempt to call state actors to account, the *Shadow Report* also put pressure on a group of underresourced newcomers to gender policy within government ministries. Three aspects of this collaboration are the coalition's use of the *Shadow Report* as a tool of what Keck and Sikkink (1998) term leverage and accountability politics, some structural challenges to the success of the boomerang effect, and internal dilemmas faced by the coalition regarding differences in expectations and priorities between academic and NGO collaborators.

Ethnographers of postsocialism have found encounters between governing bodies and nongovernmental experts to be fruitful sites from which to analyze gender, power, knowledge production, and governance on multiple scales. In the scholarship of postsocialism, the NGO often appears in the discussion of "civil society," which is often juxtaposed to that of "the state," whether socialist or neoliberal (Gal and Kligman 2000; Hann 2001). Over time, the concept of the NGO became emblematic of the notion of civil society, even as scholars pointed out the dangers of this conflation of concepts and prioritization of the NGO form over other forms of democratic action (Einhorn 2010). Concerns, such as those over the ways in which the NGO form was preempting that of the social movement (Lang 1997) or how NGOs were increasingly responsible for carrying out what had previously been state obligations in areas such as social welfare (Haney 2002), prompted the creation of a large body of analytical work on the relationship between NGOs and the state in societies in Europe and around the globe. As the work of political scientist Sabine Lang (2014) illustrates, feminist advocacy networks within the EU have to contend with governance on multiple levels, as states and supranational bodies struggle to define the terrain of gender equality. Although increased attention has been paid to women's advocacy networks within the EU, the topic of academic-NGO collaboration in and of itself has remained at the periphery of ethnographic works (Riles 2001). Along with Hana Synková's work in this volume, I bring these collaborations to the fore.

The *Shadow Report*: Leveraging Supranational Accountability

In 2004, the year the Czech Republic joined the EU, a group of six gender experts from NGOs and academia wrote and distributed a report critically analyzing the government's efforts to promote gender equality. The *Shadow Report on Equal Treatment and Equal Opportunities for Women and Men* is a comprehensive response to the official government *Summary Report on the Implementation of the Priorities and Procedures of the Government in Promoting Equality of Men and Women* from the years 1998 to 2002. The *Shadow Report* covers several years of government reports, the units responsible for monitoring and implementing gender equality policy, and a critical review of government activity in each of the priority areas in the original reports (women in politics and the labor market, violence against women, education, health care, and NGOs).

The purpose of the *Shadow Report* was to incite what Keck and Sikkink call a boomerang pattern: "When channels between the state and its domestic actors are blocked, . . . domestic NGOs [may] bypass their state and directly search out international allies to try to bring pressure on their states from outside" (1998, 12). The process was occurring at a time when the

Czech government began to be ostensibly receptive to pressure from the EU. Although the Czech Republic joined the EU in 2004, the process of alignment with EU norms began almost a decade earlier, in the latter half of the 1990s. Since then, the language of "gender mainstreaming" has increasingly inched into national policy language and has been subtly shifting cultural discourses on the question of gender equality in Czech society.

In Cris Shore's ethnography of the inner workings of the EU, he argues that, as a supranational governing body, its goal "is to create a new kind of post-national political *and cultural* order that will supersede the nation-state" (2000, 29, emphasis mine). As such, the project of "Europeanization" relies on the socialization of new member states to the norms of the larger body with the goal of creating what Shore calls a "European consciousness" (30). In turn, these assimilative processes promote not only a "sense of belonging and loyalty" to these new norms, but also lend "democratic legitimacy and authority" to the EU itself (21). As additional states are admitted, they are required to align not only their legal and economic but also their social policies with the values expressed in EU directives and communiqués (a process called "harmonization"). EU governing bodies have placed added pressure on new potential members to prove their worth through the wholehearted implementation of all of the EU's policies as part of the intense attention and scrutiny that the newest member countries received in the years preceding their entrance to the EU.[1] Due to the elements of European integration that emphasize cultural "harmonization," EU membership is fraught with significant tensions.

Despite the tensions of EU membership, women's NGOs and the field of gender studies have garnered increased legitimacy through the EU focus on gender equality legislation. One of the core planks of the EU social policy platform is gender equality. As a policy framework, gender mainstreaming calls for a reassessment and reworking of all policies so that rather than having to add women into already-existing policies, those policies are created with their relation to women's lives already in place. An explicit commitment to gender equality is emphasized throughout EU policy documents as a fundamental component of inclusivity within "European" society to such an extent that Sabine Lang argues that the EU could be considered to be a "norm entrepreneur for gender equality" (2014, 186).[2] Further, the EU, like other governmental actors, has "increasingly become dependent on policy expertise residing within the NGO sector" (25). As a result, experts on gender issues were increasingly called on to consult with and train those within the government tasked with implementing gender equality directives. This shift toward nongovernmental expertise at the supranational level provided gender experts with an opportunity to attempt to assert their influence on the Czech state and advocate for increased awareness of gender inequality in Czech society.

In the years between the revolution of 1989 and the period when the Czech Republic began retooling its institutions to harmonize with the EU in the late 1990s, ideas about gender and feminism were a source of constant controversy and a great amount of derision in public discourse. The efforts of NGOs and scholars to establish the field of gender studies got a boost as an effect of the larger process of EU accession in a number of ways. In particular, participation in the accession process meant increased access to key material and discursive resources: funding sources, legitimacy of gender inequality as a problem, and indirectly, the need for trainers, consultants, and other experts in gender issues. In a society that is skeptical of the value of the study of gender and gender relations, EU funding provided both material and symbolic support to NGOs and scholars working in what some of my cultural consultants refer to as the "gender scene."

Anthropologist Annelise Riles argues that it is important for ethnographers to attend to documents as "paradigmatic artifacts of modern knowledge practices" (2006b, 2). Riles also argues that "a failure to appreciate the efficacy of technocratic knowledge in the rush to critique it, ironically renders ethnography itself nonefficacious in the face of politics and gender" (21). In other words, documents are more than just bureaucratic detritus to be mocked for their superficiality. Rather, they are a key aspect of the ethnographic process, what Riles calls "response as a modality of collaboration" (25). Documents index the larger politics at work, in that they "anticipate and enable certain actions by others—extensions, amplifications, and modifications of both content and form" (21). The writers of the *Shadow Report* frame their contribution as "compiled by individuals from the nongovernmental sector and the academic sphere as an alternative to the governmental Summary Report on the Priorities and Procedures of the Government in Promoting Equality of Men and Women" to call to account both the official summary document and government practices as falling significantly short (Pavlík 2004, 7). They sought to provide "a critical assessment of the situation in the area of equal opportunities" (7). However, the writers also state that they intend the report to be a "constructive inspiration" for those working on these issues in the government, as well as "those who may contribute to improving the current less than satisfactory situation (legislators, members of the government and ministerial apparatuses, journalists, etc.)" (7). This particular document, which is commentary on yet another document, was born out of frustration with the way the government reported their achievements to the European Commission and Czech society at large. Using both leverage and accountability politics, the *Shadow*

Report team of collaborators was advocating for better performance of the Czech government on gender issues, as well as attempting to initiate a shift from "words on paper" to real change.

As sociologist Elaine Weiner's research shows, however, the Czech Republic has been "especially incompliant" in implementing gender equality legislation (2010, 17). She found that there was widespread prima facie compliance, but that in practice, lawyers and others addressing gender discrimination in employment were interested in presenting a nondiscriminatory image rather than actually avoiding discrimination. Weiner argues that the "language [of a labor lawyer she interviewed] suggested that the acceptable challenge for employers lies in appearing in lieu of being nondiscriminatory" (17). She locates the resistance to embracing equal opportunity legislation as being part of an essentialist view of gender that makes the law seem to be unrealistic and, as such, subject to caveats in practice. The writers of the *Shadow Report* document many instances where "the actual situation does not in any way correspond to the relatively optimistic tone of the governmental Reports" (Pavlík 2004, 7). The government report corroborates Weiner's findings, as it portrays a rosy picture of compliance, which does not hold up to scrutiny by nongovernmental actors.

One theme in the *Shadow Report* refers to the relationship between the state and NGO sectors. It points out that although the government reports give lip service to the role of NGOs in the gender mainstreaming process, the reality was less than ideal: "All Reports state that non-profit organizations are an irreplaceable part of implementing equal opportunities policies for women and men, and their activities are highlighted and positively evaluated; the 2000 Report even says that NGOs should themselves exert greater pressure on the public administration" (Pavlík 2004, 110). However, in reality, the *Shadow Report* states that NGOs have been sidelined from the process. One of the implications of this marginalization manifests in the writing of the government summary reports themselves. Since they are written by the very people who have the most interest in presenting the government in a positive light, there is no incentive to work with the NGOs that operate in the priority areas to receive and present an accurate picture of the real state of affairs. Markéta,[3] a member of the *Shadow Report* team, thinks that although the *Shadow Report* is being widely distributed, its impact may be limited: "The final product is wonderful. I really like it. It's a good quality piece of writing[;] it really reflects on the governmental work. . . . I wouldn't overestimate the impact of it. We've done our maximum to disseminate the information about it and the Shadow Report itself. We burned many CDs, sent it everywhere, publications, press release, press conference, but the thing is that it is just not the habit of those who should read it to read those things."

If it were to remain within the realm of national politics, the efficacy of the *Shadow Report* to alter policy would be restricted to the point of marginalization. The *Shadow Report* writers hoped to circumvent these national structures by including the EU as a recipient.

According to the boomerang pattern of advocacy, leveraging outside authorities is intended to trigger a response from the targeted state apparatus. In leverage politics, "by leveraging more powerful institutions, weak groups gain influence far beyond their ability to influence state practices directly" (Keck and Sikkink 1998, 23). By leveraging the expectations of the EU, the writers of the *Shadow Report* sought to put pressure on the Czech state to improve its reporting and implementation practices. In addition to leverage politics, by calling both domestic and international attention to the deficiencies in the Czech state's reporting, and also its lack of attention to gender equality goals, the *Shadow Report* also taps into what Keck and Sikkink call accountability politics: "Once a government has publically committed itself to a principle . . . networks can use those positions . . . to expose the distance between discourse and practice. This is embarrassing to many governments, which may try to save face by closing that distance" (1998, 24). The boomerang pattern described by Keck and Sikkink makes some assumptions about the power that the state has to address the concerns that the nongovernmental advocates level at them. If leverage and accountability politics are to work, the state apparatus needs to not only be sensitive to the criticism but also have the resources and human capital to successfully respond to the pressure. In the Czech case, at least in the immediate wake of the report, those who felt the sting of its criticism most keenly were the street-level bureaucrats who had been assigned to monitor and implement gender equality policy in the various ministries, the Gender Focal Points (GFPs).

Gender Focal Points: Pressuring the Powerless?

The *Shadow Report* raises a related concern about the level of expertise of those assigned to monitor and implement gender equality policy within the ministries of government. As part of its criticism of the lack of expertise in gender policy that is held by those in decision-making positions regarding it, the *Shadow Report* discusses the difficult position of the staff members assigned to these positions within the ministries—the GFPs: "Most of the GFPs are placed within the Human Resources Departments at desk officer level. That is, they are the lowest level civil servants and do not have powers that would allow them to enforce the equal treatment policy within the Ministry. They usually report to a superior who is not familiar with gender issues" (Pavlík 2004, 23). Further, the report points out that the GFPs were also at a disadvantage regarding training, since "the majority of the GFPs were first exposed to the equal treatment policy only after they were appointed" (24). Equipped with little training or authority, the GFPs were vulnerable to criticism from all sides. Although the writers of the *Shadow Report* were aware of the limited powers of the GFPs and criticize the government for not providing them with the authority and resources they need, using leverage politics meant that the brunt of the critique fell on their shoulders.

I experienced the frustrations of some of the GFPs firsthand during my fieldwork when I attended a seminar that brought together NGO members, academic feminists, and several GFPs who were charged with "mainstreaming gender" into national policy.[4] On a clear autumn day in late 2004, I traveled to the prestigious sixth district of Prague, which is known for its beautiful villas. The conference venue, an ornate but faded villa owned by the national research academy, was situated amid tall trees on the edge of a large wooded urban park. About thirty women and two men were seated around a large wooden table in the ornate conference room.

The purpose of the seminar, explained the director of the sponsoring research institute, was to present the results of a multiyear research project on applying sociological research to equal opportunity policy. Presentations included reports on research on gender inequality in the labor market, how Czech women are "harmonizing" work and family life, the use of state-allotted parental leave, and women's participation in Czech politics. The seminar audience included people I had seen at similar events (and would see often throughout the duration of my fieldwork): professors and students from gender studies departments at two major universities, sociological researchers based in the academy of sciences, and members of NGOs that focused on women's rights and gender issues. At this event, however, I also noticed a number of women who appeared to range in age from the middle of their forties to late fifties, dressed professionally in button-down blouses and suit jackets, whose faces were as yet unfamiliar to me. These women, government ministry employees representing their respective ministries in matters of the promotion of equal opportunities, were the GFPs. GFPs are responsible for analyzing ministry policies to make sure they are in line with the "gender mainstreaming initiatives" and also act as liaisons between their ministries and the government-wide coordinating body for equal opportunities. As they stood one by one to introduce themselves, the GFPs told a similar story about why they were attending the seminar. One of the GFPs explained that she was looking to "map" (*zmapovat*) the situation of women in her ministry's topic area. Others mentioned that they had been seeking "an expert" to provide them with the information, such as statistics on the number of women in various professions, that they needed in drafting government reports on the status of equal opportunity policy. In each case, their need for expert information led them to attend the seminar.

During the discussion that proceeded after the GFPs introduced themselves, it became clear that the position of GFP within the various ministries could be stressful. On one hand, there was pressure to proactively conform to and promote EU approaches to "gender mainstreaming" in an enlightened and assertive manner. On the other hand, the civil servants who were designated as GFPs often held low-status positions in ministry hierarchies, with the accompanying lack of authority to suggest programs or policies to unsympathetic superiors. They were also assigned the role of GFP as a half-time position with responsibilities over and above their existing duties, which were often in areas unrelated to gender policy. They had little or no training in gender policy analysis or gender issues more generally (some of the scholars at this conference also organized trainings for ministry employees on gender issues), and therefore sought out assistance from the academic experts in gender studies in carrying out their duties. In doing so, however, GFPs could find themselves wedged between the obligation of the state to demonstrate progress on harmonization with EU norms and the critical eye of the gender experts who were simultaneously training them and monitoring their progress.

At the seminar, GFPs expressed multiple frustrations, including inadequate pay, overwork, uncertainty about the best way to carry out their assigned tasks, and embarrassment over unfamiliarity with the discourse of feminism and gender equality espoused by EU policy, academics, and NGOs. The GFPs occupied a particularly vulnerable position within the state, one that did not always sit well with everyone. Markéta explained, "Yeah, some of the Focal Points told us that [the *Shadow Report*] undermines their work in the eyes of their bosses, although we've said a thousand times that it's not against the people, it's against the system and the results. We appreciate how hard the people work and how bad their conditions are and all that, but some of them just didn't listen to these positive things and just took the bad stuff." In contrast, Nora, another *Shadow Report* collaborator, pointed out that the increased pressure has had a positive effect on the attention the state has been paying to gender equality issues: "But there is huge progress because at the beginning those people were sitting there [arms crossed] and thinking 'this is such bullshit' and the Council [name][5] forced them to report on equal opportunities issues within their ministries and then they started to understand that there is something to it; not all of them but many of them really started to understand that it is an issue at least. Some of them more, some of them less, but the progress is here. And for example, the Ministry of Finance produced this brochure on gender budgeting. It's an amazing brochure because it's even extraordinary within Europe because when we were looking for materials, there was something here, something there, but such a brochure, such a comprehensive thing, they haven't found it." The GFP for the Ministry of Finance was mentioned by more than one of my informants as being particularly receptive to learning more about gender mainstreaming and working to bridge the gap between her initial level of training and what she needed to carry out her assigned tasks.[6]

The dynamics of the aforementioned scene demonstrate some of the tensions inherent in what Timothy Mitchell (2002) calls a "rule of experts." Although they are tasked with policy making, government workers themselves are not the authority on gender issues. They rely on the expertise of non-state actors, specifically academic experts, who can provide the state with the statistics and conceptual translations they need to present the "state of affairs" on gender equality in the Czech Republic to supranational bodies. These "knowledge workers" are themselves subject to marginalization by the very state apparatus that relies on them to provide them with training and information. Thus, calling the state to account involves much more than increased transparency in reporting on progress on implementing policy. It calls for a reorganization of the structures within which the policy is being carried out. Weiner's research finding (that gender equality is unrealistic) is only bolstered by a climate of inadequate understanding of the values and assumptions that undergird the policy conceptually. The GFPs bear the brunt of the boomerang pattern but cannot easily respond to all of the criticisms due to their own precarious positions. Part of the issue regarding this tension is a question of expertise—who has the expertise in gender issues to effectively implement EU policy? While the governmental units and heads were newcomers to the idea of gender equality policy, they were the ones who were responsible for evaluating it. The experts, however, played peripheral roles in the process as consultants or trainers or sources of research. The vicissitudes of these roles contributed not only to tensions between GFPs and gender experts concerning the *Shadow Report* but also contributed to tensions in wider collaborations between members of the academic and NGO gender scene that extended beyond the experiences of the *Shadow Report* coalition.

Dilemmas of Feminist Academic and NGO Collaboration: Advocacy and Objectivity

Academic gender studies in the Czech Republic have their roots in the nongovernmental sphere. At the same time that they were working in their academic institutions and fields to establish gender studies and feminist research, several of the founders of academic gender studies programs were also participants in the founding circle of the most prominent NGO dedicated to gender studies in the country. From its inception in 1991 as a "professional library, so-called Curriculum Center and networking site," this NGO included an academic focus (Gender Studies 2016). At the same time, some in the founding circle began to teach courses in gender studies as "travelling courses" at universities around the country (Havelková and Oates-Indruchová 2014; Šmejkalová 2004). Over the course of the 1990s, the mother organization for much of this activity retained its library and its hosting of lectures and discussions but also pursued projects related to the interests of organization leaders. After 1998, there was a shift in focus of the NGO, which resulted in increased differentiation between academic and NGO endeavors. By the early 2000s, two universities and a public research institute had established gender studies programs, as departments, or programs in collaboration with the field of sociology.[7] Meanwhile, the Gender Studies NGO, one of the larger of the many women's NGOs in existence in the Czech Republic during this time, began to focus more on advocacy. However, recent research on academic gender studies in the Czech Republic indicates that the NGO and academic spheres are imbricated in ways that challenge a sharp division between spheres—they share concepts, people, and arenas of activity (Lorenz-Meyer 2013). Nevertheless, as the present analysis illustrates, meaningful differences remain.

Despite an intertwined history and shared milieu (the "gender scene"), collaboration on the *Shadow Report* brought to the fore a number of differences between academic and NGO collaborators in expectations regarding the approach that the report should take.[8] Although some of the collaborators had experience in both sectors, the participants in the writing of the *Shadow Report* with whom I spoke each described tensions that arose between the academic and NGO members of the team. Given the interrelated history of academic gender studies and women's NGOs in the Czech Republic, this tension was surprising. Although part of the conflict may have stemmed from interpersonal issues, a set of notable themes surface in the accounts of the experiences that I collected. Markéta described the situation this way: "For example, one NGO member criticized one of the chapters that it is written in too high of language, too much expertise, that it was not possible for the people it is directed to to digest. Which is true and not true because at some point she is right because there is not a great level of knowledge and understanding of those people." Markéta described a difference in expectations between the academic and NGO members of the *Shadow Report* team. On one hand, there was a difference of opinion regarding the tone and complexity of the writing. The NGO member she referred to was concerned that the report would be too difficult to read, thus restricting its accessibility. On the other hand, she went on to explain, "if we wrote something very simple, not based on analysis and all that, it would be very vulnerable to criticism, which none of us wanted . . . especially the academic people. They didn't want that to happen because they are always subjected to such critique. The NGO would be more comfortable about some people saying 'oh it's bullshit because it doesn't have basic data and quotations and it doesn't use a certain level of language.' The NGO would take it better than the academic people. So it's a hard choice but I think that at the end it came out well." In contrast to the NGO member, the academic in Markéta's narrative was concerned that the report would not be sufficiently data driven and analytically complex. Nina, another member of the team, put it this way: "Some are more analytical, some are less analytical. . . . [Some of us] were attacked by other individuals for being too academic in our analyses, which I think is completely bullshit." From Nina's perspective, the academic members of the team were not writing at an untenably esoteric level or compromising the effectiveness of the report. Rather, as Markéta suggests, the academic team members felt that a certain level of sophistication was necessary for the report's effectiveness and its ability to withstand criticism from all quarters.

In Markéta's explanation of the dynamics of the collaboration, she linked this difference to a difference in the level of sensitivity to criticism. The academics, she suggested, are more vulnerable to criticism for a lack of rigor than are the NGO members. Because of this, they were, understandably in her view, attentive to the norms of academic communication such as data and analysis in ways that the NGO members were not as sensitive to. In her research on the creation of documents for the UN Fourth World Conference on Women, Riles found that during collaborative discussions among Fijian academics, NGOs, and policy makers around whether to use the word "gender" in the document, the academic feminist participants "felt confused by the language and objectives of the activists and bureaucrats with whom they had expected to share a great deal" (2006b, 71). As Riles found, multisectoral collaborations, even among groups whose members perceive themselves as having much in common, are subject to discursive and procedural tensions.

During the course of my larger study, I found that other academic gender studies practitioners, not involved in the *Shadow Report* collaboration, also perceived tensions between the role of the academic and that of the NGO in collaboration. One example is that of Irena, an academic gender studies practitioner who has experience collaborating with NGO members on various projects. She and an NGO worker were collaborating on a presentation of research results related to a topic that they shared an interest in. However, there was a disagreement about how to present information that might not be in the best interest of the NGO from an advocacy standpoint: "When a girl from [an NGO] and I did a presentation together, I had a terrible time writing the presentation with her because it seemed to me that she couldn't bring up some things because they weren't completely positive. But it is always a problem when you find something out from your respondents that isn't completely positive that you have to decide how to deal with. And it occurs to me that I as a researcher can't allow myself to be completely silent on these issues. And it seemed to me—and this isn't just my feeling, four of us collaborated on this presentation (three were academics, and I am a close friend with one of them so we've discussed it a lot and she had the completely same feeling) that to write [the presentation] with someone who was from the nonprofit sector was problematic." Whereas Irena expected that even results that challenged their advocacy program needed to be included in the presentation, the NGO member was resistant. In saying that she "as a researcher can't allow myself to be completely silent on these issues," Irena indicated that her expectations as a scholar were at odds with the expectations of the NGO in their advocacy for a change in society. In her narrative describing her experience collaborating across sectors, she described a position of information provider, explaining that researchers collect and interpret data and NGO members apply it according to their organizational goals. Because NGOs advocate for a certain segment of society or in favor of particular goals, she implied, they experience pressures to present themselves or their issue in a positive light, which researchers do not face or at least not to the same extent. While her colleague from the NGO found it extremely problematic to include information in their joint presentation that reflected negatively on their target group, Irena and her academic colleagues felt that it was their scholarly duty to do so. In other words, they felt they had a commitment to the data, regardless of their personal sympathies.

The issue, Irena explained, was not solely about the problem of good public relations. She felt it also stemmed from a tension between her role as a researcher and her participation in a project that was also used for advocacy: "I did some very quantitative, very sociological, research for [an NGO], simply data, data, data, no emotions. And on the other hand, out of this collaboration came a book [that] was another step [that] the NGO took that perhaps I did not completely agree with but I think that on the whole it was a very positive step. Look, the publication is really great, I like it a lot, but they explicitly recommend certain things. . . . But when I read through the publication, I noticed certain evaluations whose characteristics they got from me but to which they added plusses and minuses. . . . But this is something that is certainly activism, is something that has really changed the situation for women in the Czech Republic." Even though she was collaborating with an NGO, Irena perceived her contribution as "very sociological" in that it was "data, data, data." She characterized her NGO partner's contribution as that of recommendations, communication with the public, and as something that has "changed the situation for women in the Czech Republic." The data she provided were used by the NGO to further a social cause, one that Irena supported. However, the prescriptive ways in which they applied her data gave her slight pause. Irena explained that she perceived a difference between her role in the collaboration and felt a twinge of ambivalence; despite the fact that she considers herself a feminist and recognizes that "I basically think, of course, that no science is neutral even in the themes and methods I choose to follow. This is simply a given, in my view." While her reference to "data, data, data" suggests that her concern is with a lack of empirical grounding, her view of science as socially constructed suggests a recognition of the role of politics in knowledge production. Collaborating with NGOs on projects that advocate for social change brings these tensions to the fore for feminist academics.

Due to its emergence out of NGO activities and feminist activism, academic gender studies in the Czech context, similarly to that of women's studies elsewhere (Messer-Davidow 2002; Griffin 2005), does not hew closely to a clearly delineated boundary between scholarship and advocacy. Rather, academic feminists find themselves positioned in an intermediate space that is defined as more or less activist by the institutional context.[9] In addition to individual positions on this question, there were differences between institutions and even units within the same institution about the role of feminist scholarship in advocacy endeavors. It is possible to gain a sense of the larger contexts of institutional identity in which academics are situated through a reading of departmental websites. As Sabine Lang explains, "journalists who research issues and activities turn to web-based information from NGOs and their interlinked partners. And governments are getting clues about civic activism from the web" (2014, 191). As such, institutional websites provide clues as to how they situate themselves within the larger academic arena. For instance, the National Contact Center for Gender and Science (NKC) (2016) and the Gender and Sociology Department, both housed within the Institute of Sociology of the Czech Academy of Sciences, position themselves differently vis-à-vis advocacy. NKC describes itself in ways that emphasize both advocacy and scholarship:

> **Established in 2001, the National Contact Centre for Gender & Science (originally "for women and science") contributes to building gender equality in science and research.** We stimulate debates and **petition for measures and steps to eliminate discrimination** and gender inequalities in science. **We urge action** from responsible institu-

tions, and offer solutions to improve the professional advancement of women. **We carry out analyses** to address the asymmetrical distribution of power between men and women in science and in society in general. **We raise awareness about gender issues** in science and give visibility to women researchers and their work. We support and stimulate women's cooperation in science. We are integrated in **international networks** (European Platform for Women Scientists and ATGender) and contribute to the development of science policies. We participate in international projects and cooperate with similarly orientated support and research organizations abroad, especially in Europe. We are located in the sociology of knowledge, feminist theories and science studies, gender studies and public policy.[10]

Using terms such as "urging action" and "raising awareness" alongside terms such as "conducting analyses" and "sociology of knowledge," NKC positions itself as very much involved in the realm of advocacy. NKC is housed within an academic institute, conducts research projects and publishes scholarship, but it is also actively and explicitly working to promote gender equality in science through advocacy aimed at scientific institutions and policy makers. In other academic units, however, the mandate to carry out advocacy and academic work together is not necessarily as explicit. In contrast the Department of Gender and Sociology, also within the Institute of Sociology within the Czech Academy of Sciences (2016), presents a more empiricist image:

The Gender & Sociology department was established . . . to study the position of women in Czech society. . . . The department theoretically and empirically advances a concept of gender-oriented sociology extending to feminist sociology. Over the course of the 1990s the research team gradually expanded and today is one of the key scientific institutions in the Czech Republic that focuses on the position of men and women in society. The department combines the results of its own quantitative and qualitative research studies with theoretical research on particular issues and thus contributes to furthering the analysis of various specific gender issues. . . . The department also makes a significant contribution to the development of a multidisciplinary field of science—the gender studies, building of feminist sociological methodology and implementation of equal opportunities of men and women in the Czech Republic.

Using terms such as "empirical," "theoretical," "study," and "scientific," the Department of Gender and Sociology position themselves as data driven and scientific. While this quoted description mentions the "implementation of equal opportunities of men and women" and embraces feminist sociology, it emphasizes their scholarship and scientific approach to gender-related topics. Thus, there are nuances in the approaches not only of individuals but also academic units and institutions within the larger category of academic feminism that accompany any individual to a collaboration.

The ambiguous position of academic gender studies could be a contributing factor to the tensions expressed by members of the *Shadow Report* team. Whereas NGO members can clearly define themselves as advocacy organizations, the academics walk a finer line between scientific legitimacy and feminist activism. Further, in a field such as gender studies, which arose out of social movements or NGO forms in many parts of the world, the distinction between NGO and academic is challenged by the very nature of the field of inquiry itself. In a skeptical and positivistic climate, however, boundaries can be imposed from the outside, which practitioners have to manage regardless of their own personal perspectives. The tension around tone and approach that arose in the *Shadow Report* collaboration was one iteration of differences in the expectations of and by the collaborating parties. Elsewhere in my fieldwork, the issue of NGO-academic collaboration was also discussed in ways that echoed differences in larger institutional norms, even among feminist researchers. Although collaborators share feminist aims, political, institutional, and even departmental contexts can impact the ease with which multisectoral collaborations are carried out.

Conclusion

Hoping to tap into a boomerang pattern, the writers of the *Shadow Report* used leverage and accountability politics to put pressure on the Czech state to improve its reporting on and implementing of gender equality policy. As a new member country of the EU, the Czech government was vulnerable to criticisms levied by nonstate actors. The *Shadow Report* describes the positions of those charged with promoting and monitoring gender equality policy within the state apparatus, paying particular attention to the GFPs—under-resourced and under-trained staff members within individual ministries. The notions of leverage and accountability politics imply that once a state has experienced sufficient pressure, it will make the requisite changes. This model, however, does not delve into what happens when those responsible for making the changes demanded by advocacy networks are not provided with sufficient resources and expertise to do so. Although the collaborators with whom I spoke thought that there had been positive changes in the government, they also described some of the ways in which the brunt of their criticism was felt most keenly by the GFPs.

Scholarship relating to attempts by nonstate actors to compel governing bodies to implement social change has not paid adequate attention to the nuances of relationships within collaborations or within the state apparatuses that are their targets. The narratives of the *Shadow Report* collaboration that I collected also described some disagreements between academic and NGO members of the team over how to present the information in the report. Some of the NGO members thought that the academic members were writing at a level that would be inaccessible to their target audience in the government. Some of the academic members were concerned the report was insufficiently analytical as to withstand critique from a wide variety of national and international audiences. These tensions point to larger points of confluence and departure between academic feminists and women's NGOs in the Czech Republic that may play a part in complicating their collaboration. Institutional contexts and disciplinary expectations can impact the ease with which academic-NGO collaborations can occur, even when aims and politics are shared.

Acknowledgments

This chapter is based on ethnographic research carried out in the Czech Republic between 2004 and 2006. The larger aims of my project are to address issues of expert authority and knowledge production at the intersections of academics, activism, and social policy. Research funding was provided by a Fulbright-Hays fellowship, a David L. Boren fellowship, an IREX Individual Advanced Research Opportunity fellowship, and the University of Minnesota Alexander Dubček Fund. I would like to thank all of those who reviewed and provided feedback on this chapter, including Michaela Appeltová, Hana Hašková, Marcela Linková, and Dagmar Lorenz-Meyer.

Notes

1. For an overview of criticisms of the idea of cultural Europeanization from the perspective of the group of countries to enter the EU in 2004, which included the Czech Republic, see Engel-Di Mauro (2006).

2. For an overview of criticisms of gender mainstreaming implementation, see Kenny (2002) and Mazey (2002). For an analysis of the slippages between the terms "women," "gender," and "sex" in EU policy texts, see Kapusta-Pofahl (2008), and in Czech NGO discourses, see Kapusta-Pofahl (2002).

3. Names are pseudonyms.

4. "Gender mainstreaming" is the preferred terminology for European Union gender equality policies (see Schmidt [2005] for an overview).

5. Nora argues that the Government Council for Equal Opportunities for Women and Men has been able to put sustained pressure on the state to increase attention to gender equality issues.

6. During the course of my fieldwork I saw several GFPs attending seminars and trainings offered by NGOs and academic gender studies practitioners. Even those who had expressed frustrations at the seminar I describe participated in opportunities to increase their understanding of how to implement their objectives.

7. The establishment of academic gender studies departments began in the early 1990s with the Gender and Sociology Department in the Institute of Sociology at the Czech Academy of Sciences.

8. Despite these difficulties, the participants I spoke with expressed their willingness to undertake the project again, and some did so in a subsequent *Shadow Report* in 2006 and another in 2008.

9. While all of the academic gender studies practitioners situated within research institutes and universities that I asked affirmed themselves as feminists, there were differences of opinion about whether their scholarship was or should be also considered activism.

10. Bold in the original. NKC has been promoted to the status of a department within the Institute of Sociology as the Center of Gender and Science. This reinforces its status as an academic body, although it also carries out the advocacy work of promoting women in science.

PART II
Doing Good Work

Introduction to Part II

Life in NGOs

Inderpal Grewal

The chapters in Part II grapple with the internal and external struggles, contestations, and changes that take place within NGOs. While the context, history, and region in which an NGO is situated cannot be ignored in favor of understanding practices and processes within it, the relationship between the outside and the inside, between external forces and internal issues, is important to examine. This relationship is the focus of the following chapters.

The politics and practices of "doing good" can be understood not only through historical context but also through the relationship between state and NGO, between staff and clients, and between donors and staff. Above all, careful understanding over time of the connections between shifting practices and processes of NGOs are the means through which anthropologists are able to address the complexity of the politics and semantics of "doing good." Given that the most often cited rationale for the NGO is that it does something that other existing structures and institutions—the state, the corporation, the collective, the community—cannot, the imperative to claim a moral project becomes important. How this claim is maintained under shifting conditions of work and changing resources also requires sustained research. As states themselves shift their rationale for legitimacy from welfare to security and economic growth, NGOs stake even stronger claims to this realm of morality and welfare (Atia 2013; Elyachar 2005; Fassin 2012). In distinguishing "doing good" from governance, or humanitarianism from social justice, or even displacing rights for charity, NGOs argue for their own continued existence. The wonder is that "doing good" remains the most commonly understood notion of the NGO, even as so many other institutions have come under critique.

Yet as NGOs are created by a variety of organizations and agendas, "doing good" may not account for their goals, their affect, or the consequence of their work. There are questions about what such a phrase may mean, given the duplicity of the term that refers both to a commodity—the "goods" that it can provide—and to its claim of "doing good" as a moral project. Shifting registers of welfare linked to the moral claim need to be examined in the particular genealogies they index: Is it philanthropy, missionary work, religious injunction, community service, community advocacy, charity? Is it traditional, neoliberal, progressive or revolutionary, secular? History and context matter, as political regimes, humanitarians, NGOs, missionaries, political parties, and interests all claim that their practices are different from those in the past. The historical claims made by these NGO actors become crucial to understanding agendas and practices. As the essays in part II reveal, NGOs may suggest their projects are humanitarian rather than charitable, are based on faith rather than religion. What is clear is that there is a continual rearticulation in the face of competition from and relationships with other NGOs and institutions of the kinds of practices that constitute "doing good." The context of contending nationalisms, shifting states, ongoing wars, endemic violence, and capitalist extraction demand that what counts as "good" is always challenged and, hence, always shifting.

The politics and practices of NGOs need to be understood both temporally and spatially. There is a rich literature that has provided the tools for analysis of NGOs in the post-Cold War era, but there is continued necessity for examining the relationship between internal politics of NGOs and their external effects and relationships (Ferguson 1994; Fassin 2012; Fassin and Pandolfi 2013; Feldman and Ticktin 2010; Sharma 2008; Kamat 2002; Bernal and Grewal 2014b). First, "doing good" can manifest quite differently across contemporary societies. It can be about development, faith, religion, social justice, welfare, charity, provision, right, or duty. It can be linked to all kinds of politics, organizations, projects, and subjects, becoming meaningful and legible in changing ways. Even the terms of "doing good" need to be clarified, since moral projects are often contentious. If Didier Fassin (2012) suggests that humanitarianism signals a "moral economy," such morality encompasses a broad range of practices. Second, that the NGO participates in and becomes legible within a "moral economy" means that its transactional aspect involves a number of relationships, exchanges, and extractive and exploitative practices. The forms of power involved in those processes are critical to understanding all the projects, bodies and persons, networks, and nodes that maintain the NGO. Third, the question of politics, of intent and outcomes intended or unintended, of the politics of the organization itself and how it is perceived, within and outside, have to be examined to understand the life of an NGO over a period of time.

Studying life in an NGO is important because the NGO seems to have become a taken-for-granted form (Bernal and Grewal 2014b) even as it has become malleable and flexible enough to link itself or transform itself into other institutions and organizations. States, religious organizations, political movements, and corporate consumer cultures are just some of these entities with which NGOs have become intertwined, producing affect, activities, and ideologies that have come to resonate powerfully with the rise of neoliberal capital. But academic or scholarly researchers are not the only groups that monitor NGOs. While researchers study NGOs to examine their histories, practices, and impacts, states often have other reasons: censoring or controlling activities, especially those that are political, extracting resources, or demanding participation in transnational networks that provide cultural capital. Powerful nationalisms, as in the case of India with the Hindu-nationalist BJP government that came to power in 2014, can instrumentalize the critique of NGOs in order to repress dissent by accusing those NGOs working on civil rights of minorities of being antinationalist (Government of India, Ministry of Home Affairs 2015c; Lakshmi 2015; Outlook India 2015). The BJP government has turned progressive critique into an excuse for repression and has done so selectively to target some NGOs as foreign imperial interests. Such political exigencies emerge as NGOs become more and more powerful and some states become either hollower or more authoritarian. How the state recognizes an NGO—through a variety of regulations or through other kinds of forces—is important to the way that it works, who works there, and what its goal or agenda may be. If an organization is registered as an NGO, its visibility and viability may depend on the details of its registration. In the case of India, the Modi government built on earlier regulations to require NGOs to register online if they received foreign funds, disclose all their foreign donors, and provide personal mobile phone numbers of NGO heads. Government rules required NGOs to separate foreign funds and account for their use in detail, creating accounting burdens that are onerous for many organizations, especially those that are smaller. In a context in which the Indian government is desperate to attract foreign businesses and to privatize land for development even while decrying NGOs for their foreign donations, some NGOs are thinking of calling themselves businesses rather than NGOs. Whether they take this step will be significant. What an organization calls itself, or comes to be called, is important for the way it exists with or relates to a state, a community, a nation, and a person. This kind of identity can shape the organization, from the hierarchies within it to its mission statement, its work and accounting practices, its engagements with donors and community and with critics and researchers. Aviva Sinervo shows in her chapter that for some, one response to a variety of state and contextual demands results in the term "NGO" becoming inappropriate for organizations that see themselves as "social projects" and are run on more corporate and market-oriented terms.

The following three chapters, by Nermeen Mouftah, Aviva Sinervo, and Moshe Kornfeld, seek to understand how the concept of "doing good" comes to make an NGO viable and legible in three quite different contexts and histories. They examine the continued struggle to maintain such an agenda against a state and against other NGOs and organizations. They describe such practices as shaped through relations with other organizations, states, religious concepts and histories, neoliberal subjects, projects, and national anxieties. What constitutes these relations and how they are practiced, felt, understood, and circulated is critical for understanding not only what "doing good" comes to be but also how it becomes attached to the NGO form and how it articulates itself in a particular field and context. The essays demonstrate that the moral dimension that often seems to be the raison d'être for and legitimizes the NGO is also a domain of contestation.

As the moral and the extractive—the "goods" and the "good"—merge in capitalism and especially in its neoliberal version, it is not surprising that the two major arenas of NGO visibility discussed here, religion and tourism, emerge as the topics of the essays in this book's part II. While religion has a long history of empire, what are called faith-based organizations (FBOs) are displacing the older idea of the mission as simply a proselytizing, evangelizing, or charitable organization. Missionaries see themselves as volunteers and humanitarians, altering older spiritual and religious meanings to conform to emergent subjectivities and politics (Grewal 2016). Tourism and what is being called "voluntourism" has emerged in recent years and is a growing and changing enterprise, linking unequal subjects in new projects that aspire to evade the imperial, capitalist, and commodity form constituted by the history of tourism.

In examining these changing subjects and institutions, we need to reckon with neoliberalism and its diverse manifestations. As structural adjustment programs demanded by the International Monetary Fund (IMF) and other international financial agencies began to be implemented starting in the 1970s and 1980s in the global South and became naturalized as efficient public policy in the United States, they reduced state-sponsored welfare and opened the doors for transnational NGOs, including religious ones, to become increasingly involved in development. American evangelical churches were particularly aggressive in this regard, emphasizing free-market reforms as central to the idea of religious "choice" and adopting the language of development and human rights (Castelli 2007). They were heavily supported by the US government and by many churches and citizens (Pelkmans 2009). Islamic charities sponsored by Saudi Arabia and the Gulf states were close behind. In many parts of the world, countries such as Saudi Arabia funded religious schools, and Islamic FBOs such as Islamic Charity began to work closely with Muslim and non-Muslim governments in many regions (Benthall 2007). Local groups, individuals, and communities also began to mobilize in relation to the governmentalization of emergency (Fassin and Pandolfi 2013).

These global-historical shifts also had impacts in the United States. They provided the context for the emergence of NGOs as central to efforts in the United States at rebuilding after Hurricane Katrina when the George W. Bush administration was unable and unwilling to provide the required federal support. The retrenchment of the state in the United States, Egypt, and Peru and the emergence of more authoritarian and militarized security states are additional factors in the kinds of organizations existing in those countries, though in each country the impacts were somewhat different. Nermeen Mouftah's and Moshe Kornfeld's chapters, one on the organization Life Makers, based in Cairo, and the other on the Jewish humanitarianism in New Orleans, highlight how religious concepts and theologies, knowledges, and information circulate, producing volunteers, activists, and humanitarians as emergent subjects. The struggle over what constitutes a progressive politics for the Jewish community in post-Katrina New Orleans or a proper religious project of "faith development" in Cairo suggests that NGOs become sites where contending notions of religion and faith in their relation to welfare, charity, religious injunction and duties, public and private "good," and the frameworks of what is called social justice resonate in a larger context of geopolitics, religious movements, and neoliberal capital. These contestations bring mission statements, goals, activities, accounts, and donations under the scrutiny of both NGO staff and clients (and anthropologists), if they can be discovered. Alliances and networks (local, national, and transnational) also become contested, as funding sources and clients can be diverse and disparate depending on the local or global reach of the NGO's staff and the circuits of knowledge, identity, and power in which founders and staff circulate.

The FBO as a variant of the NGO form signals how particular religious communities are engaging with newer idea of religion, volunteerism, charity, and duty. Kornfield and Mouftah shed light on how notions of "doing good" intersect with the NGO form to shape emergent religious practices against a background of geopolitics and national politics. While so many religions and religious organizations have been involved in charity and welfare of different kinds, what we are seeing in these new "moral economies" are not only more secular forms of charity, as Erica Bornstein (2012a) reveals in her book on India and Delhi, but also more religious forms as well. As Nermeen Mouftah states in her chapter on Life Makers, the young volunteers distinguish faith from religion, and they do so through the kinds of projects they undertake in the organization, thereby rearticulating the relationship between politics and religion and taking critique out of its secular context. She sees NGOs as "social sites," relying on Theodore Schatzki's definition of the phrase (2002), through which new social meanings are articulated, and religion, development, and humanitarianism come together through separation from what is newly understood as religious tradition. The FBO does not simply have a religious or Islamic genealogy but rather reveals how "good works" reform religion through its NGO-ization.

Contested FBO politics is also the topic of Moshe Kornfeld's chapter on the post-Katrina humanitarianism of the Jewish Federation of Greater New Orleans. The chapter focuses on the organization's relationship with younger Jewish activists, who were both influenced by academic and anthropological critiques of NGOs and the desire to insert issues of race into Jewish humanitarianism. These activists drew on a history of Jewish social responsibility in debates regarding what it meant for Jews to give help to non-Jews, providing new meanings to religious terms in order to claim a social justice and progressive project of struggle against systemic racism. Notions of Jewish "social action" were recast as humanitarian projects that required the community to support those in need, especially African Americans, and to participate in social justice. In doing so, these subjects sought relevance and visibility in an altered space where service is both secular and religious and where a religious organization must alter its practices and projects to engage with a changing idea of what it means to be progressive and moral.

These accounts reveal struggles between older and newer forms of engagement with communities, altering notions of religiosity and desire to capture newer constituencies. Emergent actors come into churches and temples to understand their charitable work in newer humanitarian ways or even to separate what they do from historical Others in their religious community. Separating the political from the religious, distinguishing an older name from a newer, inserting new practices into older forms of work, disambiguating faith from religion, or turning charity into volunteerism—all of these changes are caught by careful ethnography—as Mouftah and Kornfeld describe in their chapters—attentive to the minutiae of work and debate within organizations as they struggle to remain relevant in changing and dynamic contexts. Whether dealing with slower processes of change or with catastrophic situations, we see how NGOs have to engage much more nimbly with the forces of power and support.

That FBOs also generate travel and tourism is well known, given the number of missionaries and evangelists who are on the move for short-term and long-term travel (Hefferan, Adkins, and Occhipinti 2009). Such travel combines notions of accounting and accountability as well as moral and affective dimensions. Many of those who donate to NGOs then travel to visit the child to whom or place to which their donations are directed, and they do so as much to ascertain how their money is being spent as to experience both the need that they feel they fulfill and the reciprocity demanded from their gift. While historically, religious organizations such as the Mormon church have created their own missions, more secular travel has increased dramatically as Americans (as well as Australians and Europeans) continue to travel to places that they see to be very different from their home countries and to experience and live racial, cultural, and national difference and inequality. It is this rise of what is called voluntourism, both religious and secular, that forms the context of Aviva Sinervo's chapter in the comparison of two NGOs working with children in Cuzco, Peru. Her focus is the incorporation of tourists and locals into welfare work through which an NGO can be maintained. Although it is an ethnography of two NGOs, one sponsored by the government, the other supported by mostly foreign donors, these projects are subtended by the economy of moral tourism, through which, as Sinervo argues, the "whims of NGO clients" (the tourists who are donors and staff members), as well as the regulations of the state, shape NGOs' existence and outcomes. While Sinervo shows the impact of foreign tourists and donors and state retrenchment from welfare, the other side of the picture is the increase in the number of Americans and Europeans who practice humanitarianism.

I argue that what we see is a particular Western humanitarian citizenship (Grewal 2016), in which the colonial "civilizing mission" continues as the mission to "save" distant Others and which has transformed numerous institutions in the United States: academic, corporate, state, and churches. In recent years, the numbers of Americans who travel to Africa or Asia to visit slums, poor neighborhoods, and the children or communities to whom they send money has increased dramatically, producing new itineraries and projects that combine travel with humanitarianism. What has come to be called "voluntourism" is promoted by numerous companies, colleges, and universities. College students have become a big market for these organizations, as they hope to gain skills and experiences deemed to be necessary for entry into the job market or for further study. Hardship experiences in the global South become evidence of the ability to work hard and hold down a job.

Numerous guidebooks provide information to enable such travel. Melani McAlister (2008), writing about the evangelical projects of missionary work that have emerged since the 1990s, analyzes an emergent tourist trade based upon evangelical causes to "save" Christians and Christianity around the world. The more secular versions of humanitarian tourism have also come to constitute a large market. *Volunteer: A Traveller's Guide to Making a Difference around the World* by Charlotte Hindle et al., now in its third edition; *Volunteer Vacations: Short Term Adventures That Will Benefit You and Others* by Bill McMillon, Doug Cutchins, and Anne Geissinger, which is now in its eleventh edition; and *700 Places to Volunteer before You Die: A Traveler's Guide* by Nola Lee Kelsey are just three examples of this ubiquitous and popular literature. Most of these texts provide guidance in terms of organizations to work for, types of volunteer work that can be undertaken, how to choose organizations to work with, and what kinds of "exchange" can be expected. For the most part, these guidebooks use stock phrases such as "making a difference" and "following your passion" to help readers decide where and how to volunteer, and they imply that individuals can overcome all kinds of global differences. The prevailing ideology of peer-to-peer exchange (Moodie 2013) in which power differences cannot be acknowledged seems to be one important modality of such travel and its notion of exchange implies a level field of power. Finally, the plethora of volunteer opportunities provides a wide range of consumer choices that are similar to those made by tourists deciding which country to visit for pleasure.

These guidebooks reveal that voluntourism is a large and profitable enterprise that sells particular experiences that are material and affective. The focus on individual choices and individual experience is central to this tourism. As *Volunteer Vacations* puts it, the reader must "evaluate an organization to see if it is right for me" (McMillon, Cutchins, and Geissinger 2012, xxi). Although other volunteers' personal vignettes are presented to inform the reader, and most of them claim that their experience changed their lives, the text suggests that readers must choose their own path or else the experience will not work. Because it is a project of self-improvement, such a focus is necessary, and the stories of self-improvement and satisfaction from the experience of travel are important features of these texts. All these guidebooks argue that volunteer help is needed and necessary, and that volunteers are welcome and needed everywhere. The language of exchange pervades these texts, suggesting that the notion of reciprocity as imagined by the volunteers obviates racial, class, national, or any other difference and that those regions benefit from the visits of volunteers even beyond the tourist dollars or euros they may bring.

Thus Aviva Sinervo finds that volunteers and NGOs in Cuzco, Peru, are codependent on each other, with money and emotional and pedagogical experiences being exchanged, though there are contradictions: NGOs do want to be local and self-sufficient and to serve their own communities yet find this goal impossible because of the withdrawal of the state. Sinervo's chapter reveals that the other side of this American and European humanitarian citizenship is not only the precarity of the organization sustained by it but also the possibilities created in the process. NGOs struggle not only against the state but also for tourists and the dollars they bring. This precarity is not just that of a donor-supported NGO but also that of a state-sponsored one in which there are no voluntourists with their passion for reciprocal relations in a deeply unequal context. What this chapter shows, importantly, is that consumption and charity are combined in a powerful package that legitimizes one NGO in numerous ways that are linked to the power of Western volunteers.

Together, these three chapters reveal that research on NGOs requires not simply understanding a context, historical and institutional, but also the ability to link the minutiae of internal politics and debates to broader inquiries regarding humanitarianism, tourism, consumer culture, and religion and religiosity. Without the kinds of multiscale analyses presented in these chapters, it would be difficult to make sense of the NGOs, however localized they may seem. The chapters also suggest that the anthropology of NGOs provides insights into the conditions of work and welfare that manifest in linked and diverse ways in world regions and locales. While the larger question of whether the anthropology of NGOs can lead to better practices of development or welfare depends on the consumption of the research on NGOs, it is clear that NGO studies enable a grasp of the forms taken by the neoliberal present and a greater understanding of the production of power and inequality in diverse practices across sites and scales. But NGOs are not simply informants or objects of study. Many NGOs also struggle to address these issues, a struggle that, as Kornfeld's chapter illustrates, is often hard fought and difficult. The anthropology of NGOs reveals the inseparability of political critique and ethnography, though it may be reductively absorbed into questions of policy and solution ("What should we do then, if we do not save these distant others?") in the face of the structural violence of modernity and empire. Neither can anthropology become a means to validate or legitimize particular NGOs. It would not be useful if the anthropology of NGOs becomes another Charity Watch. Rather than creating policy, this literature can create knowledge of and struggles against broader structural violence, the debilitation of rights, and an understanding of the complex trajectories of moral interventions.

6
Faith Development beyond Religion

The NGO as Site of Islamic Reform

Nermeen Mouftah

Cairo, Egypt, September 2011. The branch office of Life Makers, an NGO, pulsed with energy. When Ahmed, a twenty-three-year-old engineering student, showed up for work at noon, rail-thin and looking as though he had not slept, I mistook him for any other volunteer. He slipped into an office, and some minutes later I was told that the director of the Life Makers' Giza branch was ready to meet with me. In that first conversation, Ahmed, who turned out to be the director, explained what he looks for when he interviews potential volunteers. The concerns he brought up in our first encounter were threads that wove between our many long tea breaks together over the next four years. Ahmed said, "I want someone who believes in the idea of our organization. This is the important thing—that they truly believe in what we are doing. Life Makers is a new idea of how to do good works (*khayr*).[1] We are not like other organizations that believe in the traditional ways of doing good. Their ways are old fashioned [*taqlidi*]. They think it's religious—that they're following this path because it's how God wants us to help—but it's only repetitive. We're not a religious [*dini*] organization. We're faith development [*tanmiyya bi'l-iman*]." Ahmed underscored volunteers' self-understanding and the organization's ethic of action. He explained more than an abstract ideology: he articulated recurring debates and invocations, values and critiques that characterize Life Makers. This chapter discusses the organization's reinterpretation of the Islamic conception of "good works" (*khayr*) by investigating how they marshal "faith" (*iman*) rather than and in contrast to "religion" (*din*). Life Makers seek to redefine what constitutes Islamic good works and, more ambitiously, to reevaluate what agendas and actions are "Islamic." In this way, the NGO, rather than, say, a mosque, a religious lesson, or a religious rite, is a crucial site for the making of new forms of religious practice. For Life Makers, faith development transforms good works from the donation and distribution of goods or money to the needy, to volunteerism, where they give of their main resources: time and energy. Established in 2004 by the prominent Muslim preacher Amr Khaled, Life Makers has had a tumultuous history with Egyptian authorities for over a decade. The main source of the conflict is how the organization mobilizes Islam in their activities in a country now wary of political Islam. Life Makers offer a distinct ethics and politics of faith development, one that redefines traditional Islamic alms practices, while critiquing the entanglements of politics and religion. While volunteers, mostly youth in their twenties and thirties, distinguish their good works activities through innovative projects like building rooftop gardens and spearheading antidrug campaigns, their most potent critique of Islamic good works organizations is in their emphasis on faith rather than mere religion. Life Makers' leaders call attention to the organization's dual goals: on the one hand, to give youth meaningful work through volunteerism, and on the other, the urgent need to respond to poverty by helping disenfranchised people through charitable giving, particularly through programs that innovate.

The organization calls on its volunteers to exhaust themselves in the service of God to develop Egypt. They commonly described how through their exhaustion they were energized. Volunteers transform the practices of good works through new community projects as well as through their effort to embody the ideal volunteer, including the virtuous affects of a believing Life Maker, namely optimism.[2] I heard persistent *talk* about their work. I dwell on these self-reflective and aspirational conversations as they reveal how volunteers understood faith as the source of their action. Through their activities they sought to make faith legible. The challenge to make one's faith materially tangible was not an abstract or esoteric concern—indeed it was a major preoccupation for many Life Makers.

As volunteers worked out their values through conversations like the one I had with Ahmed, they practiced critique. Not all acts of distinction are acts of critique, although distinction is pivotal to the organization's mission. Life Makers distinguish themselves from political Islam, other iterations of Islamic good works, and what they view as the apathy of large swaths of the Egyptian public. By exploring volunteers' engagements through the lens of critique, I demonstrate how Life Makers upend assumptions of critique as necessarily intellectual and secular by tracing their activities and affects (Asad et al. 2009; cf. Said 1983). Critique is not only to question established frameworks, as Michel Foucault points out (1997), but also, as Judith Butler elaborates, it is "a mode of living and even a mode of subject constitution, critique is understood as a 'practice' that incorporates norms into the very formation of the subject" (2009, 114). For Butler, critique both questions and looks for future models of political action. Life Makers not only distinguish themselves from others but in doing so they crucially weigh in on ongoing debates in Egypt about the proper relationship of religion and politics. Significantly, for volunteers, critique is not an analytical exercise, it is to be physically *practiced* as well as *felt*.

When Ahmed said Life Makers is not a religious organization, he was not saying that it is not Islamic. As will be seen, his is not a secular critique of religion, but rather the expression of an Islamic reformulation of imagining care for the poor through an idiom of "development." For volunteers, faith is not a privatized interior condition or aspiration, rather it is what propels them to action. Their turn to faith over religion should not be likened to a Western discourse of "spiritual but not religious," but should instead be appreciated with respect to the confluence of two major trends: Egypt's Islamic Revival that began in the 1970s, as well as international economic priorities that made Egypt a strategic center for regional development (Atia 2013; Elyachar 2005). Egyptian good works organizations are profoundly shaped by these significant social and economic transformations.

In the following section I argue that the anthropology of religion and development can productively come together to shed light on the significance of NGOs in the renegotiation of religion in public life. I situate Life Makers in the context of post-Mubarak Egypt, including the organization's establishment and rapid rise in popularity, as well as its early tensions with authorities. I then examine what faith development looks like through the emergence of volunteerism as an act of worship. In the final section I examine the predominance of happiness talk as volunteers cultivate optimism as a virtuous sensibility and as the basis of personal and national progress. While positivity is often associated with new age religion, for Life Makers happiness is the virtuous expression of Islamic faith and central to their teachings, both in how they are trained to lead and in how they reach out to the people they work with. The words of two volunteers who began their work with Life Makers following the January 25 uprising, a watershed moment for the NGO, are presented. While both Amal and Umar are conversant in the language of hope and optimism, they discuss and embody these ideal affects in ways that reveal how recourse to faith is an unsettled project.

In this chapter, Life Makers is an organization, as well as the name of those who volunteer for it. While I write of volunteers as a collective, this does not imply that they were at all homogenous. The high turnover, especially for particular campaigns, means that volunteers represent a diversity of backgrounds and viewpoints. It is worth noting then that critique was especially vital among Life Makers leadership. Indeed, many short-term volunteers saw Life Makers as any other Islamic good works organization. In this way, Life Makers is compelling not because they are profoundly unique, but in many ways, because they are indicative of thousands of other religiously inspired civil society groups in Egypt today. This plurality and contestation over Islamically inspired modes of social and political intervention lead me to offer no definition or genealogy of faith, development, religion, or politics; instead, I sketch how Life Makers seek to modernize and reform good works through their conceptualization of and attempt to forge the boundaries of these spheres.

The NGO at the Intersection of the Anthropology of Religion and Development

The following discussion crystallizes the NGO not only as a site that draws on religion to motivate and mold development initiatives but also as a locus for defining, delimiting, and disciplining religion in public and political life. Drawing on Theodore Schatzki's concept of social sites (2002), I understand the NGO as a space that enables us to interpret reconfigurations of Islam through the prism of civil society. The NGO is a site where the very understanding of religion and the place of religion in the public sphere are worked out both discursively and in practice. My emphasis on the NGO as a social site builds on recent work on the subjectivities of Muslim charitable workers (Hafez 2011a, 2011b; Jung, Petersen, and Sparre 2014). While I am very much interested in volunteers' conceptions of faith and its appropriate expression, I do so by situating the NGO as a crucial site for cultivating a particular religio-political sensibility. Faith and positivity became pillars of a faith development that immunizes against political Islam.

Based on seventeen months of fieldwork between 2011 and 2015, my analysis of Life Makers is set against a backdrop of revolution and counter-revolution, the rise and fall of the Muslim Brotherhood, and the strengthening powers of Egypt's military elite. It was a period of intense contestation over what role Islam should play in charting the future of Egypt and indeed the region. My interest in NGOs during this period emerged through my fieldwork on religiously sponsored adult literacy, particularly campaigns that articulated the uprising as a watershed moment for the country to address its massive rate of illiteracy, officially some 30 percent of the adult population.[3] I set out to focus on two sites where literacy development in Egypt is concentrated: among women in a slum of Old Cairo and workers at a shipyard. While I anticipated working with Life Makers in their roles as teachers, I discovered the NGO itself pronounced on reformulating a productive Islam for Egypt's better future. I interviewed approximately forty volunteers, most of them from two branch offices in Cairo. Of those forty, about a dozen were close interlocutors who I saw every other day at regular meetings, training sessions, Islamic lessons, and a swath of social events from potlucks to birthday parties. For many, their lives beyond school and family were spent almost entirely among Life Makers. For others, they volunteered with other organizations and had hobbies and interests outside of Life Makers. I also worked with half a dozen other NGOs—Coptic and Muslim, local and international, as well as with the state institutions tasked with adult education. This perspective exposed me to outside views of the organization. Life Makers is widely recognizable in Egypt. Most Egyptians with whom I discussed my research had opinions about the group, ranging from praise for a Muslim group "doing something beneficial" to skepticism of their motives and the sort of Islam they promote through their work. Government employees questioned their efficacy and ability to carry out their work with unskilled volunteers.

Within NGO studies, the role of religion is most commonly discussed in the analysis of faith-based organizations (FBOs), while "religious NGOs" (RNOs) is the more common term among development practitioners (Occhipinti 2015; cf. Berger 2003). Still, definitional distinctions between the two are not substantive. Gerard Clarke and Michael Jennings's often-cited definition of FBO illustrates some of the conceptual limitations of studying religion within NGOs. They explain that the FBO "derives inspiration and guidance for its activities from the teaching and principles of the faith or from a particular interpretation or school of thought within a faith" (2008, 6). Faith is a self-evident category that supersedes religion. However, as I will show, by paying attention to the distinction between faith and religion we are better equipped to grasp how NGOs and FBOs, in particular, are fault lines in the contestation over how religion should best be practiced and expressed in civil society.

Studies of FBOs foreground the theological commitments of volunteers as well as the underlying motivations, agendas, and actions of organizations. These studies investigate religion in international development and yet offer limited insight into the dense interplay of how local politics shape articulations of religion within the NGO. Attention to this interplay also means detailing how the NGO shapes religious practice, and as the case of Life Makers reveals, how the NGO becomes a crucial site for reimagining Islam. Life Makers' explicit recourse to faith not only distances them from other Islamic good works organizations but situates the organization within the orbit of mostly Christian FBOs. The organization's founder, Amr Khaled, is a media phenomenon and part of a current of Protestantizing Islam within contemporary reformist movements; analysis of his media productions highlights similarities with American televangelism (Moll 2010). The study of

Life Makers alongside FBOs is therefore productive in exploring the translation of "faith" across religious traditions. The FBO literature is notable for its focus on Christian individuals and organizations in the United States (Allahyari 2000; Elisha 2011), Africa (Bornstein 2003; Freidus 2010), and Latin America (DeTemple 2005; Hefferan 2007; Occhipinti 2005), as well as on the transnational reach of the global North to the South (Bornstein 2003; DeTemple 2006). However, work on Muslim charitable, philanthropic, and development programs only occasionally refers to Muslim third-sector organizations as "faith based" (Atia 2012) but rather emphasizes "activism," "Islam," and "religion." In other words, when it comes to Muslim civil society, analysis of faith is rare. Instead, Muslim development and aid are usually associated either with the state or its opposition.

Historical work on Islamic alms draws attention to scripturally grounded ethical and legal terminologies, such as good works, giving (*birr*, *mabarra*), charity or alms (*zakat*, *sadaqa*), and charitable endowments (*awqaf*) (Benthall 2007; Ener 2003; Ibrahim and Sherif 2008; Sabra 2000). As I demonstrate, Life Makers' faith development mobilizes these terms in their plan to reform the practice of good works and to introduce volunteerism (*taw'ia*) to this critical vocabulary of Islamic giving. Studies of Muslim practices of giving are notable for their interest in the social and political history of these terms and their enactments, particularly their frictions and synergies with the state (Bonner, Ener, and Singer 2003; Singer 2008). Over the last decade, the politics of Muslim philanthropy in the post-9/11 era has given rise to Western governments' surveillance of Muslim organizations and the effects of this surveillance on Muslim charity (Atia 2007; Benthall and Bellion-Jourdan 2009; Lacey and Benthall 2014). As an organization, Life Makers illustrates the effects of the fear and censure of a Muslim FBO in a Muslim-majority country, where organizing with any reference to Islam is perceived, to varying degrees, as a threat to the state.

Insight from Egypt's Islamic Revival significantly informs theoretical debates in the anthropology of Islam and indeed of the anthropology of religion, secularism, and modernity more broadly, particularly through attention to embodied practice in the cultivation of ethics and virtuous dispositions (Hamdy 2012; Hirschkind 2006; Mahmood 2005). By moving away from what is commonly understood as religious, such as prayer, fasting, and other authorized practices within the tradition, we attune ourselves to important trends in Islamic reform. In this way, Life Makers offers a particularly rich case study to further the ongoing work of undoing binaries of the secular-religious (Agrama 2012; Asad 2012; Bender and Taves 2012; Starrett 2010). Khaled and many volunteers cite verses from the Quran and sayings of the prophet Muhammad (*hadith*) in order to explain their efforts. At other moments, they draw on UN reports that promote women's empowerment, or cite techniques of effective leadership that can be found in self-help books like Dale Carnegie's *How to Win Friends and Influence People*. These multiple references demonstrate more than a hybridity or intersection of values, rather they reveal the contemporary contours of lived religion. Life Makers undermine prevailing assumptions of secular scripts of development through definitively Islamic practices essential to their work. Recourse to faith then is at moments specifically Islamic, while in other instances it is an ambiguous gloss for hope or happiness. In this way, it is crucial to investigate precisely how faith becomes principle for the reform of religion and the best plan for developing a country. Thus, while Talal Asad cautions against a shift within the study of religion to examine faith as an interior state, Life Makers call attention to the negotiation of what constitutes faith as it is worked out through their lives and in their work.[4] For volunteers, faith can be a feeling, but it is best enunciated, whether in casual conversation or in more formalized statements of intention. For Life Makers, faith is seen through action.

Islam and Civil Society in Post-Mubarak Egypt

Since the establishment of Life Makers in 2004, the organization has calibrated its activities with the vicissitudes of a rapidly changing political climate. Following the January 25 uprising, Egypt witnessed the rise to power and later the persecution of political Islam. While a history of the post-Mubarak political landscape is beyond the scope of this chapter, a brief sketch of the regime change and laws governing NGOs offers a backdrop to understand the pressures on both religious and political spaces at this juncture and the restrictive religio-political context in which Life Makers and other NGOs operated. My point is to underline how the politics of contemporary Egypt shapes possibilities for NGOs to undertake particular projects, as well as to shape and remake individual and collective self-understandings of Islam. Following Mubarak's ouster, the country was first governed by the interim government of the Supreme Council of Armed Forces (SCAF), while newly emergent Salafi (Sunni neotraditionalist) political parties consolidated. Most notably, the Muslim Brotherhood, outlawed since 1948, gained popularity as an alternative to the old regime and formed the Freedom and Justice Party (FJP). The FJP performed well in the parliamentary elections, and in June 2012 the party's presidential candidate, Mohamed Morsi, narrowly defeated a former Mubarak-era minister. The Brotherhood's electoral success was widely credited to the popularity they gained during the Mubarak years when their welfare networks provided essential goods and services (Clark 2004; Harrigan and El-Said 2009; Wickham 2002). Yet, after a year in power widespread dissatisfaction with the Brotherhood coalesced with the June 30, 2013, protests calling for his resignation. In addition to complaints about continued infrastructural failures, demonstrators complained that the FJP put Brotherhood priorities ahead of national interests in the FJP's bid to "Islamize" the country and change the essential character of the people and state. Three days after the protests that Egyptian media reported as the largest in Egyptian history, the military stated that the president and his government failed to meet the demands of the people and removed him from power. Adly Mansour acted as the interim president, although Egyptian media lauded the minister of defense, Abdel Fatah al-Sisi, for responding to the will of the people. In June 2014 he was elected Egypt's sixth president in an election criticized within and beyond Egypt as squelching opposition voices. In the year leading to his presidency, Egypt came under fierce criticism by Egyptian civil society and international observers for the regime's massacre of Muslim Brotherhood members in August 2013 and their continued illegal imprisonment alongside unionists and leftists.

While Egypt has a long history of closely monitoring and stifling civil society, Mubarak's fall, and especially Morsi's removal, marked a sharp increase in the attack on nonstate actors. For over a decade, Egyptian civil society has been governed by the Law on Associations and Community Foundations (Law 84 of 2002). The vague regulatory laws require organizations to register with what is now called the Ministry of Social Solidarity and Justice (MSSJ, formerly the Ministry of Social Solidarity). The law does not ban NGOs outright but instead employs bureaucratic mechanisms and grants vast interpretive powers to the ministry. In 2014 the government estimated that forty thousand civil society organizations (including NGOs, law firms, and unions) were registered with the MSSJ. While numbers reported by different agencies vary, critics of heavy state regulation explain that the government inflates national statistics in order to boast that civil society is free and flourishing (Abdelrahman 2004). The political turbulence of the last half-decade has further blurred the lines of what organizing can be deemed permissible or can be deemed an affront to authorities. Indeed, many complained not of repression but of their vulnerability to navigating opaque regulations in a climate of insecurity.[5]

While both media and scholarly attention frequently cite the attacks on human rights organizations, less consideration is given to religiously affiliated NGOs, despite Islamic philanthropic organizations making up the vast majority of the country's NGOs. Despite many volunteers' attraction to Life Makers as a way to continue the revolution through nonconfrontational methods, their work is increasingly risky. As of May 2015, with the shuttering of 430 Muslim NGOs accused of being associated with the Muslim

Brotherhood (Aswat Masraya 2015), Ahmed's comments reveal Life Makers' pragmatism and flexibility for survival. So, when in 2011, he dismissed "Islamic" and "religious" charitable giving, his anxiety over the place of religion in their work anticipated a sentiment that became increasingly common. Many of Life Makers' activities in fact resemble Islamist social welfare programs like those run by the Muslim Brotherhood, yet their emphasis on faith seeks to avoid censure and court state favor.

To understand Life Makers' politics, it is important to examine who they do and do *not* critique as they position themselves beyond the fray of politics. This positioning has not always been the case. In spring 2012 Khaled launched the Future Party, with a platform that sounded like much of his Life Makers' speeches on optimism for Egypt's potential development. A year later, with the arrest of Morsi and other Brotherhood members, Khaled dissolved the party explaining that his primary work would concentrate on development through Life Makers. The following year, with pressure on religiously affiliated NGOs, Khaled resigned from his position as chairman of the organization. For Life Makers, distinction making is not exclusively a matter of ideology but is essential to their adaptability and survival. While they were keen to exercise critique of other good works organizations, and political Islam, their criticism was notably not directed at the regimes in power. Life Makers is distinct from Islamist charitable organizations who, as Janine Clark explains "attempt to create a seemingly seamless web between religion, politics, and charity and all forms of activism" (2004, 14). Life Makers, like other Egyptian good works organizations, offer services that the state fails to provide; however, this is not how they explain their work. Rather than pointing to the failure of public health and education, they work for the nation to, as they put it, "build Egypt." In this way, critique is pivotal to demonstrating who they are not—Islamists—while aligning their efforts with strategic national priorities.

The Making of Faith Development

Life Makers evolved from a nearly defunct disparate collection of activities and offices under Mubarak, into a nationally recognizable, revitalized good works organization in the wake of the January 25 uprising. The organization is the product of Khaled's television program by the same name that aired in 2004. The series sparked thousands of young people to get involved in grassroots organizing and marked the introduction of Khaled's message that civic responsibility is an Islamic duty. This shift marks a significant transformation from his previous stress on righteous etiquette (*akhlaq*). The series appealed to bored youth by calling them to replace the humiliation and frustration of unemployment with the purpose and dignity of volunteerism. Ehab, a longtime volunteer who rose through different roles within the organization before taking on a leadership position at the national level, recounted to me the earliest days of Life Makers' activities. He described how their rapid growth and popularity were a cause of concern for government officials who closely monitored their activities and posed various roadblocks. Their pilot program, an antidrug campaign, recruited more addicts for recovery than there was space available in rehabilitation centers, creating early friction with various state institutions. He and other Life Makers leaders saw the government's antipathy toward them as the result of their effectiveness through activities that unintentionally uncovered the state's shortcomings.

As one of the world's most familiar religious preachers and a leading voice in Egypt's late Islamic Revival, Khaled is best known for his propagation of Islam through his television programs that are immensely popular with young Egyptians. With no Islamic training, his mode of speaking is persuasive, and he is widely credited with making religion accessible, especially to elite classes.[6] The successful television series *Life Makers* was extended into a second season as local initiatives gained momentum and the slogan "Together We Make Life" caught on in neighboring countries.

Khaled sets himself apart from strong currents within Egypt's Islamic Revival that give great attention to the proper performance of ritual acts. Khaled's program of reform offers distinct theological and political aims for the proper Muslim subject. Still, he does not eschew ritual altogether. In fact, particular traditional practices such as supplication are central to Life Makers' activities.

Before disembarking from a bus to begin a day's work promoting their literacy campaign, volunteers paused to supplicate. With their hands raised in front of their faces, eyes steady on their palms, a group leader led the day's supplication (*du'a*). She asked God to bless and reward their effort. Those around her followed: "Ameen." They asked that their work benefit the lives of the people they were about to meet. *Ameen.* They hoped to please God in what they were about to do. *Ameen.* And be granted paradise in the hereafter. *Ameen.* This moment was essential to how they performed their work. Through supplication volunteers aimed to purify their intentions and dedicate their work to God. As one of their slogans intoned, "Makers makes us sincere" (*suna' khalitna mukhlisin*). Statements of intention and imploring God for blessings in the temporal world and the afterlife were significant to volunteers as they strived to develop their piety through volunteerism. At the same time, many critiqued Islamic charity as backward and disingenuous.

Volunteers incorporated rituals, like supplication, into their good works as a way to create an authentic Islam where one's pietistic improvement is tethered to the progress of the community and nation.

For Life Makers, faith must be made manifest in the person, and through that believer in what they do to improve Egypt. So while supplication was a critical practice of their faith work, other practices and characteristics also defined and distinguished Life Makers. The exemplary volunteer was cheerful, organized, and productive. They were meticulous in their grooming and performed their five daily prayers on time. Volunteers showed dedication to their work, but also took their family responsibilities seriously. For Life Makers, faith was in their whirr of activity: a constantly ringing mobile, running from a fund-raising meeting to a soft skills training session. The intricacies of a refined Islamic faith could be seen in volunteers' actions, and in how they imagined, hoped, and prayed that these efforts—physical and emotional—would amount to something.

The organization's agenda is consonant with Khaled's critique of traditionally trained Islamic scholars who teach "faith for faith's sake," rather than what he argues is a *truer* faith—one that seeks to do good works. In his remissive he engages a centuries-long quarrel in the Islamic tradition as to what makes an action an act of faith. The debate turns on the question of internal conviction (*tasdiq bil-qalb*), verbal expression (*iqrar bil-lisan* or *qawl*), and the actual performance of the deed (*'amal*) (Gardet 2012). In Khaled's lessons he teaches how faith in God requires the obligation to respond, not only through obligatory acts of worship like prayer but through good works as the highest act of worship, superior to mere ritual. In his preaching on the necessity of performing good works, he underlines the phrase repeated *throughout* the Quran "those who believe and do good works" (*al-ladhina amanu wa amilu al-salihat*). Volunteerism is the contemporary method of good deeds (*salihat*) and a practice of faith.

Life Makers emerged as a significant strand of Khaled's program for Islamic reform at the same time a shift was happening in national policies on charitable giving. Their activities responded to the MSSJ's appeal to charitable organizations to adopt developmental values and practices through microfinance projects, capacity building, and other methods (Atia 2007). In this way, Life Makers was exemplary, taking up the government's effort to supplant charity with development. Although the organization runs traditional good works activities, such as their annual distribution of food bags in the holy month of Ramadan, organization leaders typically background these projects to what they view as their more original activities, like their campaign against dropping out of school and their classroom visits to teach civic culture. Ehab explained Life Makers' persistence of traditional chari table activities as being in dialogue with Egypt: "We are a traditional society, and good works must function within its environment to create opportunities for giving that are familiar to Egyptians." For Ehab and other Life Makers leaders, the projects that they understood as Life Makers' signature contributions were those that departed from traditional forms of giving, but for many new recruits the distinction was not important, nor was it what attracted them to volunteer. Particularly in the days and months following the eighteen-day uprising, Life Makers offered a chance to do something, to feel connected to a project for changing Egypt.

The appeal to faith rather than religion was also an ecumenical move. Through faith, Life Makers sought to include Copts as volunteers and recipients of their programming. The organization draws on a nationalist unity discourse that promotes the values of piety and devotion rather than the specificity of a religious tradition. In this way, Life Makers appear quintessentially Egyptian in their bireligious appeal. Faith was part of an effort to integrate religious communities in social development works that are typically run separately and that usually cater to their own religious communities. Life Makers' administrators were particularly sensitive to attracting Coptic volunteers and were keen to learn from experienced Coptic social service organizations, like the Coptic Evangelical Organization for Social Services. Despite the rhetorical emphasis on religious cooperation, I did not encounter any Coptic volunteers during my research. Coexistence remained an unrealized ideal of faith development. By highlighting the resonances between Life Makers and state discourses of religious coexistence, I do not suggest that Life Makers were co-opted by the state or that their appeal to faith was somehow disingenuous. Rather, my point is to underline how appeals to faith can at moments materialize as a pliable and even cliché rejoinder, just as at other moments faith can be part of a specific vision for the reformulation of Islamic giving.

Reforming Good Works: Volunteerism

Following Mubarak's ouster, with the revitalization of Life Makers' branches throughout the country, the amrekhaled.net website—one of the most visited Arabic language sites on the web—incorporated a feature for volunteer registration. For several months, visitors to the site encountered a banner that read: "Pay your alms, donate by becoming a volunteer" (*idfa' zakatak, tabarra' tatawwa'*). The rejoinder to pay alms (*zakat*), the obligatory tithe, makes volunteering an obligatory donation. Yet, according to a jurisprudential perspective, volunteerism is not zakat, since it does not conform to the specified portion of food or money that fulfills the legal requirements.

At the same time, volunteer*ism* takes on a meaning distinct from voluntary charity, called *sadaqa*. The organization extends the language of good works beyond a jurisprudential framework of obligatory giving to include volunteerism. Through television programming and volunteer training, Khaled's audience was reminded of the right (*haqq*) of the poor and the obligation to help those in need. The necessity to respond to the right of the poor then made volunteerism compulsory, and not optional, or "voluntary." The requirement to respond to the person in need sets up a faith development that blends traditional terminology for alms with a contemporary discourse on the value of volunteerism. Their volunteerism is less about the agency of the actor, as their labor is the necessary response to encountering need. Volunteers' recourse to faith does not dispense with an Islamic vocabulary of giving but rather adapts traditional key terms and values in how they participate in good works. They make "paying zakat" not a financial responsibility but the duty of giving one's time and energy. As unemployed people with little or no income, young people are not required to pay the zakat, which makes the call to donate their available time, often through laborious physical activity, all the more galvanizing.

In Ahmed's crowded office, Maha, his fiancée and another long-term volunteer, joined us. She listened as Ahmed explained how not all good works are equal. Volunteers emphasized an ethical hierarchy of good works that placed activities that give opportunity to encounter others as superior to those that do not. For example, literacy teachers commonly spoke of learning more from their students; Ehab described the significance of working with Bedouins in a Sinai project initiated in 2014. The Bedouin, like the nonliterate or the poor, were figures for volunteers to learn from and grow through. These intersubjective encounters were essential to volunteers' understanding of what is gained through new modes of serving their communities. They sought to help others with an awareness that through these efforts they aimed to improve themselves.

As Ahmed and I reflected on this feature of Life Makers' volunteerism, Maha interjected: "Most people work here to please God and enter paradise." Maha's intervention did not undermine Ahmed's point on the social potentials of volunteerism, and yet, it exposed the critique of forms of giving that do not lead to new relationships as secondary to volunteers' primary motives. As Maha pointed out, to get carried away with critique of other forms of good works, as Ahmed and others did, was to risk losing sight of the ultimate goal. While Ahmed demonstrated shifting priorities of the ethical and practical manifestations of good works, Maha illustrated how not all volunteers espoused the dominant organization's discourse that prioritizes distinction from other Muslim organizations. The exchange was illustrative of debates about the value of good works as volunteers negotiated the significance of their actions on others as well as for themselves and in relation to God. The question of how good works should be performed, and with what intentional and material goals, raised the issue of what working for God means, and what it should look like.

Adept at recruiting and motivating his peers, Ahmed drew attention to an intersubjective value of volunteerism that while significant among Life Makers, was less prevalent in practice. In this way, Life Makers are distinct from what Erica Bornstein describes as the "volunteer experience," a secular practice, even while it resonates with religious transformative experience (2012b). Based on fieldwork in Indian volunteer organizations, Bornstein details volunteerism as a secular transformative experience, one distinct from traditional modes of donating, such as *dan* (122). For Life Makers, their self-improvement included the aim of developing their piety. As we saw with their supplication, volunteer activities were not denuded of Islamic referents but rather became a method for fulfilling a religious duty and acting for God. Volunteers understood their labor as an expression of faith that differentiated their activities from a secular organization, even when at moments their reform of Islamic practice pointed outside of the tradition.

Unlike Bornstein's volunteers, Amira Mittermaier argues in her account of charitable giving that volunteerism is distinct from a "moral economy of compassion" (2014, 518), one distinct from Christian and secular genealogies of the value of volunteerism. She describes how volunteers are illustrative of "nonliberal and nonhumanist" ideals and draws out the "Islamicness" of their work (518). Mittermaier describes a volunteerism embedded within a spiritual economy that disrupts and "radically diverges from a secular humanist ethics" (520), one that is instead part of a response and obedience to God. Like Mittermaier's interlocutors, God was central to Life Makers' volunteers, who downplayed their agency and foregrounded accountability to the poor and ultimately God. The conversation with Ahmed and Maha revealed the interplay between so-called secular humanist virtues of the intersubjective experience with volunteers' sense of duty to God. Notably, Ahmed did not object to Maha's interjection, and the conversation demonstrated a tension that runs through Life Makers' efforts that see value in immanent social relationships and yet draw meaning from a transcendent sense of working for God. Their volunteerism does not break away from a secular ethic of volunteerism that invests in the transformative experience of participating in good works, and yet at moments their God-centered orientation obscures this very desire to work with and for others. In the next section I move from volunteers' engagement qua volunteers as a critique of traditional good works to examine how faith was felt and expressed. The purpose is to render ethnographically how Life Makers assembles optimism to make faith a universal good. By investigating optimism as a feeling associated less so with *others*, and more so with *time,* we can better understand critique as an embodied dimension of volunteerism and the politics that it produces. I present two volunteers to demonstrate the ambivalence and flexibility of faith as a catalyst for development.

Faith and Optimism: Critique in Action

Hundreds of volunteers gathered in the auditorium at the National Council for Youth and Sport. Life Makers was celebrating its ninth anniversary. To mark the occasion, it held an event to recognize the major initiatives under way. Video clips with emotional soundtracks narrated their endeavors. A popular leader within the organization took the stage and the crowd cheered. She thanked the volunteers for their efforts and encouraged them in a refrain familiar to Life Makers' events: "When I first began, I couldn't believe all of the obstacles we would face. If I knew how difficult it was going to be, I might not have tried. But I was optimistic. This is our secret tool that makes us different. Don't forget your optimism. For life, and in each day. Let's keep going." The audience clapped. Although some volunteers questioned the celebratory tone of Life Makers' activities, instead preferring a more sober sense of responsibility, the organizational norm was overwhelmingly one of positivity. By focusing on their pedagogy of optimism, we attune ourselves to how Life Makers embodied and instructed feelings of happiness, optimism, and hope to motivate volunteers and propel their projects. Life Makers' promotional materials and volunteer Facebook memes repeated the mantra of these values, sometimes with "faith" mentioned alongside them, and other times when these sentiments were expressions of faith.

Positive affects were central to Life Makers' distinction from oppositional movements that gained traction in early 2011, as well as Egyptians who did not support the uprising in any way. Optimism was significant in volunteers' articulations of faith as a constructive sentiment. As Maha remarked, they did not succumb to worries and frustration and did not let anger immobilize them. This was a pointed departure from the atmosphere they worked in. Graffiti in Tahrir Square declared: "I'm angry" (*ana ghadban*) with an incitement to continue demonstrations. Evening talk shows implored their viewers to recognize various threats to the security and unity of the country. For Life Makers, optimism was not an interior state but was integral to the realization of faith through action. Volunteers drew on a wide repertoire of self-help literature, including translations of English best sellers like *The Secret*, as well as Arabic self-help books, some of which are in conversation with the Quran and the prophetic tradition, like A'id al-Qarni's popular *Don't Be Sad*. Their persistent positivity at that political juncture made their critics perceive them as naive and willfully disconnected from what was happening in Egypt.

While volunteers spoke of the more pious disposition of hope (*amal* and *raja'*), happiness and optimism were predominant. While amal and raja' describe a longing for God and the afterlife, optimism echoes trends in personal development that are aimed at improving life. Life Makers' happiness is also part of global marketing trends, and popular culture, while at the same time it emerged in a region in which, following 9/11, happiness was promoted through public relations campaigns that regarded Arab and Muslim cultures as obsessed with death. Life Makers' affective pedagogies resonated with initiatives like the 2008 "Culture of Optimism" campaign launched in Egypt (Sukarieh 2012; Sukarieh and Tannock 2011), although they were not explicitly involved in any of these internationally sponsored programs.

Life Makers' happiness contrasts with Islamic rhetorical strategies in Egypt that emphasize fear of God (*taqwa*) and fear of the afterlife (*tarhib*) through detailed images of death and punishment. Indeed, the cultivation of particular affects for ethical ends is a dominant feature of contemporary Islamic reform movements. Charles Hirschkind (2006) describes how listeners cultivate awe and fear by attentively listening to cassette sermons. The acoustic practice tuned in to the sermon's content and rhetorical styles to instill virtuous affects. My interlocutors similarly aimed to cultivate particular virtuous sentiments, although they were explicit in setting themselves apart from this major trend in contemporary Islamic preaching. So, while optimism was not unique to Life Makers, it was part of their particular critique of other reformist techniques of cultivating piety and a way of being that distinguished them from other iterations of Islam.

"Are You Optimistic?": Two Volunteers

In May 2013 I reunited with Amal. It had been nearly a year since we last met. Amal was twenty-nine when she first began as a volunteer immediately following Mubarak's ouster. She graduated from the Faculty of Law eight years prior and had since been unemployed. She lived with her mother and two brothers in a low-income neighborhood at the end of the metro line. Her family lived on remittances sent from her father who worked in Saudi Arabia. To reach the Life Makers' office near Tahrir Square, I walked past security roadblocks and wall graffiti depicting the revolution's martyrs and the latest satirizations of the president of the moment, Mohamed Morsi. As Amal and I settled into a storage room—the only available space—Amal's first question was one I hoped I would not have to answer: "Are you optimistic?" She was inquiring into something other than my opinion on politics, the subject of most of my conversations those days. As I had learned over the course of my time with the organization, Amal was asking something about me, about my faith. To not be optimistic meant that I was not a part of the same project that she hoped I had embraced through my time with her. She was asking if I shared her ontology. For Amal, to not be optimistic meant I did not believe in their vision. It meant that I was stuck in this world, with the bad news that newspapers bring.

Like Hirschkind's cassette-tape listeners, who understood fear as the appropriate disposition toward God and the next life, for Amal, optimism was both a technique to cultivate piety and essential for true faith. She embodied Life Makers' expression of faith by cultivating optimism as integral to her voluntary work. She also taught optimism in the literacy classroom. She, like other teachers, structured lessons around happiness: stressing the importance of being happy and creating happiness, as well as instructing her students in techniques for raising happy families. Yet, for Amal's students, optimism was of little interest. Happiness lessons appeared to be quaint signals of volunteers' disjunctures with their students that highlighted optimism as a classed refrain. It was not that Life Makers were among Egypt's privileged classes. Coming from an array of social backgrounds, volunteers' university educations alongside their mantra of positivity meant that many imagined themselves as upwardly mobile. They anticipated work opportunities, marriage, and other ways to improve themselves in a near future. While volunteers saw themselves as sacrificing their time, they also had expectations of how time would bring about God's reward (*thawab*) in the form of worldly blessings.

As an organization that attracted seventy thousand volunteers in the months following the January 25 revolution, not all volunteers were equally committed to its ideals. In this way, faith was less a critique of available forms of action and more of a pliable platform for positive outreach. Another volunteer, Umar, was ambivalent about Life Makers' specific faith project, while conversant in the language of positivity that intersected Life Makers' expression of faith. Umar was a photographer and a consummate observer who struggled to make decisions. He was less confident and less certain than many of his Life Makers friends. He felt caught between wanting "to do something" and not knowing the best thing to do. He explained that while Khaled "is a little bit religious," he watched his television programs because they made him feel better when he was depressed about school. When we first met, Umar was completing his studies at the Faculty of Architecture. He barely looked forward to graduation because it meant that he would become eligible for military service. He was anxious while waiting to discover if he would be enlisted. Still, it was important to him to maintain a particular form of greeting. "When people ask 'How are you?' I always say, 'wonderful.' It's a strong response to a casual question. It makes me feel good. It helps me pause to appreciate what is wonderful in my life. And it makes my listener stop and think, too." Umar's outlook resonated with many other Life Makers, and yet, he was less interested in discussions about the best way to perform Islamic good works. For Umar, optimism was not the virtuous expression of Islamic faith as it was for Amal. Instead, his repeated appeals to happiness were aloof from faith and religion. For Umar, not every aspect of life, even his volunteerism, needed to invoke Islam.

Umar's ambivalence toward Life Makers' ethic of action was not part of a discomfort with the Islamic character of their good works. For Umar, the prevalence of faith talk was redundant. As he explained, volunteerism was something he did as a Muslim, but he did not see the need to repeatedly speak of faith. "It's good to please God and get closer to Him, but that doesn't need to be so formalized." He described how he tried to make the intention to do his good works for rewards but concluded that even these statement of intention were extraneous: "People say God gives great rewards for many reasons, not just one, so it shouldn't be a problem how I do my [volunteer] work."

Umar revealed the bind that Life Makers found themselves in when faith became the touchstone of the organization's discourse—through its publicity it risked the volunteer's authenticity. Faith talk risked ossifying feelings into the dogma of religion. Umar underlined the ambiguity of faith development beyond religion. He shared the correct feeling of Life Makers' Islamic faith, one based on self-reflection and positivity, but did not share the same critical orientation. Through him, we see how within Life Makers, faith was a foil to political Islam and apathy. Amal and Umar reveal how optimism is more than an inner state but is enmeshed in the making of a particular politics, one that saw possibility in the future. Unlike other activists who spoke of anger, or other Egyptians who spoke of confusion and heaviness, optimism was Life Makers' expression of their nonconfrontational politics. Indeed, their apolitical stance was its own position.

Conclusions: The Politics of Faith

Lauran Berlant's felicitous term "cruel optimism" captures the political effects of Life Makers' affective pedagogy. For Berlant, optimism is cruel when the desire for an object impedes the very aim of initial attraction. Life Makers' optimism is cruel in how they not only refrain from critique of the state but in how their works seek to support it, despite state surveillance and regulation that makes their work precarious. Berlant explains that cruel optimism can be a "desire for the political itself" (2011, 12). Life Makers are enmeshed in a definition of the political that disciplines their work and shapes their understanding of religion as a narrow repertoire of politically exploitable practices from the past. Despite their optimism, even patriotism, Life Makers' efforts to circumvent religion and politics strengthen the boundaries they seek to undo. Their optimism is cruel in its bind to support the state through their good works, while subject to the whims of state power.

Life Makers creates a form of Islam that eschews not only political ambition but even the claim to religion. For volunteers, faith development is not only an alternative to the machinations of Islam for political power but it is an authentic version of Islam. Young volunteers reformulate traditional forms of obligatory charity to make volunteerism the most valuable form of giving. Their volunteerism straddles an idea of *voluntary* work with the *obligation* to work for others. Their reconfiguration of good works and attendant virtuous affects underline the need to scrutinize the FBO as a category of analysis. As they demonstrate, religion and faith are not synonymous. By investigating how they mobilize these categories, we attune ourselves to what is at stake in the ongoing negotiation of the role of Islam in contemporary Egypt. The story of Life Makers reveals how, when prodded by our interlocutors' terms of engagement, we can uncover the NGO as a pivotal site for renegotiating religion and politics today. Life Makers can help NGO studies develop a more precise vocabulary and analytical approach for understanding the complicated role of religion in civil society. Volunteers alert us to multiple and overlapping idioms of development from the Islamic tradition, international development, and the pervasiveness of self-help techniques in which volunteers refine and redefine themselves in close relation with notions of national progress. As Ahmed eloquently began this chapter, such an investigation lays bare the commitments and tensions, structures of feeling, as well as implicit and explicit critiques that guide not only the articulation of Islamic faith-based development but the effort to reform Islam itself.

Acknowledgments

I am deeply grateful for critical comments on this piece at various stages from Amira Mittermaier, Michael Lambek, Francis Cody, Junaid Quadri, Emmanuelle Stefanidis, Giulia El Dardiry, Alexandre Caeiro, and Elizabeth Shakman Hurd. Most importantly, I could not have begun to ask the questions I ask here, or search out their answers, without the generosity of the volunteers who welcomed me into their worlds.

Notes

1. I follow a simplified version of the standard system of Arabic transliteration used by the *International Journal of Middle East Studies*.

2. I refer to sentiment, affect, emotions, and feelings interchangeably, not as psychological states but rather as social practices (Lutz and Abu Lughod 1990; Ahmed 2004; cf. Richard and Rudnyckyj 2009). In so doing, I tend to the ways my interlocutors understand how language creates and communicates feelings.

3. For statistics on Egyptian adult education alongside other UN high-priority countries, see Huebler and Lu (2012). On the relationship between revolution and major gains in literacy, see Arnove and Graff (1987).

4. See Asad's discussion of W. C. Smith's *The Meaning and End of Religion* (1962), where Asad argues that the analytic move to examine "religion as faith" overemphasizes inner states without proper attention to practice (2002).

5. For an account of the effects of changes to the NGO laws, see the International Center for Not-For-Profit Law's analysis of Egypt (2013).

6. Popular media and scholarly publications alike describe Khaled as an influential Muslim reformer representative of devolving Islamic authority, particularly among affluent urban youth (Haenni 2005; Moll 2010; Sobhy 2011; Winegar 2014).

7
Interdependent Industries and Ethical Dilemmas

NGOs and Volunteer Tourism in Cusco, Peru

Aviva Sinervo

In Cusco, Peru—a city where the yearly tourist population exceeds the local residents threefold (DIRCETUR 2007; INEI 2008)—the popularity of volunteer tourism has been increasing steadily throughout the last decade. Volunteer tourism is a growing global industry wherein tourists combine travel, leisure, sightseeing, cultural exchange, and language training with opportunities to assist local communities as unpaid laborers (Wearing and McGehee 2013). Volunteers in Cusco work in a variety of sectors, including construction, health care, community development, and formal education. Yet the projects drawing the most support are run by NGOs that provide aid to children. There are more than a dozen local language schools that teach Spanish to short- and long-term international tourist volunteers, while also facilitating their placement into more than a hundred different aid projects targeting so-called poor, abandoned, or working children. The scale, scope, and diversity of volunteering programs and child-focused NGOs are difficult to quantify, as they are continually on the rise and not all are officially documented. However the economic, political, and affective dimensions of the NGO and volunteer tourism phenomena are deeply entangled, often with ethical consequences for NGO programs and staff, volunteer tourists, program child recipients and their families, industry intermediaries (such as Spanish schools providing tourist language instruction and volunteer placement opportunities), and government officials.

Cusco's plethora of NGOs is partly a response to high rates of poverty combined with government retreat from social assistance in Peru. Indeed the global proliferation of NGOs follows these trends (Lewis and Kanji 2009; Riddell 2007). Though the nation's official poverty rate stood at 24 percent in 2013 (World Bank 2015), down from the 45 percent reported in 2008 (UNICEF 2008), the Peruvian state has withdrawn funding for many services that might help Peru's poorest to cope with widespread job insecurity, rising food prices, and significant inequality. With such an obvious need, publicly manifested in high incidences of visible child labor (Bromley and Mackie 2008; Campoamor 2012), there is a ready NGO focus on providing resources for vulnerable children. Yet economic necessity and poverty are only one possible reason for the emergence of a prominent NGO community in Cusco. Another piece of the equation requires attention to the particular arrangements of NGO financial, social, manual, and emotional support.

This chapter draws on ethnographic portraits of two children's after-school centers to analyze how the NGO sector has grown in relation to Cusco's economic dependence on tourism and the Peruvian government's disappearing or nonexistent investments in social assistance regarding poverty alleviation and childhood well-being. The NGO case studies—Children for Change and Centro de los Niños—have been chosen to highlight the diversity of mechanisms by which overlaps in aid industry and tourism industry interests allow for creative possibilities for NGOs.[1] These possibilities include soliciting donors' hands-on involvement, relying on volunteer labor instead of paid employees, and creating programming that builds on tourists' cultural capital and diversity. While Children for Change was founded by an independent local entrepreneur with a vision for using foreigners as "friends" to educate Cusco's youth and expose them to alternative models for self-betterment and care, Centro de los Niños was founded by a local police officer and the project was eventually incorporated under national police force jurisdiction. Technically, Children for Change is an NGO par excellence—yet its director rejects this labeling and prefers to call his after-school center a "social project." In contrast, Centro de los Niños is officially a government program—yet its staff members capitalize on its legibility through the NGO frame to position the organization within this classification. Both programs are read as NGOs by tourists and are similarly positioned within the broader volunteer tourism industry in terms of their roles in providing assistance to poor children in Cusco.

I use these contrasting NGO examples to argue that, alongside the provision of necessary funding and infrastructure, the coconstituted nature of the volunteer tourism and NGO industries generates moral and logistical contradictions for all participants. Highlighting the entangled relationship between NGO viability and touristic consumption practices allows for an analysis of the ways that NGOs must employ certain discourses and strategies in order to negotiate economic and political considerations coming from the global tourism industry alongside national and international aid communities. In this endeavor, I build on scholarly insights on the ever-changing roles of NGOs vis-à-vis state forms of public divestment and authority (Bernal and Grewal 2014b; Schuller 2007 and 2009). Moreover, situating NGOs within the internationally booming climate of volunteer tourism (Mostafanezhad and Hannam 2014; Vrasti 2013) prompts reflection on how aid subjects are constructed not just by governments or NGO staff, donors, and recipients but also by tourists.

In many Cusco-based NGOs for children, volunteer tourists occupy the role of financial donor but also act as economic and affective clients. NGOs are dependent on volunteer labor and donations but also must provide their volunteers with "rewarding experiences" in return. Tourists are both workers in, and patrons of, the NGO industry. In straddling the divide between the corporatization of the volunteer tourism sector and the widespread emotional appeal of helping needy children, NGOs find themselves reworking the assumptions, categories, and meanings that underlie their missions and practices.

The Intertwined Growth of Volunteer Tourism and NGOs

Cusco's NGO Boom

Child-focused NGOs in Cusco have grown in both number and importance. In the absence of an official list by which to document their scope, in 2008 I began to compile my own database of local NGOs, pieced together from information from volunteers, Spanish-language schools for tourists, and policing, judicial, and development government offices.[2] Governmental and nongovernmental assistance programs include educational preparatory programs, orphanages, dormitories, feeding programs, penal institutions, and after-school centers.

With a process of governmental decentralization under way (Ballon 2011; McNulty 2011) and in the wake of perceived state disorganization and retreat from social services, the challenge of taking care of local children has progressively fallen to the NGO community. While in Cusco during a period of global recession, I spoke to several nascent NGO directors who thought that the state was not responding adequately to the needs of their communities.

NGOs might arise to fill a need that the state has never addressed, or they might be created following the state's withdrawal from a specific neighborhood or sector of aid provision. Both of these factors were in play in 2005 when Rodrigo[3] (a middle-class, local Spanish teacher for tourists) began the process to open his own NGO elementary school and communal dining room, in the absence of a neighborhood public school and after the closure of a nearby government-run dining program. By 2010, Rodrigo had purchased property and begun construction on an official school building, had paperwork in place to apply for government status as a certified school, and had a cadre of devoted volunteers raising funds internationally and traveling to Cusco to work for his program. Volunteers provided labor and donations and also acted as creative partners, generating suggestions for new structures, promotional campaigns, and longevity planning.

Rodrigo's case illustrates how NGOs come into being not just to cope with governmental absence but also to deal with state restructuring that leaves vulnerable populations without adequate social support. Rodrigo's connections with a population of foreigners during his time as a Spanish schoolteacher enabled him to upgrade his NGO's services gradually to meet the needs of his community. My interviews with parents and children attendees of such programs also pointed to how NGOs have become a popular means for alleviating economic hardship and replacing previous government services. For example, twelve-year-old Lucia explained that she used to attend a governmental dining facility, but since its closure, she attends lunch at a program run by a group of nuns.

NGOs in Cusco are a relatively recent phenomenon, as most services not being provided by the state used to be fulfilled exclusively by the Catholic Church. In an interview with a past director for the Red Semilla Nueva— a network of state and nonstate organizations that work with "at risk" children—he explained that during the 1990s, NGOs proliferated in Cusco and grew in prominence and power. In large part, they augmented church services, such as offering assistance to the poor and placing orphaned children in adoptive homes. The director emphasized that there was no governmental oversight or control during this period. NGOs were officially supposed to be registered, but "no one ever bothered." It is worth noting that this early period of NGO growth coincided with the state's focus on combatting the Shining Path, a Maoist extremist group promoting violence in the 1980s (Stern 1998). Years of civil unrest had led to economic depression, but the slow return of tourists to Cusco throughout the 1990s, blossoming in the 2000s (Steel 2008), led to new configurations of NGO autonomy and economic power linked to the reinvigorated tourism industry.

The government is complicit in the growth of opportunities for NGOs through tourism, not only because of its inability or unwillingness to provide social services but also through its participation in international frameworks of development and campaigns on poverty and childhood. The state officially promotes tourism as one of the main pathways to economic development in the region (PEDRC 2008).[4] In recent years, the state has additionally reasserted itself as the political authority in charge of mediating how aid reaches Peruvian children.

Peru is a signatory to the 1990 UN Convention on the Rights of the Child and clearly is aware of the international community's gaze in terms of regulatory expectations to produce quantifiable and transparent improvements in national childhood well-being.[5] In addition to participating in campaigns with international partners like UNICEF, the government has responded by instituting new mechanisms of oversight over the NGO community. Since 2007, the state has legalized a standard record-keeping process, requiring all children's NGOs to submit organizational plans and social goals, employ a team of state-certified experts (such as psychologists, lawyers, and accountants), and quantify the number of children it can serve. In 2008, I interviewed a Lima-based federal official who was in charge of compiling this new registry. She claimed that these registers for child aid legibility at the institutional level, requiring organizations to categorize themselves and classify their participants and methods, are geared toward enabling transparency and good governance—and encouraging continuity—in the NGO sector.

Moreover, it is worth noting that before the 2007 law, registration was required only for children's organizations providing residential services. This previous loophole in jurisdiction allowed a range of NGOs to escape state monitoring, by catering to an aid subject that was not defined within the parameters of state purview. The state encourages foreign spending through tourism, while at the same time ceding international humanitarian obligations regarding childhood and poverty to NGOs. While state investment in this sector is limited, the state can still use its regulatory arm to claim involvement in these processes and outputs, thereby appearing to be active participants in meeting international development and well-being goals surrounding childhood and poverty.

Cusco as (Volunteer) Tourist Destination

While all forms of tourism in Cusco are on the rise, volunteer tourism has developed quickly within the already popular model of using the city as a site for language immersion and instruction. Spanish schools catering to foreign tourists often coordinate the placement of volunteers at local NGOs. Schools collect volunteering fees, a portion of which is sometimes passed on to the NGO partner to fund aspects of their aid agendas.[6] Not all NGOs work with Spanish schools to obtain volunteers; an NGO might also solicit its own "direct" volunteers and request that donations are made directly to the project.

The majority of Cusco's current NGOs rely heavily on foreigner funding through Spanish school fees and independent, individual donations. Although likely representing a small portion of the overall tourists in the city, the subset of foreigners who seek to combine travel and sightseeing opportunities with volunteering are generous in donating money, time, and energy.

Volunteer tourists are part of a global trend placing value on service-oriented experiences that coincide with broader development initiatives (see Butcher and Smith 2010). In Cusco, they primarily come from North America, Europe, and Australia, although the number of Latin American tourists is on the rise. Mirroring worldwide trends (Vrasti 2013), these volunteers are predominantly middle-class young adults in their early twenties. Many arrive with intentions to spend part of their trip volunteering, and a high percentage of these tourists are placed in projects in advance of their arrival. Others end up volunteering on a whim, switching projects, or staying longer than originally planned. Length of placement, degree of advanced planning, skills (including Spanish proficiency), and cost for volunteering fees all vary considerably, yet tourists fulfill key parts of after-school center missions. In addition to their pivotal economic role, many project staff members believe that volunteers bring social and cultural diversity to a program environment by exposing child attendees to other languages, traditions, and ways of living. In interviews, volunteers were adamant about being valued primarily for their social and emotional—not financial—investments.[7]

Despite a dependence on tourist wealth, we must consider the "local" qualities of Cusco's NGO phenomenon. Many children's aid centers are founded and directed by foreigners, but there are also a significant number of home-grown organizations. I was privy to the passion and dedication of several local Cusco residents, Rodrigo included, as they built NGOs from the ground up—even abandoning other promising career opportunities to pursue social projects that might improve the nutritional, familial, and educational prospects for children in the region. Some projects reject charging volunteer fees for foreigner participation and develop models of financial sustainability that are not rooted solely in international funds. Focusing only on the profit engine of volunteer tourism, or the absence of a public social safety net, is misleading if it overshadows attention to the intense local desire to mitigate problems of poverty that seem to be addressed best—from a moral and educational standpoint—during childhood.

Ethical Dilemmas

From this brief historical profile of NGO and tourism growth over the last twenty-five years, it is clear that the sector's newfound breadth and capacities are connected not just to poverty and state absence or retreat from social service provision but also to the dynamics of tourism in the region. The markedly symbiotic relationship that exists between children's NGOs and the global volunteer tourism industry has led many locals to question whether NGOs have proliferated as a means of profiting from the tourist market. For example, the moral dimensions of NGO existence as a direct response to changing touristic consumption practices was discussed by one Spanish school volunteer coordinator in terms of a "prostituting" of Peru's poor children to generate business wealth (see Sinervo 2015, 166).

Volunteer tourism is a profit-generating industry (Lyons and Wearing 2008), and the affective tenor of childhood readily makes children into attractive aid subjects for foreign donation and investment (Huberman 2012; Mostafanezhad 2014; Stephens 1995). The underlying subtext of this coupling generates concern. Are Cusco's children's organizations brought into being to service tourists' desires to work with poor children? Are children themselves being used as an affectively instrumental demographic whose needs are promoted to align with volunteering tourists' expectations of their own role (as wealthy foreigners) in meeting such needs? Are tourists, perhaps unwittingly, actively involved in producing the visible "need" they want to help alleviate? Is the creation of aid opportunities in the form of NGOs driven mostly by potential income from the tourism industry? Or are there so many programs catering to Cusco's children because the population has particularly defined and significantly scaled needs?

With these questions in mind, I explore how the evolution of Cusco's NGOs, in its intimate ties to the growth of the tourism industry, has created an interdependence with ethical consequences for local and foreign participants, as well as for the volunteer tourism industry and the NGO sector more broadly.[8] The growth in the number of NGOs comes from a complex variety of factors and agents, relating to an influx of willing donors (individual tourist volunteers), an interest in meeting children's needs through NGOs (as seen with local NGO directors), a compelling target group ("poor children," real and imagined), and an opportunity created by a unique set of child assistance industry relationships (enacted by Spanish school businesses, government entities, and international agencies). I subsequently highlight the dynamic of intersecting NGO and volunteer tourism interests within two after-school centers (Children for Change and Centro de los Niños) where I conducted ethnographic fieldwork—and worked as a volunteer—between 2006 and 2008.[9] In both cases, organizations must grapple with how to accomplish their day-to-day operations and set their long-term visions when considering an absent state and an increasingly commodified form of aid provision for Cusco's children.

Meanings, Contexts, and Motives of NGO Positioning

These two children's after-school centers do not comfortably fit the label of NGO.[10] Yet, they are both an integral and well-known part of the landscape of children's social assistance in Cusco, and both might be readily termed NGOs by unsuspecting audiences. As an independent nonprofit,

Children for Change seems to resemble an NGO by all definitions and is officially registered as such; yet, its leader publicly insists that it is not. Centro de los Niños is a government program and thereby *not* an NGO; yet, it embraces the potentiality of NGO positioning. While these after-school centers are similarly situated by the global volunteer tourism industry—as enacted through the volunteer coordinators who place tourists in the programs and the tourist volunteers who seek enriching experiences of "making a difference" (Butcher and Smith 2010; Simpson 2004; Sinervo 2011 and 2015) with poor children—the directors and staff members narrate the programs quite differently based on the desirability of certain kinds of foreigner involvement.

In both instances, deployments of the label NGO refer less to an organization's roots in civil society, degree of independence from the government, or lack of political or profit-based motivations (see Lister [2003] on the issue of NGO legitimacy) but instead signal divergent visions for situating one's organization in a competitive, NGO-rich environment, enmeshed in the politics, economics, and emotions of the volunteer tourism industry. While NGO is well documented as a slippery concept that resists categorization and homogenization (Hilhorst 2003), in Cusco we must consider the surrounding bureaucratic framework of volunteer tourism, and the raison d'être, for many such programs in the first place: not only to provide aid to Cusco's poor children but to do so through tourist dollars in a way that also commodifies and markets an experience for foreigners. Whether NGO is a derogatory or celebrated category depends on a shifting framework of responsibility, not just for Cusco's children, but also for the stability of the NGO form as related to the region's access to development aid generated by the tourism industry.

Children for Change: The Social Project That Is Not an NGO

Children for Change is an integrated "social project" founded and run by a local man named Aron, who is in his mid-thirties. Aron was raised by a single mother, yet his family is economically well-off by Peruvian standards. An active participant in the local nonprofit scene, Aron espouses a philosophy that he terms "economic justice" and "antiwelfarism": he is insistent that social projects should be self-sustaining, not reliant on individual, foreign donations, and that children attend his program for motives that are social and cultural, not solely economic.

In 2006, two years after Aron started a children's after-school center with his own savings, he opened a restaurant in order to provide the organization with a constant source of funding. He claims to favor this coupling of business and aid program because he has seen too many projects close due to an abrupt change in foreign interests, and he wants to promote the local economy and be a model for self-sustainability. Yet he also advances an agenda that advocates neoliberal values as he encourages the children participants to be self-sufficient, build self-esteem through good deeds, and avoid an attitude of dependency on international aid.

Aron boasts that he pays his restaurant employees a living wage and offers them health and education benefits. He also continually reminds the project's tourist volunteers and local children about their achieved economic autonomy by underlining that Children for Change is a "social project": it docs not receive any money from the government, the Catholic Church, or from volunteer fees, and it is *not* an NGO.[11] NGOs in Cusco, Aron explained to me, must be registered with the government so they may receive tax and import/export benefits. The phenomenon of NGOs, moreover, is intricately intertwined with the boom in foreign interest in Cusco. But Children for Change is Aron's attempt to create a "cultural socioeconomic system" that makes lasting projects—something he does not believe is possible if one must rely on the whims of foreigners who are socially conscious but have short philanthropic attention spans. Additionally, NGOs are problematic models because not every local with a valiant idea is able to solicit international involvement. Being an NGO is not bad, Aron said, "but why not create a system that also would be easy to access for people who do not have foreigner contacts and cannot make an NGO?" He continued by emphasizing his broader plans for promoting economic justice and long-term social change through children's projects:

> You have to keep thinking in relationships. "Bubble" projects, there are many projects that last some years, but what happens with these youth when they leave the project, they go to the streets, return to the real world, return to look for work, and they find the same, corruption, bad salaries, a lack of respect for their dignity. Therefore, what real change? We simply gave these youth illusions that afterwards they cannot use in the real world. Therefore what is the problem? The problem is the real world, and what is the real world in Peru? Money, businesses, capital. If we could with each social project also change the economic system, have a restaurant, an agency, whatever thing that apart from funding the project, also appreciates its workers, pays them well, gives them social services, serves Peruvian products, pays its taxes. I am an ambitious person, I am not going to stay in my little social project: I, with this project, in three years, will offer franchises!

This long excerpt is characteristic of Aron's oratory style and global envisioning of revolution within the NGO and commercial sectors. He critiques projects that do not expose children to strategies for ethical and practical survival in the "real world," and he sees his approach as broadly replicable by other NGOs. He hopes that his project will serve as a business role model for the children while also making concrete changes in business practices. (He also once told me that he hopes the children in his program will grow up inspired by his example and later start their own social projects to help others in turn.) Aron does not just resist the NGO framing because he sees NGOs as problematically dependent on foreign capital; the NGO label also does not feel appropriate because he runs his program like a corporate venture, complete with business language ("franchises"), marketing ("social project" rather than NGO), and financial strategies (the affiliated restaurant supporting the children's center).

When I asked Aron why he started using volunteer labor to run the center, he emphasized the importance of exposing children to global values, cultures, and peoples. He therefore embraced the potential of the tourism industry to provide him with opportunities to access cross-cultural perspectives to share with Cusco's children, even as he rejected the discourse that might frame the economic viability of his organization's growth in terms of touristic trends. While Aron initially envisioned his project in terms of its independence from foreigners, Children for Change has grown in size and success thanks to the dedication and passion of the many "friends" who have volunteered there over the last two years.

A Canadian named Rebecca, the most senior volunteer when I first arrived at this project in 2007, emailed her entire family right before Christmas, asking them to all make donations to the project that had become "like family." When first arriving to Cusco, Rebecca had only planned to stay for one month out of her year-plus of backpacking around Latin America, but it was five months before she could "pull away." Julie and Erling, two other volunteers from Denmark, had raised money among friends and family back home to help purchase the furniture for an expansion of the center, which had multiple rooms leading from two secluded patios. Like Rebecca, they were spending a year in Latin America, although their specific goal—in taking a year off from their paid jobs—was to volunteer. Rebecca was taking time off from college to decide about her long-term career orientation.

Their personal stories of encounter with Children for Change—heard through word of mouth or by meeting people eating at the affiliated restaurant—and motivations for undertaking volunteer tourism in Cusco were representative of the volunteer population at the center. This was especially the case since Aron rejected working with Spanish schools and international sending agencies due to his belief that charging volunteer fees went against the spirit of the endeavor. As the project grew, his website and word of mouth created an international buzz. Travelers went home and continued talking about the program (and in some cases sending donations), which helped maintain a steady stream of volunteer participants. Most volunteers would advertise the restaurant to other travelers they met and would frequent it themselves as their preferred place of drinking and dining. So in many ways, the volunteers do support the project economically, either directly by making donations or indirectly by patronizing the restaurant. Many of them expressed how important it felt to be able to contribute some money, even as they admired the project for Aron's ideals about economic justice and independence.

Furthermore, Aron valorizes affective and intangible resources over economic assistance, especially as he critiques the kind of aid that other children's projects distribute. Children for Change prioritizes children's agency and self-esteem, whereby children are prompted to focus on self-betterment and self-management, long-term future stability as opposed to short-term gain, global responsibility instead of dependency, and how to help others in lieu of expecting aid for themselves. Instead of seeing themselves as *pobrecitos*, poor children in need of assistance (see Sinervo 2013), Aron connects deservingness with responsibility, and responsibility with care, to teach children to be teachers, leaders, and givers. He consequently reshapes what children are supposed to appreciate and value.

Eschewing the provision of material resources as a central goal, Children for Change uses tourist volunteers to funnel sociocultural resources to the children: education, emotional support, opportunities for cross-cultural exchange, and friendship. Aron calls these "gifts you can't touch." In an early conversation about the center's goals, Aron elaborated on this aspect of his philosophy:

> The biggest challenge is to keep [children] coming, because their parents are not that interested and do not offer much consistent support. Poverty is this relative thing and the government responds by giving out money. But that is not what we do here. Here at Children for Change, we put systems in place for people to learn about the values of their lives and good ways to live better. Perhaps we can teach children to live better. Most parents would like their children to go to projects where they will be taught about Catholicism and they will receive things like clothes and food. But here, we are nonreligious—we teach the children about all world religions—and we don't believe in *asistencialismo*.[12] We help the children to make their own future better.

The four-hour center program involves two components. From three o'clock to five o'clock in the afternoon children arrive; wash, receive hand lotion, and greet all volunteers with hugs and kisses; and then are sent to one of four different activities. There is a playroom with games and toys that spill out onto the patio and an art room providing themed projects. There is a library, where children cyclically receive one-on-one attention practicing their reading. Finally, there is a study room, where all children who have homework must start their afternoon. Volunteers are stationed in each room, and Aron or the lead volunteer distributes the children and rotates them accordingly. Sometimes volunteers with interest in leading workshops will create additional rotations, such as karate, dance, yoga, meditation, animation, or baking classes.

At five o'clock Aron calls the children together into a circle where he discusses a value that he wants to emphasize that day. From five until six thirty the children are divided into volunteer-led classes that focus on a theme chosen by Aron that is taught for two weeks to a month. Topics for these classes range from world religion and languages to social values. At six thirty the children receive a warm drink made on-site with milk, oats, chocolate flavoring, and sugar. When classes are dismissed, children and volunteers say goodbye with affection similar to that they have exchanged throughout the afternoon, and sometimes children receive vitamins as they depart.

Monday through Wednesday, volunteers teach classes based on Aron's curriculum. On Thursdays classes prepare a presentation for Friday's fiesta, where the whole school gathers to share what they have learned that week. Volunteers help children put together plays, songs, artworks, dances, or poems on that week's topics, which each class presents in turn. On Friday evenings volunteers meet with Aron for their weekly meeting.

Aron relies heavily on volunteer contributions to make the project run. The "gifts you can't touch" that volunteers give to children include supporting their formal education and development through study room tutoring and activities, providing educational enrichment through classes that are geared toward cross-cultural awareness and global citizenship, and establishing affectionate friendships and mentorships that promote feelings of shared love and investment. Moreover, volunteers, in their global mobility and cosmopolitanism (not just their wealth), are uniquely positioned to provide children with this window into the wider world.

While volunteers are officially acknowledged for these nonmaterial inputs, and the project tries to pursue tenets of economic independence, there are contradictions in the ways that Aron frames self-sufficiency and local anchoring at the same time that he promotes connection to the international community through volunteer tourists. He wants the project not to rely on foreign spending and donations, yet he recognizes the importance, currency, and value of the social, cultural, and affective assets of tourists. Even as Aron tries to reject tourist economic resources—going so far as to not accept volunteers from sending organizations that collect fees—he cannot escape the reality that in Cusco, even a for-profit business operation like his restaurant is reliant on the tastes and desires of customers, who, in his case, are foreigners who want to help needy children. Aron also cannot completely control the inclinations of his volunteers, many of whom desire to give physical gifts to the children and donations to the center.

As he rejects the label of NGO, Aron distinguishes his program from other children's organizations and advances an ideological model that he believes is replicable and might help Cusco's growing number of NGOs achieve independence from direct foreign donations or volunteering fees. In his mind, NGOs problematically represent limited social vision and a type of welfarism that he does not want to teach the children in his program to expect. Pursuing "economic justice" therefore entails folding his social project's future into the future of his business ventures. Yet Aron is also strategic in how he harnesses the possibilities of volunteer-child interaction across divides in nationality, culture, class, and age. As much as he would like to shelter his program from reliance on foreigners, the presence of volunteer tourists in Cusco is key to both the economic and the social strategies enabling the organization's success.

Centro de los Niños: The Government Organization Mimicking the NGO Model

In contrast to Aron's ambivalence, Centro de los Niños is an after-school center that eagerly solicits the involvement of foreigners as economic contributors. In fact, this program could not survive in its day-to-day functions without explicitly drawing financial and labor support from its volunteers directly, as well as from the Spanish schools that send volunteers and might provide the center with some small segment of their volunteering fees.

Founded in the mid-1990s by Roberto, a local police officer, the project was integrated into the national police shortly thereafter. Roberto was still the main director of the project when I first began volunteering there in 2006, but during my 2007–8 stay in Cusco, another police officer was in charge. The national police send a rotating staff of officers to open the center's doors each weekday—official hours are from three thirty in the afternoon to seven thirty in the evening, although these are not adhered to consistently—and staff members oversee the program from a desk in the corner. Police officers are assigned to the project for brief periods that usually do not last more than a couple of months. Although technically a national government program, the only support that Centro de los Niños receives from the state is in the form of this transient staff. The building itself is loaned to the police by the municipal government, although this arrangement is the source of many complaints and much uncertainty, as the municipality constantly threatens to revoke the permit for the space, which is ill-equipped to handle the numbers and needs of the children, staff, and volunteers. For example, the center space is small, divided into two rooms with no outdoor play space except the street. There is no running water or bathrooms, although there is a propane stove and staff members could choose to haul water down from one of the storefronts up the road.

Unlike at Children for Change, programming at Centro de los Niños is inconsistent and sporadic, although there are typically diverse efforts under way by staff, volunteers, or the current director (who may or may not be a presence on a daily basis) to generate a lasting routine.[13] Sometimes the children are provided with an evening meal. This seems to depend on the flow of resources to do so, as well as the will of the police staff members to do the cooking and cleanup. Children are offered homework help, although there is no system in place for ensuring that children focus on schoolwork or complete it. Volunteers often complain that they are not equipped to help the local children with what the volunteers perceive as complicated schoolwork exercises across a linguistic divide.

One successful routine that became entrenched during my second period of volunteer work in 2008 was holding birthday celebrations for children and goodbye parties for departing volunteers. Everyone seemed to look forward to, and enjoy, these events despite their occasional nature; they had the aura of an emerging tradition, and volunteers used the framework to be especially generous with the specific children with whom they had formed deep attachments. The lead-up anticipation was almost as exciting as the actual occurrences.

In contrast, during my volunteer work in 2006, disillusionment ensued from a failed attempt to establish a routine. Volunteers often arrived with aspirations to teach English classes, as this kind of interaction with local children fit into their ambitions for connection and impact, and they believed that English was a useful linguistic skill. Even though volunteers might not have had any formal training as language teachers, they, as native speakers, nevertheless felt equipped to model and explain grammatical rules and verb tenses. Police staff members, eager to keep volunteers happy and not usually invested in creating their own programing alternatives, encouraged this practice. When putting this trend alongside the often short-term nature of touristic volunteering stints (and the subsequent high turnover of volunteers), the result was that the center's children learned vocabulary for colors and numbers and how to conjugate the verb "to be," over and over again. The children would grow disinterested and act out, while the volunteers were disappointed that their experiences did not match the romantic visions of engagement they arrived with.

Situations like these led to frustration on the part of volunteers, who saw the center as a poorly run one that did not make adequate use of their contributions, as donors or workers. When volunteers complained to their Spanish schools, the schools might revoke or restrict funding, causing significant reduction in benefits for the child participants and compromising the project's long-term viability. Irregularities in defining and meeting assistance goals therefore generated continued dysfunction, as the center had to ensure it could satisfy its tourist support network, whose negative judgments—as clients—could perpetuate already chronic problems stemming from a lack of funding.

The police and the supporting Spanish schools took turns blaming each other for the deficiencies in the center's daily operations. There was suspicion and accusations of corruption—mainly resource pocketing—on both sides. Police asserted that Spanish schools were not meeting their obligations when they delayed funding and that such delays impacted their ability to provide food, school supplies, and promised extracurricular activities such as fieldtrips. In an interview with Nina, a police officer placed at the project for four months in 2008, she recounted that "recently, the [program director] went to [the Spanish school] to request [the money] because they asked us for a letter explaining all that we needed for the children. There is a budget of 2,000 soles [approximately $700], but it is a bit aggravating because they have not given us a response. They said that they lost our letter and I gave them a copy and now they say that there is no money, or maybe they will send the money. This is discomforting because I thought that this money [from the volunteer fees] was earmarked for the children and we need these supplies most urgently." In this same vein, the project's police staff members would regularly denounce Spanish school owners for their greediness, claiming that the owners were making money on their participation in the lucrative volunteer tourism industry and were not passing enough of the revenue on to the aid project and children.

Spanish schools, for their part, were critical of the project, asserting that funding depended on the police's capacity to make transparent statements about what items were needed and that donations would be disbursed only when accounting records were in order. In an interview with the volunteer coordinator at the same school that had been accused of losing the Centro's request, I was told that the program had not been making regular requests until recently, and that the director and staff members did not seem to understand or respect the school's processes for donation disbursement. Volunteers and school coordinators alike confided their suspicions that the police officers were taking home supplies for their own children or for use at the police station; foreigners lamented that the government did not do more to support its own program directly in the face of "urgent needs."

The uneasy codependent relationship between Centro de los Niños and its affiliated Spanish schools continues, even in the face of widespread discontent. Police staff members develop ways to subvert the Spanish school channels, for example by directly petitioning volunteers for extra donations. This often works, as volunteers come and go regularly, and so there are usually freshly sympathetic donor targets for specifically framed and obviously needed requests. These range from in-the-moment needs, such as for bread, jam, or oats for the evening meal, to larger investments, such as replacing a stolen propane gas tank. During February and March, volunteers are always asked to contribute school supplies for the children's individual use in their upcoming school-year classrooms.

During my interviews with police staff members, they indicated that the goodwill of tourist volunteers provided the only avenue for continuing the program. In the absence of foreign support, the national police department would likely allow the center to close. This upset the individual police staff members who came to care for the children under their watch, although they also defended and rationalized their own best practices as officers of the nation. Spanish school volunteer coordinators narrated their frustration with the project and its processes, yet continued sending volunteers to this project because of its central location and its desirable profile in terms of helping an urban group of child workers. Being seen as an NGO is therefore an advantage for this program because of the access it creates to foreigners, particularly through tourism. Police try to downplay their role as much as possible, not only eschewing financial responsibility for the program's success but also by removing themselves from much decision making about the day-to-day routines at the center. It is left to the tourist volunteers to assist children with their homework, suggest what games or activities to undertake, purchase needed goods to cook dinner or host a birthday party, and petition their Spanish school volunteers for additional oversight or funding.

Dilemmas of NGO and Volunteer Tourism Industry Entanglement: Practice, Morality, and Discourse

Children for Change explicitly denounces the designation of NGO as part of a broader mission for economic independence from foreigners. Yet Centro de los Niños clings to the same decried economic dependence despite evidence that program dysfunctionality stems from limited state inputs coupled with uncertain reliance on well-meaning foreigners, whose interest in providing aid might spontaneously disappear. There are obvious contradictions in nomenclature here: Children for Change is actually a model NGO, while Centro de los Niños is a government organization that wants to capitalize on the tourism industry to make up for state disinterest in financially supporting its own program. In both cases, collaboration between locals—whether an individual like Aron or a collection of police staff members trying not to represent official government channels—and foreigners produces dilemmas of engagement. Aron is uneasy with how he might best take advantage of his project's positioning in a global tourism hub like Cusco. He has come to rely on foreigners to a large extent, despite his efforts to achieve self-sufficiency. Meanwhile, national police eagerly accept fraught relationships with Spanish schools in order to fund and run a program they can no longer economically maintain.

These dilemmas, as outlined comparatively between a program created and maintained by a local entrepreneur versus a program run under the auspices of a state office, highlight a tug-of-war of responsibility around the provision of care for local poor children, as well as the role of tourism in creating access to economic and affective resources for delivering this care. Moreover, they draw our attention to the creative spaces enabled by the NGO discourse in a place where global money circulates alongside intimate sentiment.

There are practical limitations of the mutual dependencies between NGOs, volunteer tourists, and the corporate mediators that participate in their engagement. I have illustrated many of them here: control over resources, being at the mercy of tourist "clients" who have the power to affect the supply of aid, concerns with sustainability, the impossibility of achieving desired distance from foreign wealth, the resulting dangers of welfarism, the difficulties of soliciting direct volunteers, aid chains gone awry where middlemen get the money intended for poor children, and the short-term nature of volunteer tourist labor. In the case of Children for Change, Aron does not desire volunteer tourism aid; and the case of Centro de los Niños nicely illustrates its capricious and inconsistent nature when flowing through Spanish school intermediaries.

I conclude by raising problematic moral dimensions of these interdependencies, which, while providing genuine improvement in the lives of both children and tourists, also highlight key elements of the NGO form, responsibility for aid, and commodified experiences of "doing good" through both NGOs and volunteer tourism. In relation to the role of volunteer labor in the Hurricane Katrina recovery, Adams writes that "volunteering to help people creates opportunities for the creation of large social networks and for people to connect with others through a shared sense of purpose that in the end displaces claims about rights and expectations from the state" (2013, 150). Poppendieck (1998) raises a similar concern in her discussions of how private charity threatens an end to social justice and entitlement and, in fact, distracts us from the systemic structural inequalities that create poverty in the first place. It is dangerous to transfer the burden of public social welfare onto the private volunteer tourism sector, not only because of the opportunities for multiple levels of corruption, which muddy the efficacy of the aid chain, but also because private service providers or contractors cannot be held responsible for overall population well-being in the same way that the state should be accountable to its citizens.

It is equally morally suspect when we realize that children's NGOs dangerously walk the line of exploiting portrayals of need in order to justify their own existence. Answering the questions posed at the start of this chapter, NGOs *do* participate in the commodification of childhood poverty in order to attract volunteer tourist benefactors. Moreover, so many NGOs have been able to thrive in Cusco because there is such a surplus of interest in this form of aid from the touristic sector. This can result in NGOs focusing on pleasing their tourist clients rather than meeting the needs of their child recipients (allowing volunteers to teach the same English lessons repetitively, for example). Finally, as illustrated by Aron's narratives, this issue is not just a struggle for economic means but one focused on social values, sense of identity, and conceptions of Peru's place in the world vis-à-vis wealthy outsiders.

Despite these concerns, seeking aid from within the parameters of the burgeoning tourism industry may be the only viable alternative if the state remains ambivalent about providing assistance to vulnerable local populations. Following Aron who wants Peruvian society writ large to transform into one in which assistance programs are not necessary, it is useful to remember that it is often the practices of NGOs that lead to changes in state and international assistance policies, not necessarily the other way around (Mosse 2005). In the meantime, foreigners are eager to take on the task of supporting Cusco's poor children, even as they might struggle with how to do so in ways that enable long-term sustainability and even short-term functionality.

The critiques described here should not detract from the fact that NGOs and volunteer tourism *are* indeed doing good—together and separately—in Cusco. Tapping into the volunteer demographic might be in the best interests of the region more broadly, whose future is very much based on the success of multiple sectors of tourism. It is also important to realize that even as NGOs use children to motivate the aid impulse for potential project donors and individual benefactors, children rely on the material, social, and emotional resources of NGOs and volunteers to cope with the shortcomings of state assistance.

For instance, child after-school program attendees endeavor to establish longer-term godparenting relationships with volunteers. Children, program directors, and staff solicit specific donations of food supplies or school materials. In essence, children attend after-school programs not only to access the program's resources but also to draw on potential affective individualistic relationships to produce a reliable safety net that is personalized. The exchange facilitated by these programs can include friendship, affection, and love. Given the ambition of volunteer tourists to do good for a *universally* legible aid recipient (a poor child), in a particularly *personal* way, children and NGOs actively cultivate opportunities for emotional and economic connection. They creatively use tourists to fill in the social welfare gaps left by the retreat of the state.

In Cusco, a significant portion of development aid is executed with tourist dollars and interests at play, even though the government may proclaim resounding new successes in improving the situation for children in the region. In this landscape of merged aid industry and tourism industry interests, taking care of children necessarily involves taking care of the foreigners who want to help these children—those who come to Cusco seeking a particular type of traveling and volunteering experience. The designation or brand NGO itself becomes caught up within these changing dynamics of how states, tourists, or aid organizations are expected to take care of Peruvian poor children within an evolving marketplace of tourism, volunteerism, childhood poverty, and NGO growth.

Acknowledgments

I am grateful to Amy Cox Hall and Jason Rodriguez for feedback on early drafts of the ethnographic material presented in this chapter. Thanks also to Steven Sampson and Heather Hindman for organizing the panel on NGO elites and labor where it was first publicly shared. Many of the theoretical ideas were solidified in a later presentation on the politics of doing good, organized by Jason Rodriguez and Naomi Glenn Levin Rodriguez, where I further appreciated how Heather Hindman's discussant comments helped push this work forward.

Notes

1. These two organizational names are pseudonyms.

2. My ethnographic research in Cusco spans eighteen total months between 2005 and 2014 (including thirteen consecutive months in 2007–8).

3. The names are pseudonyms.

4. The "state" here refers to all levels of government: federal, regional, and municipal. The broader retreat of social services partly resulted from the constant re-

organization and decentralization of Peruvian state responsibility between these scales. As the federal government turned over tasks to regional governments, which turned over tasks to municipal governments, inevitable gaps in service provision emerged. Fiscal decentralization also lagged because of political and administrative decentralization due to shifting federal priorities and election outcomes (Eaton 2010, 2015), resulting in mandates that lacked funds to support delegated subnational responsibilities.

5. See Newberry (2010) on transnational governmentality regimes around childhood and see Aufseeser (2014) for an example of the Peruvian case in particular.

6. Not all Spanish schools distribute money to their NGO project partners or have the same system for distribution. In some cases, schools pay on a one-to-one basis: each volunteer placed at the NGO merits it a fifty-dollar donation from the school, for example. This has created problems in that NGOs will request more volunteers than labor needs require, in order to receive the financial credit for additional volunteer placements. Schools might make bulk donations of cash or supplies, or they might pay for an added program feature at the NGO, such as English classes, psychological evaluations, or breakfasts. Spanish schools thereby are responsible to both their own volunteer tourist clients as well as the NGOs with whom they partner. In turn, Spanish schools might receive their volunteers from international sending agencies, who do the fee collection and pass a portion of each fee on to the Spanish school itself. See Sinervo (2015) for a discussion of the complex intermediary role played by Spanish schools in the volunteer tourism and aid industries.

7. For additional analysis of the opinions, desires, and motivations of the tourists whose dollars and energies are so important to NGO success, as well as the perspectives of the child recipients and their families who accept, appropriate, or resist the ways that their poverty is framed in order to attract a demographic of wealthy, do-gooder foreigners, see Sinervo (2011, 2013).

8. In the vast literature on the ethical relationship between (both alternative and mainstream) tourism and development, the role of NGOs as actors has occasionally been highlighted. For example, see Wearing, McDonald, and Ponting (2005, 427) for a celebration of NGOs as creators of sustainable tourism practices that prioritize social ethics, community empowerment, and equitable access—in sum, "socially appropriate tourism." On the critical side, and interested in development and NGOs but not tourism, see Bebbington (2005) for a look at how, in Cusco in particular, NGOs often fail their targeted populations because of misunderstandings of need. Differing from both these approaches, this chapter is interested in the codependence between NGOs and volunteer tourism and how this plays out on the ground ethnographically within Cusco-based NGOs, with consequences for the very meanings and functions of NGOs as a salient form. While important, I am not interested in debating whether NGOs (or volunteer tourism, for that matter) are good frameworks for enacting development.

9. Readers may note that one NGO portrait is more comprehensive than the other. This follows from different degrees of coherence and accessibility within each site's NGO discourse and practice during fieldwork.

10. The school day in Peru is divided into morning, afternoon, and evening shifts. What I here call "after school centers" service students attending the morning school shift. Sometimes afternoon students do show up to the tail end of a program. Parents rely on centers for childcare, tutoring, and meals, although children in Cusco are reasonably autonomous and most attending such programs are responsible for their own activities and movements while their parents are working.

11. While Aron pays his restaurant staff, at the time of my fieldwork, he had only one paid staff member for the after-school center, whom he fired after six months due to what he described as "unethical" practices relating to her clandestine collaboration with an international volunteer placement agency.

12. *Asistencialismo* means something akin to welfare or welfarism.

13. For another discussion of practices at this project, see Sinervo (2013, 403–4).

8
Rebuilding Justice

Jewish Philanthropy and the Politics
of Representation in Post-Katrina New Orleans

Moshe Kornfeld

Taking one exchange between a group of activists and a mainstream Jewish philanthropic agency as its core example, this chapter traces intra-Jewish discourse about politics, antipolitics, and representation. I examine the consequences of the World War II-era development of a representative (i.e., political) function for Jewish philanthropic organizations. Considering the often explicitly political nature of Jewish philanthropy, I analyze intra-Jewish discourse that emerged when the Jewish Federation of Greater New Orleans claimed that its aid to non-Jewish Katrina victims was politically neutral. I situate the ensuing exchange between the NGO and a group of Jewish activists in relation to (1) a World War II-era debate about the institutionalization of Jewish philanthropy's representative function, (2) contemporary debates about the meaning of Jewish ethical texts, and (3) discussions within the anthropology of development and humanitarianism regarding politics and antipolitics. Taken together, these analytical approaches reveal that, within American Jewish culture, NGOs create a framework where the meanings of American Jewish identity and social responsibility are negotiated, debated, and imposed.

As in most Jewish communities in the United States, in New Orleans, Jewish philanthropic efforts are coordinated by a central Jewish philanthropy agency, the Jewish Federation of Greater New Orleans. The federation, working with its national coordinating partner, the Jewish Federations of North America (formerly United Jewish Communities), organized what might be described as the official Jewish communal response to Hurricane Katrina. For the first four years following the 2005 storm, this response focused primarily on aiding the Jewish community and secondarily on participating in broader rebuilding and recovery efforts. In order to consolidate its giving to non-Jews, in 2009, the Jewish Federation of Greater New Orleans announced a partnership with the St. Bernard Project, a rebuilding agency that formed in response to the storm. The partnership would direct funds and volunteers from the Jewish community in New Orleans and from around the country toward this particular rebuilding organization. In pursuing this partnership, the federation intended to make visible (even if only to concerned Jews) the Jewish contribution to the broader effort of post-Katrina recovery. This partnership led to an antagonistic exchange with a group of young activists who were concerned about the specific agency chosen for the partnership.

The study of humanitarian organizations and initiatives presents anthropologists with a number of methodological and ethical problems (Lashaw 2013; Fassin 2011; Redfield 2011). How does one critique an industry whose practices are grounded in explicitly moral claims? How does one engage in the study of actors who are skilled at representing themselves and who claim to inhabit an ethically privileged space? These challenges are further highlighted when we consider that those who study humanitarianism tend to be former and sometimes current aid practitioners. Didier Fassin suggests that scholars inhabit "an epistemological position that can be described as distanced interiority," that is, a position that might enable the production of an engaged critique that does not entirely reject or accept the premises under which aid agencies operate (2011, 38–39). Amanda Lashaw suggests a second approach that considers how activist norms are challenged by competing activist groups with alternative views on how to further causes (in her case, the school reform movement). Lashaw writes, "Comparing the two [activist] worlds allowed me to decenter . . . and recast progressivism as a field of struggle in which the meaning of progress itself is open for contest" (2013, 518). In this chapter, I build on both approaches, drawing on my personal experiences to describe Jewish philanthropy as a discursive field where the nature of Jewish social responsibility is debated and contested.

I use the term "philanthropy" in a rather expansive sense to refer to the dense network of Jewish agencies that define the American Jewish collective. For American Jews, philanthropy has long been oriented not only toward a variety of charitable causes but also toward the project of Jewish unity and Jewish identity. This is to say that a thick matrix of Jewish NGOs—and in particular the system of Jewish community federations—has unified American Jews across class and religious and political divisions. In fact, the very notion that one can speak of a mainstream American Jewish community, as opposed to a series of American Jewish communities, is a product of American Jewish philanthropy's unifying role. Writing about Jewish ethnic identity, historian Joshua Zeitz notes that Jews "erected an enormous philanthropic network that set much of the tenor of Jewish identity in the postwar period" (2007, 12). Commenting on the system of Jewish community federations, J. J. Goldberg (1996), a journalist who reports on Jewish life, pronounces Jewish philanthropy as the locus of Jewish power in the United States. Lila Corwin Berman (2015) describes Jewish philanthropy as a "complex," that is, as the vital force at the center of American Jewish life. Additionally, in the postwar era, Jewish philanthropy integrated a representative political role that led scholars of American Jewish philanthropy to describe this field as a polity (Elazar 1995), as a Jewish public sphere (Cohen 1980), as a form of Jewish civil religion (Woocher 1986), and as assuming statelike functions (Kelner 2013). In other words, Jewish philanthropy has played and continues to play a central role in the cultivation of what Benedict Anderson ([1983]1991) might describe as an imagined American Jewish collective. While not entirely distinct from religious expressions of Judaism, the Jewish NGOs that make up the field of Jewish philanthropy constitute a primarily secular, cultural expression of Jewish collective identity.

This chapter is ultimately about discourse and about the role that Jewish NGOs play in structuring intra-Jewish debates regarding Jewish social action and Jewish political identities. While religious and theological ideas play a role in these debates, I argue that the historical development of a representative function for Jewish philanthropy accounts for the ways in which young Jews express seemingly secular political identities in Jewish terms and in relation to Jewish philanthropic organizations.

To participate in American Jewish life is also to live—to some extent—within the frameworks established by American Jewish philanthropy. I grew up in a traditional Jewish family and attended a variety of institutional Jewish programs up to early adulthood. These diverse experiences—which included an interfaith summer program focused on progressive political activism, a year of study in an all-male religious Zionist seminary in the West Bank, employment with an environmental Jewish nonprofit organization, and three months of volunteer work with a community of converts to Judaism in Uganda—ultimately led me to view Judaism from a culturally relativistic perspective and to question the truth claims of any particular Jewish group, religious or secular. While I have progressive political leanings, my objective in this chapter is not to favor the progressive activists or to defend mainstream Jewish philanthropy—rather, I aim to situate and unpack the role Jewish NGOs play in defining the nature and tenor of intra-Jewish politics.

Historicizing the Politics of Jewish Representation

In the 1920s, Jewish philanthropic organizations around the United States, many of which had formed to provide aid to Jewish immigrants, were joining local Community Chest agencies, effectively ceding Jewish community control over fund-raising for local social services (Freund 1931, 30). This development deemphasized Jewish particularity and applied a supposedly rational approach to social services that favored efficiency and economies of scale (Seeley 1989). By the late 1930s and early 1940s, Jewish communities began to mobilize in support of their suffering coreligionists in Europe. World War II and the Nazi assault on European Jewry created new challenges for American Jews and led to a countermovement that would increase the scope of Jewish philanthropy and redefine its mission to focus on Jews in need, wherever they might be located.[1]

Debates within the Jewish community about how best to represent community interests at this moment of crisis led to the formation of community councils empowered to speak on behalf of Jewish communities in the public sphere. The creation of these secular bodies concretized the idea that Jewish charitable organizations would not only focus on raising and distributing funds for a variety of charitable and educational causes but could also enact the equivalent of Jewish public policy. While first formulated at a moment of crisis, this institutional concretization would lead to the widespread perception that Jewish philanthropy represents the American Jewish community and would have far-reaching consequences for Jewish life. This is to say that the perception that Jewish philanthropy represents American Jews has been the source of American Jewish solidarity and has sometimes led young Jews to turn their social critiques toward the institutions that claim to represent them.

On December 18, 1941, a committee of three rabbis and four lay leaders convened in the offices of the New Orleans Jewish Federation in order to consider the formation of a body that would represent the New Orleans Jewish community. Advocating for such a community council, Rabbi Uri Miller, an Orthodox leader, mentioned two examples from the New Orleans Jewish community's responses to the war in Europe that, he argued, demonstrated an urgent need for a representative body authorized to speak on behalf of New Orleans' Jews. Miller described how a debate emerged in response to a Jewish Federation contribution to a campaign raising funds for the "purchase of an Ambulance for Great Britain" and the question of the gift's designation as "a Jewish contribution." Those in opposition to this designation wanted to avoid differentiating between Jews and non-Jews when participating in broader wartime efforts. A community council, argued Miller, could mediate and resolve such debates and "express the community attitude" (Jewish Federation 1941). While this situation is not entirely analogous to the situation of Jews in post-Katrina New Orleans, this example illustrates some of the intracommunity tensions that emerge when Jews and Jewish institutions respond to humanitarian disasters that affect both Jews and non-Jews. In particular, such circumstances highlight questions regarding whether Jews should differentiate themselves from the broader community when aiding non-Jews.

Miller also described a boycott of German-made goods that had been proposed several years prior. Without a council authorized to speak on behalf of the Jewish community, Miller asserted that "there was always the danger that some irresponsible individual or group of individuals might speak in what purported to be the name of the Jewish community," potentially undermining the boycott's efficacy (Jewish Federation 1941). Extrapolating from these examples, we can surmise that Miller envisioned a community council that might achieve both inclusive and exclusive objectives. In the first example, Miller asserted that the council might incorporate divergent positions regarding how best to present Jewish community actions; in the second, he argued that a community council might neutralize wayward, minority voices that might otherwise undermine the community consensus.

Responding to Miller, S. Walter Stern, a member of a prominent, wealthy New Orleans family, expressed opposition to the council's formation on ideological grounds, arguing that Jewish philanthropic organizations should not have a representative function. Stern held that Jewish philanthropic agencies should not claim to speak on behalf of the Jewish community. Meeting notes describe Stern's strong dissent: "Mr. Stern however, stated that he was opposed to the Community Council, because he felt that no organization no matter how representative could speak in the name of the Jewish people of New Orleans. He felt that if a controversial issue finally came to a vote in such a body the minority or many members thereof would not want to be bound by the majority opinion. He felt that if the matter did come to the community the people that were in favor of the given line of action could call a meeting of those interested and have it determined what the attitude of that particular group should be, leaving other groups in the community free to adopt whatever other opinion appealed to them" (Jewish Federation 1941). We can understand Stern's argument as an insistence that Jewish philanthropic organizations should focus on their particular social, educational, and religious missions and should avoid taking on what might be construed as a political or representative function. Stern further argued that, while the idea was to achieve unity, the council would likely disillusion those whose opinions were overruled by the council's majority.

Arguments in favor of the formation carried the day and the committee passed a resolution recommending the establishment of a community council. This development, alongside the founding of community councils throughout the United States, institutionalized Jewish philanthropy's representative function. In fact, in the seventy-five years since this meeting oc-curred, the idea that Jewish philanthropic agencies, and especially the Jew-ish Federation system, represent American Jewry has been widely accepted both within and outside the American Jewish community. Resulting acts of representation tend not to be grounded in explicit religious or theological positions; rather, they tend to enact what might be described as Jewish pub-lic policy based on a broad sense of Jewish community interests.

I call our attention to this development in the history of the New Orleans Jewish community, and to Stern's opposition in particular, because it sug-gests a number of questions about the field of American Jewish philanthropy with contemporary relevance. What are the possible consequences of Jew-ish philanthropy assuming a representative and political role for American Jews? And what happens when there are those who oppose the actions and policy decisions of Jewish philanthropic organizations? More specifically, I argue that this earlier historical moment can help us understand contempo-rary debates regarding how official Jewish community positions are formu-lated and contested. Turning to my case study, this history helps us under-stand why a set of Jewish activists focused their attention on critiquing the Jewish community when they could simply have joined the broader activist community critique of St. Bernard Parish.

Ultimately, the establishment of community councils was part of a rapid expansion of the scope and function of Jewish philanthropy during and af-ter World War II. Transcending religious, economic, and political differ-ences, mainstream Jewish philanthropy thrived from the immediate post-war years through the early 1990s, when sociologists note the beginning of a decline (Cohen 2011). Starting with the countercultural movements of the 1960s and 1970s, progressive Jews began challenging this postwar sta-tus quo, asserting a Jewish politics that integrated Jewish identity and a va-riety of progressive political positions. What originated as expressions of Jewish counterculture at the margins of Jewish life have since emerged as a competing model for what defines Jewish social action. Organizations such as the American Jewish World Service and Bend the Arc: A Jewish Partner-ship for Justice were founded in the 1980s and achieved mainstream status by the first decade of the twenty-first century. The ideological positions rep-resented by these NGOs coalesced in the formation, in 2008, of the Jewish Social Justice Roundtable, an umbrella agency that provides an alternative model for Jewish social action focused on leveraging Jewish political, social, and economic resources in order to aid those outside the Jewish commu-nity. Applying a humanitarian logic, these efforts assert that giving to needy non-Jews should be prioritized over supporting Jewish communities. This is because Jewish progressives now perceive Jews to be in positions of power, both in the United States and in Israel.

In the post-Katrina era, Jews and Jewish institutions struggled to balance normative Jewish positions focused on Jewish needs with advocacy on behalf of the non-Jewish communities most intensely affected by the storm. Despite the growth of Jewish social justice organizations, the postwar status quo and its primary focus on aiding Jews remain dominant in the field of Jewish philanthropy and characterize the response of the Jewish federation network, which directed the majority of the post-Katrina funds it raised to affected Jews. Paradoxically, it was at the moment when the New Orleans federation attempted a corrective measure that they were most directly criticized by a group of young Jewish progressive activists.

Visualizing Jewish Aid

On August 11, 2009, three weeks before the fourth anniversary of Hurricane Katrina, Michael Weil, the executive director of the Jewish Federation of Greater New Orleans, sent an email announcing a federation partnership with the St. Bernard Project, a rebuilding agency that was established in the years following the storm. Weil's email explained that a primary motivation for establishing the partnership was to present the Jewish community as making a visible contribution to the broader humanitarian project of post-Katrina rebuilding and recovery. The letter stated that despite having "sent thousands of volunteers and millions of dollars to help rebuild the Gulf Coast," the Jewish community's response was impossible "to measure" and "visualize." By directing Jewish relief efforts to a particular rebuilding agency, a partnership between the federation and the St. Bernard Project would "allow any Jewish individual or organization, regardless of affiliation who wishes to help rebuild the Gulf Coast, to have a central Jewish volunteer location where our joint efforts can be measured" (federation email, August 11, 2009). In language reminiscent of the World War II-era meeting that recommended the formation of a unifying community council, Weil's email reflected a desire to represent efforts sponsored by American Jews in support of the broader project of post-Katrina recovery as a "Jewish contribution."

This email and partnership suggest a number of questions. What might account for this Jewish community concern with visibility? Why did the Jewish community wait until the storm's fourth anniversary to consolidate their rebuilding efforts for non-Jews? In contrast, a number of Christian denominational networks including Presbyterian Disaster Assistance, Catholic Charities, and Lutheran Disaster Response played an early and central role in coordinating post-Katrina aid and recovery efforts (Erdely 2011, 6; Adams 2013). Most central to the concerns of this chapter is the question of why the federation partnership elicited such a strong negative response from a group of young Jews, most of whom were recent transplants to the city.

With the support of national and international Jewish philanthropy, Jewish New Orleans transitioned from post-Katrina despair—many lost homes and businesses and the community shrank by more than a third—to poststorm renaissance. Bolstered by Jewish philanthropic support that flowed primarily though not exclusively to the Jewish community, by 2009, the New Orleans Jewish community was enjoying a flurry of activity, a collaborative spirit, and new leadership. The spirit of collaboration was most evident in the relocation of an Orthodox synagogue, whose building was destroyed by the storm, to a building belonging to a Reform congregation.[2] The sense of revitalization was also reflected in the arrival of a cohort of young, charismatic rabbis across the various denominations, who were drawn to the challenges and opportunities of post-Katrina rebuilding efforts. Having mostly secured its own recovery, the New Orleans Jewish community was in a good position to reorient itself outward toward the broader project of helping others in the post-Katrina rebuilding and recovery process.

Poststorm recovery was an unequal process that proceeded differently in different parts of the city and for different ethnic, racial, and socioeconomic groups. While New Orleanians of all socioeconomic classes were affected by the storm, African American communities who tended to live in low-lying areas faced significant structural barriers to recovery in the post-Katrina era (Flaherty 2010; Finger 2008). Vincanne Adams (2013) argues that, as a result of the application of neoliberalism to the project of poststorm recovery, government-sponsored aid efforts were privatized and prioritized profit over providing effective aid. Faith groups thus played a disproportionate role in what was a profoundly unjust process.[3] As a result of this widely recognized governmental failure, socioeconomic factors played a significant role in the recovery process. Outside donations given specifically to the New Orleans Jewish community facilitated this community's recovery in the poststorm era. Likewise, a tight-knit, low-income Vietnamese American community centered in the east New Orleans neighborhood of Versailles leveraged its social capital in order to advocate on its own behalf and to raise the community's profile in the post-Katrina era (Campanella 2006, 143).

Judaism has classically favored providing social aid to fellow Jews, but Weil's email also reflected an anxiety regarding whether the American and New Orleans Jewish communities had contributed sufficiently to the project of post-Katrina recovery and rebuilding. This anxiety would be felt acutely at a moment when the Jewish community was transitioning from post-Katrina

recovery to post-Katrina vitality. Weil's email and the partnership it announced addressed this concern by establishing an institutional framework
within which the Jewish community could symbolically and tangibly contribute to the broader project of post-Katrina recovery. Concern that Jews
had not participated sufficiently in broader recovery efforts was also a product of emergent ideologies devoted to reframing Jewish social action as a
humanitarian project. During a postfieldwork interview conducted in New
York, Ruth Messinger, a prominent advocate of Jewish humanitarianism, former Manhattan borough president, and, at that time, the president of American Jewish World Service, suggested to me that many Jews who contributed
to the federation's Katrina fund were under the impression that they were
donating to the broader project of poststorm recovery, when, in fact, the
funds were mostly directed toward Jewish aid recipients (Ruth Messinger,
interview by Moshe Kornfeld, December 2013).[4] This critique, expressed by
a prominent advocate for Jewish humanitarianism, illustrates intra-Jewish
tensions regarding the nature of Jewish social action and suggests a discon-
nect between the leadership of the largest Jewish philanthropic institutions
and many individual Jewish donors. With these factors in mind, I suggest
that we view the partnership as a corrective measure meant to assuage Jewish donors and community members who wanted to see greater Jewish involvement in the broader project of post-Katrina recovery. When they chose
the St. Bernard Project, a widely praised rebuilding agency with a Jewish co-
founder, the federation and its leadership were surprised to find themselves
challenged by a group of Jewish progressive activists.

Challenging the Federation

Upon receiving Michael Weil's email, a number of youth activists also became concerned with the issue of visibility, but from a very different perspective. The activists were concerned that, as a result of this partnership,
the Jewish community might become implicated in a series of racist housing policies that St. Bernard Parish had enacted since the storm.

St. Bernard, a low-lying parish bordering New Orleans to the east, was
hit hard by the storm.[5] In the second half of the twentieth century, the parish experienced dramatic population growth as a result of working-class
"white flight" that first began with the desegregation of New Orleans public schools. Census data records a population of eleven thousand in 1950, a
number that grew to over sixty-five thousand in 1980 (US Census Bureau
1995). Roughly seventy thousand residents lived in the St. Bernard Parish in
2005 when Katrina struck, and virtually every building in the parish was either damaged or destroyed. The magnitude of the damage in the parish led

Liz McCartney and Zack Rosenberg, post-Katrina transplants from Washington, DC, to found the St. Bernard Project, a rebuilding agency whose work initially focused exclusively in the parish. The agency that McCartney and Rosenberg established "became one of the highest-profile initiatives in the region, with millions of dollars in corporate and individual donations and thousands of volunteers" (Flaherty 2010, 130).

While the St. Bernard Project was achieving national fame for its efficiency in rebuilding homes damaged or destroyed by the storm, the parish after which it was named attracted negative attention for its racist housing policies. In particular, the parish passed a "blood relative" ordinance that made it illegal for homeowners to rent to anyone who was not a blood relative, effectively restricting African Americans from moving to a parish that was 85 percent white before the storm (Flaherty 2010, 129). Even after federal courts struck down the ordinance, the parish was held in contempt of court on numerous occasions for pursing racially discriminatory policies (Alexander-Block 2013).[6] While Rosenberg (who is from a Jewish background) and McCartney did not intend to align themselves with the parish's racist policies, they also were not willing to critique the parish publically, insisting that their work was apolitical and focused on getting Katrina victims back home (Flaherty 2010, 131).

The St. Bernard Project's increasing prominence provoked a chorus of activist voices calling on the agency to challenge the parish's policies. On September 10, 2009, local activists posted an open letter on the blog of the Louisiana Justice Institute challenging the parish's discriminatory policies. The letter was signed by many progressive agencies involved in post-Katrina rebuilding as well as by many individual activists, including a number of local rabbis. A day after the broader activist community posted this letter, a group of Jewish activists sent a protest letter to the Jewish Federation of Greater New Orleans. The letter, which was ultimately signed by thirty-four young Jews living in New Orleans, ignited an antagonistic exchange with the federation and the establishment of the NOLA Havurah, a short-lived progressive Jewish group formed by the letter-writers that defined itself in opposition to the Jewish Federation of Greater New Orleans.[7]

While the federation's email emphasized a desire to establish a visible and measurable response to Hurricane Katrina, in their letter, the young activists expressed concern with how this relationship might be understood by the African American community: "We worry about the ramifications this partnership could have on our Jewish community and our relationships with communities of color. For example, if the Federation does not actively and publicly oppose St. Bernard's racist policies, will the public assume that the Federation (and by extension the Jewish community) supports them?" (activist letter, September 11, 2009). The young Jews felt compelled to challenge an agency that claimed to speak on their behalf. Mirroring the efforts of the broader activist community, the young Jews were loath to become even implicitly associated with what they perceived as structures of inequality. This youth activist challenge to the federation appears to affirm Stern's prediction decades earlier regarding the consequences of empowering Jewish philanthropic organizations to enact Jewish public policy, that is, that vocal minorities would not accept the majority position.

In their letter, the young activists explained their concerns regarding the partnership and their sense that it did not emphasize or advance "equity" in the rebuilding process: "We are troubled by S[aint] B[ernard] P[rojects]'s refusal to make any public comment on St. Bernard Parish's racially discriminatory housing policies, or to inform volunteers about these policies, despite requests from a growing number of Jews and non-Jews in New Orleans and across the nation. . . . Our Jewish values and history remind us that silence in the face of injustice is tantamount to complicity." The nonsectarian letter that emerged from the broader activist community makes a similar point regarding the implications of silence: "With the benefit of hindsight, we now know that St. Bernard Parish officials interpreted silence as consent, which has now emboldened them to pursue other means to deny the Fair Housing Act" (Louisiana Justice Institute 2009). By reframing the struggle against St. Bernard Parish in relation to Jewish history, the activists resituated this local issue as part of national, intra-Jewish debates about the nature of contemporary Jewish social responsibility. And while I could find no evidence suggesting that the federation partnership with the St. Bernard Project received much, if any, attention outside of Jewish circles, the discourse generated illuminates intra-Jewish tensions regarding the nature of Jewish social responsibility as well as the role Jewish NGOs play in such debates.

Although St. Bernard Parish was not particularly concerned with activist opinions from the parish next door, the federation was quite sensitive to critique from local Jewish constituents. Even though only eight of the thirty-four signatories were former program participants and the activists described themselves as an independent group called the NOLA Havurah, Weil insisted that they were representing and were represented by Avodah, a Jewish service corps that had just started its second program year in New Orleans. Weil called both the local and national directors of Avodah to complain about the youth activist challenge, claiming that the program was radicalizing its participants. By contacting Avodah, Weil situated the debate within an institutional context and insisted that the organization was in some sense responsible for controlling and channeling Jewish activism in New Orleans. We might also think of Weil's response and of his emphasis

on institutional affiliation as a reflection of the notion that Jewish philanthropic organizations serve a representative role within American Jewish
life. Weil's decision to contact Avodah discursively reframed this local debate
in relation to broader trends in Jewish philanthropy defined by the emergence and growth of Jewish social justice organizations. Within this broader
framework, Weil's actions reflect the sense that Jewish social justice efforts
in general, and youth activism in New Orleans in particular, should not involve explicit critique of the mainstream Jewish community.

Discussions of this episode periodically arose in casual conversation. At
the end of a Sunday trip to a festival hosted by A Studio in the Woods, an
art-based retreat and learning center, a group of young activists gathered
for a potluck dinner celebrating Sam's birthday.[8] Sam was an alumnus of
the first Avodah cohort and remained at his original placement, the Lower
Ninth Ward Center for Sustainable Engagement and Development, for three
additional years after the conclusion of the program year. Over pizza, Noa,
one of Sam's housemates and an Avodah alumna from the second program
year, asked me if I had met Michael Weil. This question led Sam, a central
member of the NOLA Havurah, to share his perspective on the episode
and his sense of frustration at how the debate ultimately took place. Sam
emphasized that the youth activists did not oppose the partnership per se
but wanted to encourage the federation to take a public stance against St.
Bernard Parish's racist policies.

Sam described how, following a meeting between the leaders of the NOLA
Havurah, Weil, and the federation's public relations official, the agency posted
a statement to its website expressing opposition to housing discrimination
in general. The federation did not single out St. Bernard Parish for its racist
housing policies or critique the St. Bernard Project for its quiet complicity,
as the activists demanded. The statement, which mirrors the categories protected in the Federal Fair Housing act, included the following text: "The Jewish Federation of Greater New Orleans is committed to help post Hurricane
Katrina regional rebuilding efforts. An integral part of this mission is opposition to any and all housing policies that are discriminatory in action
or intent. Specifically, the Jewish Federation opposes housing discrimination on the basis of race, national origin, religion, ethnicity, gender, sexual
orientation, and/or disability" (Jewish Federation 2009). Although it is not
surprising that an NGO would avoid a political debate unrelated to its core
mission, the activists were disappointed with this outcome. Sarah, one of
the initial letter writers, reported that she understood this statement to be
"vague and not meaningful" (interview by Moshe Kornfeld, September 11,
2011). She further reported that those involved in the original protest letter

ultimately decided that the federation was irrelevant to them and that they had wasted their energy by trying to engage the federation in serious debate. Although Sarah's disassociation from the federation was particularly intense when compared to some of the other activists, there was a general sense that their efforts did not yield any measurable results and ended in frustration.

The debate between the young activists and the federation also revolved around competing notions regarding the meaning of *tikkun olam*, a term that directly translates to "repairing the world" and that has become a central concept within the American Jewish community over the past quarter century. *Tikkun olam* is not found in biblical sources; rather, the term first appears in the Mishnah, a second-century legal text in which *tikkun ha-olam* is used to describe the result that comes from the enactment of *takkanot*, a type of rabbinic legal decision. Both *tikkun ha-olam* and *takkanot* share the same root, which means to fix or repair. The term *takkanot* refers to rabbinic legislation meant to enact basic equality and fairness. In the mishnaic context, *takkanot* almost always deal with divorce law and with rabbinic injunctions meant to secure the economic and social welfare of women after the dissolution of marriage (Rosenthal 2005, 217). A similar concept is found in medieval rabbinic writings, in which the term *takkanot* refers to new rules enacted for the welfare of society. In the medieval context, *takkanot* are not limited to divorce law and extend to other social issues.

The traditional context in which the phrase *tikkun olam* is best known is the *aleinu* prayer. Written in the third century and recited since the early fourteenth century after each of the three traditional daily prayers, *aleinu* includes the following passage: "We therefore hope in You, O Lord our God that we may speedily see Your glorious power, when all the abominations will be removed from the earth and all the idols will be abolished; when the world will be mended and improved under the kingship of the Almighty, and all creatures will call upon Your name and the wicked will turn to You" (Rosenthal 2005, 220). The Hebrew words *le-taken olam be-malkhut Shaddai*, translated to mean, "when the world will be mended and improved under the kingship of the almighty," represent the most well-known use of the term (220). Lastly, in a kabbalistic context, *tikkun olam* has a mystical meaning. Beginning with fourteenth-century kabbalistic thought, the concept of *tikkun* came to refer to the repairing of the celestial world through religious and spiritual actions. While Gilbert S. Rosenthal asserts that contemporary, universal understandings of the term are rooted in the mishnaic and rabbinic *takkanot*, most scholars understand the term's contemporary meaning as a modern Jewish formulation (e.g., Kranser 2013). Jonathan Kranser writes that "the contemporary connotation, with its emphasis on human agency in bringing about God's kingdom on earth, represents both a synthesis and reinterpretation of earlier conceptual frameworks and a response to the perceived failure of the modern Jewish experiment" (2013, 60).

In Weil's original email announcement, he wrote, "We intend to visibly demonstrate how Jews come together to care for others in need, which is the embodiment of *tikkun olam*" (federation email, August 11, 2009). Weil's usage of the term reveals an understanding focused on Jewish giving to non-Jews. Defined in this way, *tikkun olam* is an expansive term that refers to any Jewish community effort to aid non-Jews and that signals a departure from normative Jewish community concerns. The implied meaning conveyed by Weil's use of the term does not differentiate between social action, defined by efforts that address immediate and often individual needs, and social justice, defined as systemic social change.

Responding to Weil, the activists' letter suggested a conflicting definition of the term *tikkun olam*. Drawing on an article written by Jane Kanarek (2009), a faculty member at Hebrew College in Boston, a progressive rabbinical school, the activists distinguished between acts of *chesed*, a traditional Jewish term sometimes defined as righteousness, and *tikkun olam*. Acts of *chesed*, they argued, involved aid to individuals, something akin to charity, whereas fulfilling the idea of *tikkun olam* demanded a focus on social justice, on working toward systemic change and against inequality and racism. The activists' letter included the following passage: "Caring for others in need is indeed a *mitzvah* [commandment], but is it truly the embodiment of *tikkun olam*? The St. Bernard Project works at the level of individual homeowners. It has a big impact because it is well organized and is able to affect the lives of many individuals in need, but as an organization it has not taken a stance on systemic issues that determine where and how individuals are able to live. According to Rabbi Jane Kanarek, acts that benefit individuals but do not transform society are better classified as acts of *chesed* (loving-kindness), rather than *tikkun olam*" (activist letter, September 11, 2009). Despite having used the term in his original email, Weil criticized what he perceived to be a left-wing appropriation of the term by sending the activists an article titled "How Not to Repair the World." In the article, Hillel Halkin (2008), a prominent Jewish intellectual, challenges the association of Judaism (and *tikkun olam*, in particular) with progressive political positions: "Health care, labor unions, public-school education, feminism, abortion rights, gay marriage, globalization, U.S. foreign policy, Darfur: on everything Judaism has a position—and, wondrously, this position just happens to coincide with that of the American liberal Left. . . . Judaism has value to such Jews to the extent that it is useful, and it is useful to the extent that it can be made to conform to whatever beliefs and opinions they would have even if Judaism had never existed." While on the surface it may seem as if an initiative (the federation partnership with the St. Bernard Project) designed to showcase Jewish involvement in broader rebuilding efforts was reframed as a rigid and binary left/right, liberal/conservative political divide, a further exploration of this exchange suggests that we consider how claims regarding politics and political neutrality are often enacted strategically (Redfield 2011, 68).

The Politics and Antipolitics of Jewish Aid

Over the past quarter century, development and humanitarian aid have become defined by what Stirrat and Henkel (1997) describe as a "new orthodoxy" that celebrates "the role of the nongovernmental organization (NGO) as the primary agent in its vision of development" (67). The ideologies that support the NGO-ization of development and humanitarian aid posit that, once removed from explicitly political entities (i.e., governments), aid regimes would enact apolitical and more efficient forms of humanitarian assistance. Anthropologists have critiqued this depoliticization as masking and obscuring the inherently political contexts in which aid is given and received (Mosse 2006a).

In line with this development orthodoxy, the federation's choice of the St. Bernard Project emphasized market-based metrics focused on efficiency in the provision of aid. Weil's initial email highlighted this aspect of the St. Bernard Project's reputation: "The St. Bernard Project has already rebuilt over 220 houses since it started working in 2006. They are doing it on a mere $15,000 per house and a build time of 8–12 weeks" (federation email, August 11, 2009). In seeking out the St. Bernard Project, the federation sought to maximize the return on the funds and labor they wanted to invest. Analyzing the federation's choice of the Saint Bernard Project in the context of ensuing debates, we see how a supposedly apolitical emphasis on making the Jewish contribution to poststorm recovery "visible" involved partnering with an agency with strong tangible outcomes (220 houses) while ignoring the less visible sociopolitical contexts within which this work was taking place. By contrast, the young activists insisted that the federation envision the symbolic and political implications when deciding how to reach out beyond the Jewish community.

In a review essay, "Doing Good? The Politics and Antipolitics of NGO Practices," William Fisher (1997) notes that "the development industry's view of NGOs as efficient new instruments of development largely ignores, downplays, or attempts to co-opt the political role of NGOs. Through depoliticization, NGOs are in danger of becoming the new attachments to the 'antipolitics' machine of development" (445–46). Similarly, writing about Hutu refugees in Tanzania, Liisa Malkki (1996) argues that aid efforts often reflect an understanding of refugees and displaced individuals as dehistoricized subjects whose reason has been compromised by trauma (384). According to Malkki, aid givers often perceive refugees as beings whose bodies tell better stories than any utterance they might articulate. Refugees thus possess a basic, raw humanity that triggers the responses of humanitarian organizations. By contrast, Malkki argues that effective aid regimes must account for specific political and historical contexts and perceive refugees as agentive subjects in order to provide aid and assistance more effectively (378–79). In light of these anthropological interventions, we can understand the young activists as accusing the federation of engaging in a problematic form of antipolitics.

During an interview conducted a number of years after the incident, Weil explained that the federation is not a social action group and that his agency was not prepared to oppose St. Bernard Parish. It is the policy of the federation, Weil explained, not to take a political stand on issues (Michael Weil, interview by Moshe Kornfeld, February 20, 2012). St. Bernard Project took a similar position in response to their critics; project leaders contended that they were not an advocacy organization but simply an agency helping people get back into their homes (Flaherty 2010, 131). These claims take the political neutrality of humanitarian action for granted. By emphasizing issues of race and systemic injustice, the young activists countered this apolitical stance by insisting that post-Katrina rebuilding had to occur within a necessarily political framework in order to move toward justice.

The federation's stated commitment to political neutrality is situational in nature. During the interview mentioned, Weil also described how the federation was considering public support for a school voucher program that might aid the community's struggling parochial school. In contrast to the ideological position asserted in defense of the federation's decision not to denounce the St. Bernard Parish, this move suggests that the federation assumes a position of neutrality when engaging in humanitarian aid to non-Jews but may in fact take a political stance if Jewish community interests are involved.

Within this framework, we might understand Weil's claim that the young activists were overly political in light of Peter Redfield's view that claims to political neutrality can be enacted strategically within humanitarian contexts. Commenting on Doctors without Borders/*Medecins Sans Frontieres*'s inconsistent approach to humanitarian norms that emphasize political neutrality, Redfield writes, "In the end, I suggest, MSF's inconsistency provides a more revealing reference point for principles such as neutrality. Yes, neutrality is a fiction and often a thin one. But the very inconsistencies of its practice recall that neutrality is also a strategy, one whose effects vary in different contexts" (2011, 68). Building on this analysis, I suggest that we consider Jewish community attitudes toward politics and political neutrality as strategies in a contested field within which competing views of Jewish social responsibility are posited and debated. The question at hand is not about whether to help non-Jews but rather about the politics and antipolitics of reaching beyond the Jewish community.

Conclusion

This chapter is ultimately about intra-Jewish discourse and about the role that Jewish NGOs play in structuring debates regarding the nature of Jewish social action and political identities. I argue that the development of a representative function for Jewish philanthropy provides a historical context for the phenomenon, in Jewish youth culture, whereby young Jews frame seemingly secular political identities in Jewish terms. Questions about the politics of Jewish representation and about the politics of Jewish aid become proxy debates for questions regarding what it means to be an American Jew. Both during the World War II era and in the post-Katrina era, questions about how and whether to make Jewish aid visible were ultimately about the extent to which Jews imagined themselves as a distinct political group and about how Jews imagined the responsibilities that such collective identity might involve. Transcending reductionist understandings of Jewish giving that often describe a distinction between universalism and particularism, giving to Jews versus giving to non-Jews, my analysis reveals a more subtle intra-Jewish distinction—expressed through discourse—about the role of the political in aid to non-Jews. This more nuanced approach is the result of pairing the contemporary ideological debates I observed ethnographically with debates I read about in the archives. Considering contemporary debates alongside an ethnographically attuned reading of microhistorical exchanges is shown to provide yet another entry point to the critical study of NGO worlds.

Notes

1. Traditional approaches to Jewish charitable giving, as described in Jewish legal texts such as Maimonides's *Code of Jewish Law*, emphasize that Jewish responsibility to Jews takes precedence over Jewish responsibility to non-Jews.

2. While the various liberal denominations (Reform, Conservative, Reconstructionist, and Renewal) often coordinate with one another, interdenominational collaboration between liberal and Orthodox congregations is increasingly rare.

3. For more discussion of the problematic imposition of neoliberalism in the aftermath of Hurricane Katrina, see Naomi Klein's (2007) *The Shock Doctrine: The Rise of Disaster Capitalism* and *The Neoliberal Deluge: Hurricane Katrina, Late Capitalism, and the Remaking of New Orleans*, a volume edited by Cedric Johnson (2011).

4. Based on a report published by United Jewish Communities (2007), a central Jewish philanthropy coordinating agency, I calculate that, in the immediate aftermath of the storm, the Jewish community provided 68 percent ($2.74 million) in aid to the Jewish community and 32 percent ($1.268 million) to those outside of the Jewish community. Though federation allocation of funds in the first few weeks following the storm was heavily skewed toward the Jewish community, when compared to long-term giving in response to Hurricane Katrina, it reflects the federation system's moment of greatest commitment to helping those outside of the Jewish community (UJC 2007, 8–9). Calculating the financial support allocated for long-term recovery efforts, the percentage given to Jews increased to 83 percent ($9.6 million) as opposed to 17 percent ($2 million) that was distributed outside the Jewish community (UJC 2007, 10–11).

5. On account of its Catholic past, Louisiana uses the term "parish" to describe what is in other states called a county. The City of New Orleans and Orleans Parish cover the same geographical area.

6. While this episode was unresolved when I first drafted this chapter in early 2014, by December of that year, the nearly decade-long case was settled and the parish agreed to "establish an Office of Fair Housing, hire a fair housing coordinator, and engage in a three-year marketing campaign to attract renters and developers of multifamily rental housing to the parish" (Alexander-Bloch 2014). Additionally, the parish agreed to pay $1.8 million in legal fees as part of the final settlement.

7. The term "havurah" connects the activists to a grassroots movement, started in the 1960s, devoted to creating alternatives to institutional Judaism. For an ethnographic study of the early Havurah movement, see Riv-Ellen Prell's (1989) *Prayer and Community: The Havurah in American Judaism*.

8. The names of all youth activists included in this chapter have been changed.

PART III
Methodological Challenges of NGO Anthropology

Introduction to Part III

How to Study NGOs Ethically

Erica Bornstein

Anthropological loyalties usually lie with those we research, and our disciplinary guidelines articulate responsibilities to our informants.[1] Some of these social obligations are forged in the practice of ethnography itself: the processes through which we build bonds of trust and friendship are not taken lightly; the relationships are hard-earned. How does the ethnography of institutions such as NGOs differ from studying other social groups? Nonprofit organizations such as NGOs offer ethnographic challenges that may be unique to the nonprofit sector due to the institutional orientation of our informants vis-à-vis the causes they champion and the relation of funding streams to NGOs in the global economy. NGOs are, ideally, not in it for themselves; they ostensibly work on behalf of other, usually more vulnerable populations—whether the poor, needy, downtrodden, or marginalized.[2] As not-for-profit institutions, NGOs occupy a space supposedly devoted to public good. Working on behalf of others, NGOs depict themselves as representing others, much like anthropologists do. Some NGOs structurally embody this intermediary position by acting as brokers (Lewis and Mosse 2006; also see Lemons, this volume), liaisons, and nodal sites of funding and information (Jakimow 2012; Sharma 2008).

NGOs themselves may become "the field" for anthropologists, comprising a target site for research, providing a wellspring of informants, and producing the "cultures" anthropologists seek to comprehend. Because of these structural realities, when we study NGOs our loyalties to our informants may extend well beyond the brick-and-mortar boundaries of the offices we visit and the populations whom NGOs serve. This often distinguishes our work from ethnography in other types of institutional settings, such as corporations or governments, where loyalties may lie with populations affected by institutional policies or practices instead of with the institutions themselves. Thus, for ethnographers of NGOs, loyalties may lie with the NGO, extend to the NGO workers and to the vulnerable groups NGOs serve and represent (i.e., the beneficiary groups), and may even include donors who support NGOs, and the social causes that NGOs champion more broadly. One could say our loyalties are oriented to a chain of people and institutions, some known and others more distant and abstract. Loyalties can also be divided, or change during the fieldwork process, and some ethnographers may not be compelled to even consider where their loyalties lie. Although we do not want our anthropological engagement, including our published writing, to hurt our informants, loyalty is not defined by the absence of critique, here understood not simply as assessment, but as analysis of NGOs as social actors and social sites in relation to particular theoretical questions.

Increasingly, NGOs are called upon to address the world's problems. They inhabit highly moralized zones that at times may appear immune to critique, or "untouchable" (Fassin 2011). NGOs may be considered saviors (Redfield 2013); they may merge with the military (Fassin and Pandolfi 2010) or even the state in welfare provision (Sharma 2008). They may also merge with powerful capitalist interests (INCITE 2007). Most anthropologists studying NGOs realize that pigeonholing NGOs into dichotomous, moralized categories of good or bad is not theoretically productive. NGOs, like other types of institutions, operate in the gray area of real life where people do their best, face limitations and obstacles, and encounter unforeseen circumstances, further muddling dichotomous understandings of their efforts to "do good" (Fisher 1997). NGOs invariably produce unintended consequences, notably in humanitarian contexts (Bornstein 2005; Terry 2002; Ticktin 2011) where their presence is itself a political act (Redfield 2013).

In the contemporary global economy, particularly post-9/11, NGOs have not only been honored for their work, they have also be vilified, demonized, and considered threatening by states, governmental bodies, and those who oppose the causes and populations that NGOs serve. There is evidence to suggest that NGOs face a shrinking global space for dissent and critical engagement in relation to the nation-states in which they operate (International Center for Not-for-Profit Law 2013; Rutzen 2015). NGO efforts to promote change or public critique are increasingly constrained through national laws, which seek to limit internationally funded rights-based agendas, or NGO project activities, in the name of national sovereignty and security. For example, governments may declare NGOs as "foreign agents," as in India and Russia, where new laws regulating foreign donations to civil society groups restrict their political activities and add extra layers of bureaucratic, governmental surveillance monitoring their efforts (Bornstein and Sharma 2016). In this global world of rights-based activism, it has become a common refrain for governments to question where NGO loyalties lie and to interrogate whether NGOs are accountable to their donors or to the populations they serve (Stein 2008). Concerned about what they view as antinational activities and issues of accountability, governments ask, "Who will watch the watchdogs?" (Bornstein and Sharma 2016). Following this line of thought, if NGOs are the watchdogs of civil society, and we anthropologists study the watchdogs, the academic world and beyond watches us. As we observe, analyze, and participate as ethnographers in political spaces of dissent with our anthropological gaze we too are open to scrutiny and we may decide to self-censor as we write, to protect our informants and their associated communities. These are consequences of studying all politically charged ethnographic contexts, not just NGOs.

How do anthropologists maintain professional and personal ethics when studying NGOs? Here, loyalties to protect one's informants, who may include donors, NGO workers, and beneficiaries, and anthropological loyalties to justice more broadly, often exist in volatile environments. Although we cannot control how our writing will be used or interpreted, I have often worried about the political effects of my writing and pondered the possibilities of governments using my carefully crafted ethnographic critique to close down an organization. NGOs, like any organization, are filled with visionaries, incompetent staff, and people who do excellent work in between. I think that most anthropologists would agree that exposing internal politics is not worth the risk of getting an organization defunded, since when an NGO loses its funding, those who are dependent upon the NGO, and who are usually more vulnerable, also lose access to resources. Here we see how responsibilities to a chain of loyalties can affect ethnographers of NGOs.

While writing my last two books, in which NGOs featured prominently (Bornstein 2005, 2012a), I thought about how my work might be interpreted and even possibly misunderstood. With my work on World Vision, a Christian humanitarian organization that operates worldwide in its mission of social justice and poverty alleviation, I belabored the question of whether or not to use its name or a pseudonym. Eventually, I decided that since it was the largest Christian NGO in the world at the time and since I was not writing anything I anticipated would injure the institution or its staff, I should use its real name. For employees, however, I gave pseudonyms. I determined my ethnographic loyalties were to the NGO staff members not the institution itself. After the book's publication, I worried about the reception of my work by the NGO, which was sadly met with silence—a cruel reality for anthropologists but mostly a hazard of academic writing. There was no explanation for this silence, and I knew not whether my work had been read or if there was simply nothing the NGO wanted to say. NGO staff members rarely have time to read academic publications, which is why I sometimes present my work orally to the organizations I study, saving people the experience of slogging through journal articles and books.

Before leaving World Vision in Zimbabwe in 1997, I presented my work to a group of executives and managers. A rousing debate ensued as they discussed my findings and observations. This was the spirit of the institution I had come to know, and I found it helpful and satisfying as I prepared to write up my material. Though it took me years to write the book, once it was published, I dutifully sent copies to my key informants at World Vision and Christian Care (the other organization featured in the book). To my dismay, I received the copy I had sent to Christian Care returned and unopened. It turned out my key informant and friend had tragically met with a fatal car accident. Nobody else in the organization seemed to care until many years later, when I received a request for the book via email for a library, and I happily sent it along. As to World Vision, there was no response to my writing for many years. When I did receive a response, it was a frantic phone message from an employee of World Vision Australia who wanted to use my work to make a point in a meeting. His copy of my book had been stolen from his car, so I emailed him the passages he wanted to use.

A few years later, I received another frantic call—this time from the press representative of World Vision France. Someone had reviewed my work in a French magazine, to which she had been alerted, and she was concerned that the reviewer's interpretation of my analysis of their evangelical efforts could be used against the organization in the Muslim contexts where they operated. I tried to explain to the representative that my research for the book was conducted in an earlier decade, in a different context (Zimbabwe), and on a different part of the continent from World Vision France's current projects. My explanations failed to reduce her anxiety. I emailed her passages of the book with explanations of the context in case she was ever in a position to defend the role of religion in World Vision's work. I was never sure whether my attempts to clarify the context of my research assuaged her anxieties about its interpretation. Cognizant of this, I was thoughtful about these issues as I wrote my next book, focused on religious ideas of philanthropy and humanitarianism in India, and I spent an extra month crafting a particular passage about Hindu philanthropy and global giving, hoping that political and religious Hindu extremists would not misinterpret my work as supporting their agenda.

My point is to emphasize that one cannot control how one's work is used, who reads it, or how it is understood. As we write our ethnographies, all we can do is clarify our political positions as ethnographers and identify the audiences for whom we write. Different forums exist for different types of writing, and if we anthropologists really want to matter in a utilitarian manner or to be read by NGO folks or policy wonks, then we should consider writing reports and blogs instead of ethnographies. This is not to say that our informants do not read our books—some of them do, and they may have a lot to say about them, not always good (cf. Mosse 2006a), which is another professional hazard or a boon depending on one's perception.

With loyalties so diffuse and political allegiances so volatile in the contexts that NGOs operate, how does one proceed? Perhaps we should not see ourselves as truth tellers but as analysts of social life. As such, we can self-censor and modify our message, constrained by the supposedly "pure" moral space and political realms in which NGOs operate, and we can write with political sensitivity about what we observe, while being aware—though not in control—of the potential consequences of our writing. This does not mean we write or tell "everything" about the institutional contexts within which we engage. It means we are strategic about where we publish and the audiences for which we write. It also means we trust our ethnographic method to make larger theoretical points about big topics using the small details of life. The two ethnographers in part III of the volume, Katherine Lemons and Amanda Woomer, offer two divergent approaches to dilemmas anthropologists face when studying and writing about NGOs.

Divergent Approaches

In "The Anthropologist and the Conservation NGO," Amanda Woomer advocates for activist engagement instead of distanced observation when conducting research with NGOs. She identifies this as an ethical pursuit in itself, full of limitations and partially mapped out. Based on work with environmental, international NGOs in Tanzania, she explores how anthropologists are not only critics—they are also participants, educators, and advocates. Organizations such as the international NGO with which she worked are intersectional, and as she clearly demonstrates, they inhabit social spaces encompassing technical experts, heterogeneous beneficiary groups, conditional donor funding, and need. Rather than run from the ethical entanglements she encounters, Woomer advises us to confront them head-on. We see how the idealism of anthropology (and ethnography) can be constrained by the reality of NGO work, including such limitations as a paucity of funding, excess bureaucracy, and paternalism. NGOs tend to be practical, focused on getting things done, even in less than ideal circumstances. Woomer takes up this stance as well, maintaining her idealism regarding activist engagement in order to advocate persistent involvement. In other words, even though an ethnographer's idealism about the cause an NGO supports might be a mismatch for NGO realities, Woomer urges us to carry on and work within the NGO to make change, to blur the lines between academic and activist, research and volunteer. Woomer asserts we must continue to try to effect change while being conscious of the complex limitations of ethnography, which include ethnographic timeframes too short to effect change and which continually position the ethnographer as an outsider.

For Woomer, activist work with NGOs involves moving beyond critique to action, but she is also aware of the limitations of this approach. Anthropological engagement is political, and in the field of environmentalism she asserts that all ethnography may have policy implications. Given these impacts, Woomer suggests that anthropologists consciously mediate their engagement, and she considers this form of ethnographic engagement more fruitful than distanced critique. Conscious engagement has its own ethical dilemmas, but she advocates that they be confronted directly in the ethnographic process itself. Woomer's study calls on us to dive into the NGOs we study. We cannot simply observe; we have to be involved in action—to do what they do—to try to effect change. Whereas Fassin (2011) recommends anthropologists maintain a space "on the threshold of the cave" of critique, both inside and outside the institutions we work with, in order to maintain critical distance, Woomer pushes us in. Critique, she asserts (citing Brosius), is a luxury that neither conservationists nor anthropologists can afford. By dismissing mere observation and mere critique, we encounter the anthropologist as NGO activist.

Lemons offers an alternate approach, and in reading the next two chapters side by side, we can conclude that ethnography with NGOs can take divergent approaches. In "The Ethics and Politics of NGO-Dependent Anthropology," Lemons deconstructs her fieldwork in women's community organizations in India, which was overseen by an NGO. The NGO in this instance was a gatekeeping mechanism for Lemons's ethnographic research. It provided access, became an object of critique, and presented questions of political loyalties. Lemons tells a story of symbiotic influence, whereby NGOs are dependent on anthropologists for critique but in so doing they co-opt anthropologists, who risk adopting NGO perspectives as their own. As much as anthropologists depend on NGOs, NGOs also use anthropological findings to make cases, to assert legitimacy with donors, state agencies, and other NGOs.

Lemons ponders the question of how to maintain a critical perspective as an anthropologist in this complicated environment. In radical opposition to Woomer, who urges us to dive in and push past mere critique in order to make change and to challenge the NGO itself, Lemons argues that anthropologists need to maintain their inquiry apart from the "interests" of the NGO (cf. Fassin 2011). She identifies a distinction between knowledge with goals (which are purposive and produced inside the NGO, as in Woomer) and the type of critical inquiry of anthropology (which has the potential to be more unbounded). Lemon's view of NGO-based ethnography cautions against "diving in" and warns against the very activist stance that Woomer advocates. The institutional goals of NGO-based knowledge production, Lemons notes, are instrumentally produced descriptive acts. She contrasts this type of representation with that of ethnography, which is descriptively critical. Lemons cautions us against mimetic adoption of an NGO's perspective—something Woomer touches upon briefly as well. NGOs are mediators, gatekeepers, door openers, and keys to research settings. As Lewis and Mosse (2006) contend, NGOs are brokers and translators, not only for beneficiary communities and states but for anthropologists as well. Lemons suggests we use the categories offered to anthropologists by their NGO interlocutors as "categorical fictions" to be investigated, analyzed, and not taken for granted. As much as anthropologists are interpolated by NGOs, anthropologists must become aware of this social mediation. Not only are NGOs shape-shifters (Bernal and Grewal 2014a), they are also shape makers, Lemons contends. If we are to meditate upon the boundaries of an NGO being studied, Lemons suggests we include its group-making capacity in our analysis, specifically its Foucauldian, discursive power to make certain populations visible. Lemons suggests we turn to this as our prime arena of analysis.

What are we to do with these two opposing models? One is action-oriented, educational, and activist in its stance. The other is distanced but leaves no social process outside of its analytical net. I suggest we select our approach based on our own disposition as anthropologists and the contexts in which we work. There is no solitary correct way to study NGOs ethnographically, though some approaches may be more appropriate for certain situations and ethnographic affinities. This is where one must also consider the audience of our work, and the form of knowledge production we employ in our ethnographic process. For reports and blogs, an activist stance may be more suitable. Garnering more space and length for analysis, an ethnographic monograph might be a more practical format for nuanced critique. Different ethnographic settings might inspire the use of an approach as well, demanding and encouraging a distinct ethnographic tool set. One can also write different texts for different audiences; writing an ethnographic monograph does not preclude writing a blog or a report.

Seven Challenges

In this section are seven challenges I have encountered while conducting ethnographic fieldwork with NGOs. Though not unique to the study of

NGOs (they may also be relevant to other ethnographic contexts that involve institutions), they form a scaffolding for NGO-based ethnographic engagement. Because NGOs are flexible shape-shifters, they are intensely social environments where people work with passion and sometimes low or no pay. To work in an NGO can sometimes feel like participating in a dysfunctional family, though unlike family membership one can walk away from an NGO. The sensitivities one encounters in NGO-based ethnography can be political and personal.

1. *Getting in*: An NGO landscape may consist of intersecting communities of beneficiaries, staff, boards of directors, governmental liaisons, and donors. Where does the anthropologist begin? How does one define the boundaries of an organization? Although studying an NGO may not entail an exotic locale, we can deploy our tried and tested ethnographic techniques as we identify the group and trace its lineage, its social and political economy, and its ritual practices. Though social life in NGO offices may not be very eventful—in fact it may often be tedious—as Lemons notes, we tend to merge with the NGO we study. NGOs are staffed by individuals much like anthropologists: reformers, cosmopolitans, elites, and brokers. Yet in the end, their project is not our project.
2. *Gaining trust*: In my ethnographic work with NGOs I have been frequently mistaken for a journalist and have had to convince NGO staff members, particularly those in authority, that I am not planning to write an exposé. I've done research with large transnational NGOs and small advocacy NGOs, and in both cases on different continents the NGO directors were suspicious of my intentions. In each setting, one must work very hard to gain a degree of trust or, at least, to reduce the understandable suspicion that an outsider may gain knowledge of an organization's inner workings.
3. *Making oneself indispensable*: This can be done by being useful: writing reports, being a part of the organization as a volunteer or otherwise as an unpaid employee, doing what others cannot, and by being dependable and depended on. When one does this, one is "in."
4. *Knowing too much*: Once you are in (hooray!), the situation offers a new set of challenges. Suddenly, you may find yourself overworked and party to gossip, backbiting, bad management, and the intricacies of poor organization.
5. *A question of audience*: One must decide in which theoretical debates to participate and for which audiences to write. Our audiences include our eloquent and intellectually astute informants/interlocutors (for some, collaborators), many of whom write theoretical analyses of their own.
6. *The politics of anonymity*: When do we change the names of the NGOs we

study? When do we decide to use their names? Are there different ethics in play for big or for small NGOs? Due to current trends in transparency in the NGO world, it is becoming increasingly common to use the names of NGOs in ethnographic writing, though this issue should probably be evaluated in each setting and in consultation with the NGO. Anonymity should not be a substitution for research ethics, as disguising names will not resolve political dilemmas.

7. *The unsaid*: Once we gain trust, we cannot write about certain things. We are in a bind of knowing too much. What if the unspoken is an important part of an ethnographic story, for example, about practices of internal governance? In most societies, the unsaid, the taboo, the silent is a core aspect of social life; so it is with NGOs, especially when we observe everyday routines, governance, competition over funding, struggles over transparency, institutional democracy, hierarchies, and the darker sides of organizational life. The unsaid is important because NGOs inhabit a protected moral space due to the nature of their work and the causes they champion, which many of us ethically support. As researchers, we do not want to damage the causes by critiquing the NGO. But failing to present critique also poses an ethical challenge. What are the ethics of not writing about certain things? What are the ethics of silence? This is an ethical question that anthropologists in and of NGOs face each time they write.

On Ethics and Unintended Consequences

A few months ago, I encountered a disturbing citation of my work: *Disquieting Gifts* was used in a US Supreme Court amicus brief to make an argument respecting anonymous donation in political contexts in the United States. When I wrote my ethnography about giving practices in New Delhi in 2005, I never anticipated that it could be used in debates over super PACs (and, for the record, I do not support anonymous donations for political campaigns). The strength and danger of ethnography is that it is deeply context specific; it can always be taken out of context, and one never knows where one's ideas will travel. Perhaps this is more of an issue for those of us who "study up" (Nader 1972; Gusterson 1997) instead of studying those without power. That said, I am not writing a prescription for studying those with whom one agrees. If all knowledge is situated and partial (Haraway 1991), then an ethical understanding of knowledge production also allows for and accepts its limits. To expect an all-encompassing and totalizing view, a God-trick, as Haraway so rightly wrote in the 1990s, is to efface the politics of knowledge production. One must not shy away from messy ethnographic situations—quite the contrary! That is where the action is.

Within the two approaches I have outlined, the critical approach (as in Lemons, this volume) is not apolitical. One's work will be used, and the political economies of its use are beyond the author's control. Alternately, one can roll up one's sleeves and dive in as a politically engaged actor, struggling for the political aims of the NGO with which one works. Both perspectives engender political consequences. Neither is outside a political zone and neither is neutral. Where one stands vis-à-vis a research approach may largely depend on the context (the tried-and-true basis for our thick description) and the constitution of the ethnographer. I do not believe that one approach is ethically superior to the other. Each has limitations. One must question which approach is most suitable for a particular setting and/or its unique set of theoretical inquiries. This, in fact, is what determines the ethnographic, and ethical, tools for the study of NGOs. Readers may argue that I am sitting on the fence here or that my political stance is not strong enough. However, I will argue in response that not all tools are appropriate for the same task. Would one use a hammer to cut bread? A wrench for brain surgery? How about a tweezer for felling a tree? I, like many of my anthropological colleagues, would like my work to be relevant in the world. The greatest compliment I receive is that my work is useful. Yet, one cannot control how one's work is used, and this is the ethical terrain that one enters when researching NGOs. Because NGOs are often engaged in ethically sensitive terrain—of social justice, human rights, humanitarian relief—the misappropriation of ideas can seem unjust. This, however, is not a reason to discontinue our work as ethnographers of sensitive topics, ethical issues, and nongovernmental worlds. It is all the more reason to pursue our work.

Critical and Anticipatory Ethnographies

As anthropologists, we are trained to document empirically and meticulously, the activities, experiences, and structures of social lives; this is ethnography. Through human experiences, we build analytical architecture and create theory through ethnography—whether about NGOs or any other social institution—and theory can be used as a predictive mechanism: it can potentially analyze social action in other, future contexts.

During an ethnographic project studying activists in New Delhi, I was frequently asked how I could contribute action-oriented research, and I found myself perplexed by the request. Though I sought to be part of the activities of the NGO I was studying in order to better understand it (as in, participatory research), I knew my time as an NGO-worker—in this case, writing reports and analyzing data—was limited. It had an end point, at least a temporal one. Though I am in touch with my interlocutors and follow their activities, I am no longer in the office doing the work. I have left the field and reentered my primary job, as a university professor who spends her days teaching, researching, and writing. Many days I find myself buried in the very same type of office struggles I encountered in the NGO field, though I face them in my university setting. In other words, my context has changed, as has the primary site of my action-oriented work. Even if I were to consider myself an activist-oriented anthropologist, my activism flowers in my writing and my teaching. I am not an NGO worker by profession, at least at the moment (and, full disclosure: I have worked in the nonprofit sector in previous professional incarnations). There is a form of anthropology that is analytical/predictive, which constitutes an action-oriented perspective. It is geared toward the future of the NGO (see Woomer, this volume). This type of ethnography is anticipatory; it aims to change the future of the causes championed by NGOs that are ethnographically studied, and it is here that we anthropologists encounter sensitive ethical terrain as we ruminate over whether our job is to critically document the world or to change it. I suggest that we move beyond this simple binary to explore how critical and anticipatory ethnographies are analytical and predictive. While anticipatory, action-oriented ethnography seeks to change social practice, critical ethnography seeks to develop theory and change thought. Both, in different ways, aim to impact the context being analyzed. If ethnographic relations are also power relations, we must also remember Foucault's lessons: the micropolitics of power are neither simply good nor bad; they are productive, and as ethnographers our primary responsibility is toward the production of knowledge with all of its associated ethical tangles.

Acknowledgments

I would like to thank the Jawaharlal Nehru Institute for Advanced Studies for a 2012–13 resident fellowship at Jawaharlal Nehru University in New Delhi, the University of Wisconsin–Milwaukee for a sabbatical grant the same year, and all the NGOs and NGO workers that have welcomed me into their worlds.

Notes

1. See the American Anthropological Association (AAA) ethical guidelines and blog at http://www.americananthro.org/ParticipateAndAdvocate/Content.aspx?ItemNumber=1656 (accessed March 23, 2017).

2. Though this is an ideal, NGOs have been critiqued for not living up to this ideal and being focused instead on their own self-promotion and institutional growth (for examples, see INCITE 2007).

9

The Ethics and Politics of NGO-Dependent Anthropology

Katherine Lemons

NGOs are a significant part of work for many, if not most, anthropologists. This is especially true of those whose work touches on women's perspectives. As Victoria Bernal and Inderpal Grewal have succinctly put it, NGOS are "now well established as an institutional form across the globe, especially in relation to questions of women's welfare and empowerment" (Bernal and Grewal 2014a, 1). This is in part because feminist NGOs were included in the UN conferences on women in 1975, 1985, and 1995, rendering NGOs recognizable as institutions capable of responding to "grassroots" needs and to informing policy debates (Bernal and Grewal 2014a, 11–12). This chapter reflects on my fieldwork with a women's community organization in India directly overseen by an NGO to elaborate a phenomenon that I call "NGO-dependent anthropology."

While I will argue here that there is something new about anthropologists' dependence on NGOs, I do not wish to imply that anthropologists were previously *in*dependent. Lila Abu-Lughod (1999) begins her now-classic *Veiled Sentiments: Honor and Poetry in a Bedouin Society* with an account of how her father accompanied her to the field (10–16). In doing so, Abu-Lughod interweaves the introduction to her fieldwork with an analysis of the vehicle that enabled it. Her Jordanian, Arabic-speaking father introduced her to the Bedouin family with whom she lived, thereby demonstrating to them that Abu-Lughod was cared for by her kin and suggesting, implicitly, that she required a similar measure of care by her adoptive kin. This introduction, in other words, situated her as a daughter, subject, as a result, to all the restrictions and possibilities that attend such status in a "society where kinship defines most relationships" (Abu-Lughod 1999, 15). The reflexivity of this opening narrative consciously and conscientiously posits the anthropologist as positioned, nonomniscient, and changeable—susceptible to being made over by relationships. Abu-Lughod is able to understand her position because of her ability to recognize the inherent oddity of being introduced by her father: "I suspect few, if any fathers of anthropologists accompany them to the field to make their initial contacts," she writes (11). This recognition of uniqueness descriptively and argumentatively serves as the anchor that enables kinship to become central to her analysis: introduced as kin, this is what she becomes; thus related to as kin, the resulting kin expectations, and possibilities for their disruption, are what she learns. And because of her dual status as both kin and anthropologist, she recognizes the way her vision is made and remade by her position in the family.

For many anthropologists—including, at times, myself—the NGO has become the analogue of this fatherly introducer, albeit one distinctive in significant ways. Indeed, the introduction I received to the women's arbitration center, or *mahila panchayat*, I discuss here was effective because it was made by NGO members, referred to as "aunties" rather than by a father. Many anthropologists now enter new fields—especially those deemed "classically anthropological" (such as the village, the neighborhood, and the community)—through the mediation of an NGO. NGOs offer ways of mapping the field—as I experienced—or direct introduction to the field in question (Perwez 2008). The attendant resources can be advantageous. Often being taken on by an NGO entails introduction to those identified by the NGO as community leaders, offers of places to stay, interlocutors to speak with, and approval by local authorities and even something to do, such as taking notes, writing reports, and participating in the life of the office. But a crucial difference exists between the introducing NGO and the introducing father of Abu-Lughod's account. Often the NGO does this work of introduction in a way that masks their quality of *positioning* introductions, replete with evaluative frames and ready-made descriptive accounts. Moreover, since this form of introduction is anything but unique, its significance is routinely obscured by its pervasiveness. In cases where the NGO does not itself become an object of research, and even in those cases where the NGO plays only the most limited of roles in the way fieldwork unfolds, these introductions spill out into more general anthropological methods of inquiry: fortifying the significance of particular networks, instantiating some expectations over others, and enabling some observations while foreclosing others. As I discuss in this chapter, my NGO-assisted introduction to the mahila panchayat shaped my understanding of it, providing certain terms in relation to which I worked to see and describe it—and also instantiating particular expectations about my aims in observing its work.

Here, I focus on three ways that NGOs and anthropologists intersect in the field and in ethnographic writing. The first aspect of this relationship concerns access: anthropologists are increasingly reliant on an NGO for contacts or introductions in their fieldsite. This appears to be a straightforward, pragmatic form of dependence: NGO workers have ties to the types of subaltern or marginalized groups, communities, and life-worlds that traditionally interest anthropologists.[1] Second, by being so intimately involved with the object of anthropological analysis, NGOs are themselves nominated for ethnographic scrutiny (Bernal and Grewal 2014a; Hemment 2007; Hodžić 2014; Riles 2001; Sharma 2008). Third, NGOs and anthropologists both seek ethnographic data and in many ways share an epistemological framework, raising the question of what the difference might be between these "co-ethnographers" (Dzenovska 2015, 192). NGO dependence is contextualized and made visible by analysis of the involved NGOs' goals, practices, technologies, and coarticulations with state formations and projects. Each of these relationships entails certain ethical and political demands, some of which are readily attended to and others of which are notably neglected. The aim of this chapter is to open up some questions about these demands and to inquire into what is being produced by discourses that focus on certain aspects of NGO-dependent anthropology while eliding others. At the end, I return to some texts in the history of anthropology to ask what resources they have to offer as we consider our NGO dependence.

NGOs in the Field

The problem of NGO-dependent anthropology came to my attention through my fieldwork on nonstate institutions of Islamic family law in Delhi, India. In 2005, as I began my research, I conducted a survey of the institutions involved and quickly discovered that two major sets of actors are engaged in such legal interventions at the local level: religious leaders and NGOs. The religious leaders ran *dar ul qazas* (usually translated as "sharia courts"), gave *fatwas* (authoritative Islamic legal advice), and engaged in informal dispute adjudication in mosques or homes. The NGOs were predominantly feminist organizations aiming to educate poor women in Delhi and neighboring villages about their legal rights regarding marriage, divorce, and domestic violence. Another increasingly active type of NGO offered advice to women facing domestic conflict and held formal (if not legally binding) arbitration hearings with the women's families.[2]

The seeming saturation of poor Delhi communities by NGOs should not come as a surprise. Delhi is still in the midst of an NGO "boom" (Alvarez 1999). Indeed, the presence of NGOs throughout India has dramatically increased since the 1980s, with roughly two million NGOs registered with the Home Ministry at the beginning of the twenty-first century (Kamat 2002;

Sharma 2008, 41). In Delhi alone the government lists 3,822 NGOs as part of its new "partnership system" (Government of India 2016), and there are undoubtedly many that remain unregistered.[3] NGOs in Delhi work in an environment where the state is simultaneously omnipresent and absent, a situation conducive to NGO flourishing (Dave 2012, 22). NGOs are able to build niche partnerships with state apparatuses, rather than displacing them, a process that signals a neoliberal shift wherein welfare provision is handled by nonstate organizations rather than state ministries. This shift is not, however, totalizing. Indeed, Aradhana Sharma shows that the relationship between state welfare programs and NGO interventions is one of "complementarity" (2008, 43): the state continues to oversee and regulate NGOs even as it positions itself as a "separate and superior actor."[4] Delhi occupies a particularly good site for elucidating this boom. Erica Bornstein has shown, for example, that Delhi has a large network of NGOs involved in collecting and dispensing humanitarian gifts, even as NGOs are broadly distrusted (Bornstein 2012a, 59). Dave describes Delhi as a "city of hope" that is also, as a consequence, "a city of frustration and misery" (2012, 21). In this context, direct-action NGOs find many opportunities for their largely middle-class employees to offer services to the urban poor. Disparities between the wealthy and the poor are especially visible when considering Delhi's Muslim population to be 1,163,934 strong, based on the total given for the National Capital Territory (NCT) of Delhi, including urban and rural residents (Government of India 2011). Disproportionately poor and marginalized, they occupy the shadow of what Zamindar calls the "long partition" (2007, 2).[5]

The Delhi-based NGOs I called as I began my research were welcoming, inviting me to attend their workshops and onsite legal training sessions, browse their libraries, talk with their staff, and even accompany them on their drives to day-long legal trainings in villages in the neighboring states of Haryana and Uttar Pradesh. In conversations, the staff members of these NGOs generously offered their analyses of the challenges facing poor women in both urban and rural settings, in addition to their insights regarding the intersecting forms of disadvantage (class, caste, religion, gender, family structure) that produced these challenges. Of the six or seven such organizations I contacted, one drew me into significant research engagement: an NGO-run women's arbitration center, called a mahila panchayat, located in an eastern Delhi resettlement colony (a neighborhood constructed to house those displaced by government development projects in other parts of the city).

Mahila panchayats are local-level arbitration centers designed to enable local women to hear and adjudicate cases of domestic conflict.[6] At the time of my initial research on mahila panchayats, an NGO called Action India oversaw a branching structure of thirteen other NGOs and sixteen community-based organizations (CBOs), each of which was responsible in turn for over-seeing at least one mahila panchayat.[7] The leader of each mahila panchayat was trained by Action India but ran the mahila panchayat independently, alongside volunteers from the neighborhood. At the time, there were forty-four such panchayats operating in *bastis* (slums) and resettlement colonies throughout Delhi. Although the mahila panchayats' judgments were non-binding and unenforceable by the state, in 2001 Action India began to re-ceive funding from the Delhi municipal government with the promise that an expanded network of mahila panchayats could alleviate stresses placed on state courts by domestic dispute cases.

I was introduced to Delhi's regional legal rights NGOs not by a father fig-ure but through friends and friends of friends—lawyers and activists work-ing on issues of law and gender inequality—and through Internet searches—even very small NGOs in Delhi often have some web presence. Action India staff members introduced me to the mahila panchayat: I visited the NGO's office and spoke with the staff, attended the monthly meetings of local ma-hila panchayat leaders held at the office, and was subsequently invited to at-tend the oldest and most well-established mahila panchayat to observe pro-ceedings. Finally, I was directed to the mahila panchayat in east Delhi where I chose to pursue my research because of its location in a predominantly Muslim neighborhood and its all-Muslim leadership and clientele. With this introduction to the east Delhi mahila panchayat, my research acquired two distinct but related objects: Action India and the mahila panchayat. In other words, the NGO shifted from being simply a possible object of analysis to being the vehicle to the fieldsite toward which my research interests in law drew me—the mahila panchayat. As I illustrate through the ethnographic sketch that follows, it was the difficult but necessary demand to consider Ac-tion India as both object and vehicle that generated many of the questions propelling this chapter.

NGOs as Objects of Analysis

Inasmuch as Action India constitutes an object of anthropological analysis, this analysis must reflect on the place of the nongovernmental in the admin-istration of local justice in India. From this perspective, mahila panchayats can be regarded as an extension of the state's welfare system. The specific type of welfare work they perform is that of mediation. The east Delhi ma-hila panchayat primarily heard cases involving marital breakdown, domes-tic tension, and violence perpetrated by spouses, in-laws, and, sometimes, adult children. By offering women-run adjudication processes as an alternative to the failed or insufficient legal mechanisms of the state, Action India, through the mahila panchayat, can be seen as playing a corrective role.

Yet looking at the process and outcomes of mahila panchayat cases, they appear to mimic the courts' often-inadequate responses to alleged domestic conflict—shoring up, rather than disrupting, normative familial relations (Sunder 2003, 165–66; Basu 2015, 103). Action India founded and funded local mahila panchayats, and it was also responsible for training mahila panchayat leaders to hear cases. The effect of this common "paralegal" training was evident in the uniformity of process and results in mahila panchayats across Delhi (Grover 2011). Hearings followed a regular protocol: a neighborhood woman involved in a domestic dispute would be engaged in an informal consultation and invited to submit a formal complaint. A case file would be opened, whereupon the other parties to the dispute were called to a hearing mediated by the leaders and volunteer members of the local panchayat, in which each party was asked to give an account of the situation. A typical hearing was spread across several meetings. Upon concluding, the mahila panchayat's leader would draft an agreement stipulating each disputant's responsibility and a commitment to return for further mediation should the problems continue. This document was signed (or fingerprinted) by each party. This formal consistency was matched by an equally consistent outcome: spouses and in-laws forged reconciliation agreements in nearly every case of domestic violence I observed or studied, with the effective result of returning women to the dwellings of their husbands, often shared by their in-laws. In this way, the adjudication process consistently reproduced and naturalized the idea that even in the face of ongoing violence a woman belongs in her husband's household. By favoring reconciliation, even in cases where spouses and in-laws are acknowledged to be violent, the mahila panchayat, like the Kolkata family courts Srimati Basu (2015) has studied, "view ensuring strategic survival within an existing marriage as their most valuable service" (103). Women unwilling to reconcile were left with few options.

The tensions between Action India's claim that the mahila panchayats offer an alternative to state courts and their seeming reiteration of the state courts' approach to marital dispute make up one aspect of the anthropological analysis of the NGO. Action India could, in such an analysis, be regarded as "limit[ing] the play of meanings," as AnnJanette Rosga (2005, 277) has described it, intentionally seeking results that could be framed as "success" to the Delhi Commission for Women (DCW), funding partners, anthropologists and sociologists, documentary filmmakers, and others. Action India reports picked out cases of "happy endings"—reconciliations accompanied by an end to violence. Similarly, the DCW's glossy newsletter included a one-page synopsis of the mahila panchayats and a case to illustrate their success. This analysis fits Action India's work into the "paradigm of NGOization," in which feminist scholarship criticizes increased NGO participation in women's movements and issues as depoliticizing co-optations of feminist agendas (Hodžić 2014, 222–27). After all, Action India depicts the mahila panchayat's reproduction and naturalization of the family as success, even in the face of domestic violence, thereby receiving support from the state. That is, rather than doing work readily recognizable as grassroots and movement based, their work appears to be driven by the kinds of interventions that can secure funding from and support of the state and development agencies. Within the paradigm of NGO-ization, there is an anthropological imperative to critique.

However, I would like to suggest that remaining at the level of critique of the NGO, which is one effect of limiting one's analysis to examining the NGO as object, not only fails to account for the ambiguity and ambivalence of NGO practice (Hodžić 2014) but elides significant obstacles to writing ethnographies cognizant of NGO dependence and its effects. The remainder of this chapter elaborates the problems of collaboration and mimesis, two core sources of NGO-dependent anthropology's ethical and political conundrum obscured by overemphasizing the problems of NGOs themselves.

Collaboration and Mimesis in Anthropological Knowledge Production

My position in the mahila panchayat renders questions of collaboration and mimesis unavoidable. As I note, Action India is, like other Indian NGOs, answerable to the government and funding agencies. One practical aspect of these relations is that visitors to the mahila panchayat are common. While Action India staff members regularly attend mahila panchayat meetings for "site checks," there were also visits from employees of the DCW, members of other mahila panchayats, reporters, and social scientists. After my first few visits to the mahila panchayat I was reintroduced and surprised to discover that I had been identified as an affiliate of the DCW. Another time I was identified with Action India. So despite my efforts to clearly explain my role as researcher with no affiliation to these organizations, I was nonetheless placed—because I was not local and because I took notes, asked questions, requested to copy files, I suspect—in the same category as other "outside" observers. In many ways this continued misidentification was helpful: as they would for these other observers, the leaders of the mahila panchayat provided me with case files, let me copy case lists, talked to me about their aims, expectations, and successes, and unhesitatingly allowed me to observe the hearings and meetings. But this also meant that my questions were always interpreted within the frame of the DCW and Action India; any information and case analysis I was provided with was always shaped by understandings of what it was these organizations wanted to see and hear, based on a preconception that my aims and interests aligned with those of the introducing NGO. Put otherwise, the intersubjective "liminal mode of communication" that, according to Paul Rabinow, defines the fieldwork encounter was displaced and overwritten by a different encounter, between the mahila panchayat and its managers (1977, 155). By placing me in the same category as the DCW and Action India, the mahila panchayat members implicitly suggested that I and these other institutions were united in our search for ethnographic data—and that difference was something I would have to produce (Jean-Klein and Riles 2005, 185).

The need to produce difference in response to appeals for collaboration was further evident in my conversations with Deepa in the summer of 2013. One of the founding members of Action India, Deepa currently heads the organization. Our conversations illustrated the struggles characteristic of so much of the NGO work that is aimed at improving women's lives. I asked Deepa how she responds to the allegation that the mahila panchayats betray their feminist origins by so systematically advocating reconciliation—even when domestic violence is alleged. Her response was telling. Some feminists, she said, indeed think that this constitutes a betrayal. But given that most women are unable to provide for themselves and their children through their own means, living with a marital family that can be persuaded both to improve their behavior and to provide financially is preferable to returning to an equally impoverished natal family that does not think caring for a married daughter is its responsibility. Ultimately, however, she was ambivalent about this argument and, as if by way of illustration, told me about a case in which a woman wanted to leave her husband and children for her lover. Deepa convinced the mahila panchayat members to support the woman's wishes against their belief that the desire was shortsighted and likely to end in hardship. Both of these positions—the one that proposes to support what women want and the one that works to persuade women that they should limit their desires to what the mahila panchayat members understand to be realistic aspirations—are framed by what Marilyn Strathern might phrase as a shared stake in "the promotion of women's interests" (1988, 23). Although the assessments of what constitutes women's interests are in conflict, and indeed generate discontinuities in approach in different mahila panchayats, this shared aim constitutes the groundwork for a feminist debate within the NGO.

Deepa was eager for anthropological voices to join this debate. As she made clear, she looks to social scientific analyses with interest. When I asked her what she thought about the heavy presence of anthropologists hovering over Action India's work, her answer was frank: "We understand that people come in the form of journalists, researchers, etcetera, and want to interview us," she said. "We also cater to sensitive filmmakers. We actually like it when people write about us seriously. The five or six serious studies that have been done about the mahila panchayats have been done by anthropologists and sociologists. Now, I couldn't have written those; so it's good. We welcome it." Deepa suggests that part of her work is opening the NGO to analysis and engaging with insights—including critical ones—articulated by various experts and social commentators.

The very openness of NGOs like Action India to anthropological analysis and feedback poses a challenge to the anthropologist. In and through this openness, NGO workers constitute themselves as part of anthropology's reading public, becoming partners in framing research and even writing ethnography. Those like Deepa running NGOs are also working to understand what is happening on the ground and how their work impacts everyday lives. Notably, Deepa's interest in anthropology is premised on the difference between anthropological analysis and her own, a difference that makes this analysis useful to her. In one way, this interest complements a long-held goal of anthropology: enabling us to involve our interlocutors in the process of analysis. But in another way, it frustrates anthropologists' ability to distinguish themselves from their objects of study, as NGOs share many of the epistemological frameworks foundational to anthropological research.

For example, I struggled with how to frame my analysis as distinct from the NGO's, and the mahila panchayat's, categories: education, empowerment, rights, and "what women want." These are all instrumentalized categories, rubrics through which success or failure can be assessed and measured. While it is the mandate of the NGO to determine whether the mahila panchayats are succeeding or failing in relation to these goals, ethnographic analysis has other investments. It is for good reason that anthropologists do not usually traffic in evaluations of success and failure; yet in a field so thoroughly overdetermined by the logic of the NGO, the implicit demand of such valuative language is difficult to avoid.

The NGO's presence in the field thus raises practical and philosophical questions about the roles anthropologists can or should adopt in relation to such NGOs, coconstituted as part object of study and part coethnographer. How does one write and think in the context of NGOs without falling into the logic of the organization under study—without reproducing their logic in the resulting ethnographic analysis? Some anthropologists engaged in studying organizations and expertise have argued that one aim of such anthropological research is to "merge" anthropological thinking with that of "its found counterparts" (Deeb and Marcus 2011, 52). I argue instead that anthropologists need to consider how to maintain the specificity of their inquiry as distinct from the interests of such organizations, which are both subject to study and integral to making that study possible. Anthropologists produce not truth but *anthropological representations*, which are only possible if they do not collapse completely into the terms of their object of analysis. The work of anthropology, it seems to me, rests not in "merging" but in maintaining a certain "incongruity" (Miyazaki 2003, 255).

Jean-Klein and Riles address an analogous concern about the potential collapse of anthropology into its object of analysis in human rights anthropology. They write, "If at times it seems there is no difference between anthropological practice and human rights practice, then perhaps difference . . . must be produced, as an effect, not simply found in the world" (2005, 188). This project of producing difference is shared by differently positioned anthropologists—whether "local" or "foreign," anthropologists work to produce anthropological difference as a precondition for description and for critical intervention. Aptly picking up Marilyn Strathern's argument that anthropology must hold to its own disciplined and disciplinary practice in its engagement with feminism, Jean-Klein and Riles suggest that a similar dedication to anthropology's own practices is necessary if it is to remain distinct from and therefore capable of meaningfully analyzing human rights practices. The difference that anthropology can produce must be an effect of its own practices, practices that include decisions about when to engage and when to hold back, which alliances to build and which to let go, which discursive framings to accept and which to challenge (2005, 186). In relation to NGOs like Action India, which function as self-critical sites of knowledge production and intervention, the question of how to remain anthropologically disciplined presents a similar challenge. Maintaining a commitment to its own methods of inquiry may enable anthropologists to produce anthropological representations that are both descriptions and critical engagements— representations that neither completely distance them from NGOs but that nonetheless resist being instrumentalized by them. One way to maintain such a commitment may be to recognize that anthropological knowledge is "incompatible" with development practitioners' knowledge as with interlocutors' knowledge because these different knowledge claims emerge from "incompatible interests."[8]

In this section, I have suggested that the saturation of NGOs in at least some anthropological fields renders NGOs themselves and the individuals who constitute them both necessary objects of analysis and a recognizable readership. I have argued that the NGO framed as both object and audience raises questions for anthropological modes of analysis. Implicit in this claim is the suggestion that when anthropologists produce knowledge with an understanding that it will be shared with goal-oriented practitioners—such as those aiming to improve women's lives—they do something different from when they produce knowledge and share it with an otherwise complicit object of study—such as when Abu-Lughod showed her research to the Awlad 'Ali Bedouin family that was both her host and the object of her study (Abu-Lughod 1999, xxv–xxvii). The content of this distinction is, perhaps, unexpected. In the case of the Bedouin family, the implicit question is whether the anthropologist succeeded in saying something recognizable to those she studied, regardless of whether this recognition generates applause or critique (Abu-Lughod 1999, xxiv–xxvi). In the case of the NGO, however, the anthropologist is aware of the hope that she will say something both recognizable to the NGO *and* useful toward the aim of improving women's lives. The question, in other words, is whether the anthropologist's *descriptive* account will enable better *outcomes*—whether it can be put to use because it is recognized. This usefulness test, however, assumes both that anthropologists and NGOs share common interests and that they share a common audience—neither of which holds, as Englund has shown (2011, 71–93). Thus, along with Jean-Klein and Riles, I have suggested that to maintain anthropological fidelity requires displacing the question of usefulness in favor of the act of description, suggesting that the aim is to resist epistemological mimesis (Jean-Klein and Riles 2005, 186). In the next section, I turn to the question of how to contend with the mimesis into which we are propelled because of the frames through which the field presents itself to us as a field.

NGO-Dependent Anthropology: Framing the Field

NGO discourses may shape our analytic categories, but they also produce the fields we encounter, bleeding discursively familiar analytical frameworks and agendas into our own, and thus shaping the contours—often invisibly—of our fieldwork. In the case of my research with the mahila panchayats, my direct object of analysis was not, in fact, the NGO (Action India) but the locally run, semiautonomous arbitration forums (mahila panchayats) funded by the NGO. As a result of this framing, I came to see that the mahila panchayat's arbitration practices, and the discourse surrounding it in the local community, regularly exceeded the frameworks formed by the dominant discussions in the NGO. And yet, my attempts to understand and contextualize these discourses were impacted by the received knowledge of Action India's overarching aims and struggles. Any attempt at understanding the mahila panchayat on its own terms, or through other frameworks, was subsumed under the shadow of the NGO's understanding. The following overview of a particular case in the east Delhi mahila panchayat illustrates both the ways in which this mahila panchayat's practices can be seen to exceed the NGO's terms and also the ways in which an anthropological inquiry remains susceptible to adopting these terms in its own analysis.

The mahila panchayat in east Delhi hears the same sorts of marital disputes and domestic violence cases found in other mahila panchayats (Grover 2011), but because of its location in a predominantly Muslim neighborhood, the mahila panchayat in east Delhi is run by Muslim women and hears cases brought by Muslim disputants. The discourse of this community differentiates it from the guiding principles laid out by the NGO, nominating it as a site where the overarching goals of the overseeing NGO can be isolated and examined. One good example of this arose in the adjudication of Saida's case.

Saida came to the mahila panchayat dissatisfied with her seven-month-old marriage. She was the second wife of her husband—a fact she was unaware of at the time of her marriage, and a major component of her complaint. In India, Muslim men are legally entitled to marry up to four wives, but doing so is only socially acceptable in certain circumstances. One such circumstance is when a first wife is unable to have children, which was the case with Saida's husband. While at the outset of the case, Saida stated that she wanted to find a way out of the marriage, but through the process of adjudication she was convinced to instead work toward improving her marriage.

The mahila panchayat members took up several arguments as they adjudicated the case, and while many of the arguments were standard to other such organizations, another—unique to this panchayat's demographic—took the form of religio-legal argumentation. Relying on an analysis of the Quranic injunction that a polygynous man must treat multiple wives equitably,[9] the mahila panchayat members elaborated the entitlements of marriage. Sufiya, the head of the local CBO that oversaw this mahila panchayat, interpreted the demand for equity to mean that men must provide for all women in a polygynous marriage equally. This provision, she argued, is not only about material requirements for life such as food, shelter, and financial support for the wife and the couple's children. A husband, she argued, must also be able to provide emotionally for all of his wives, spending time with each of them. She insisted that ensuring such equality (*barabari*) among his wives is a husband's duty. Sufiya did not contest the legitimacy of polygyny when a first wife was unable to have children, though she was skeptical about the feasibility of treating multiple wives equally. This interpretation of the Quranic injunction augments legal and social considerations regarding normative marital relationships with a religious-legal argument. When combined, the two argumentative frames functioned to strongly support the mahila panchayat's view that Saida should learn to inhabit her marital relationship as a precondition for household harmony, and that this marital construct offered Saida the best hope for some measure of independence.

While this is clearly a case in which it matters that the disputants are Muslim and the resources they draw on are religious, here I am interested in this line of reasoning as an indication of the specificity of arbitration in one local mahila panchayat. Most mahila panchayats do not serve Muslim women and most mahila panchayat leaders, according to the directors of Action India, are not equipped to engage with matters of Muslim Personal Law (law governing Muslim family disputes). This approach to dispute resolution offers one example of the incompleteness of the success-oriented discourse and resources proffered by the overarching NGO. It is possible, then, that looking past the limits of the NGO's discourse we can discover an ethnographic strain that remains relatively autonomous to their overarching goals and agenda. And yet, in analyzing this dispute it is impossible, and unproductive, to ignore the NGO infrastructure that funds, trains, and monitors the mahila panchayat.

While this mahila panchayat draws on the sources of Islamic law to ground reconciliation, other mahila panchayats similarly draw on Hindu law, or general principles of or truisms about familial harmony. The goal, however, remains the same, and it is typically steered by the backing of the NGO. Prior to the hearing itself, Action India has framed this field by training mahila panchayat members to find cases and encourage women to approach the mahila panchayat and holding information sessions to inform the community about the mahila panchayat's existence. In so doing, Action India has helped produce a group of women who understand themselves as in need of arbitration (rather than running away, staying with natal kin, or continuing to live in and with violence). Put otherwise, in diagnosing needs and implementing responses, Action India has produced collectivities that have become legible through these needs. Importantly, these collectivities do not only include women who actually come to the mahila panchayat to have their situations translated into "cases." Instead, by making it clear that those who come forward are but a small portion of a broader group waiting to be found, the participants come to stand in, metonymically, for poor, urban (Muslim) women more broadly. The difficulty of producing difference at the level of analysis, then, is one inherent to the fieldsite, which has been brought into being by these very categories of analysis.

Writing NGO Dependence

At the start of this chapter, I recalled Abu-Lughod's fatherly introduction to the field, suggesting that it provided her with insights both into her position and her object because of its odd form. Through an analysis of my research in the mahila panchayat I have tried to show how NGOs have taken over this role, presenting the anthropologist to the field and the field to the anthropologist. Further, I suggest that NGOs have prior to but also through these introductions constituted the very fields under study. In this final section of the chapter, I turn to several texts in the history of anthropology to ask what resources it offers to address the problem of how to write this new form of dependence.

In considering the NGO as ubiquitous father, interpretive collaborator, and safeguard, it is impossible not to revisit critiques of colonial ethnography and ask what makes this moment of NGO-dependence new. In Talal Asad's introduction to the edited volume *Anthropology and the Colonial Encounter*, he writes that colonialism "made possible the kind of human intimacy on which anthropological fieldwork is based, but ensured that that intimacy should be one-sided and provisional" (1975, 17). Certainly, NGOs now provide this kind of intimate access; and inasmuch as they are the ones maintaining connections to the communities with whom anthropologists work, they can enable a provisional intimacy. It is nonetheless tempting to suggest that because of the frequency with which NGOs *do* become objects of anthropological analysis and because of the self-consciousness with which we have learned to approach the relations of power that enable our research, Asad's concern has been addressed by the discipline. Indeed, the recognition, by some, of NGOs' cyborg qualities—their internal struggles, ambivalences, and transgressions of a purported state/nonstate border—becomes a good example of the ways NGOs have been engaged and addressed (Hodžić 2014, 231–32; Haraway 1991). But this attention to NGOs as anthropological objects is distinct from analyses of how they shape anthropological fields, even when they are not the direct object of analysis.

It is more difficult to dispense with another of Asad's (1975) arguments: that colonial power relations affected "the theoretical treatment of particular topics" (17). This concern is one that has been effectively addressed by numerous critics of anthropology's continuing colonialism. For example, David Scott has shown that the anthropologist indelibly shapes the field by deploying received categories, producing it in such a way that resulting analysis can only be articulated in relation to the categories adopted. Scott proposes that colonial problematics—"the interrelated set of distinctive ideological or discursive presuppositions that establish the contours of visibility of native practices as objects of Western discourse"—thus remain undisrupted (1992, 301). The field is made and is made visible via presuppositions that anthropologists ought to interrogate, he argues. The point here is not that NGOs are analogous to colonial power but rather that they participate in complex and shifting mechanisms of government that simultaneously shape anthropological fields and anthropological perceptions and analyses of them. NGOs' premises and their modes of knowledge may be multiple, they may shift, they may be internally contested, but they nonetheless frame fields by means of reports, interventions, and aims.

Taken together, Asad and Scott lay out the workings by which anthropological presuppositions are obscured by and through established relations of power. They invite anthropologists to interrogate and disrupt the received categories that do the work of obscuring these power relations. Thus, the categories themselves are nominated as objects worthy of analysis, that anthropology might "abandon altogether its faith in the assumption of a fixed and transparent relation between itself and its objects" (Scott 1992, 319). As Scott acknowledges in a footnote, Asad's genealogical treatment of such anthropological categories as "religion" and "ritual" offers one example of how such an approach might be productively engaged (319).

While a genealogical approach, which traces the contexts of a concept's emergence and uses, can certainly function as a crucial method for opening up and contesting anthropology's received categories, thereby exposing how these categories make the field, it needs to be coupled with another approach in order to move from critique of anthropological categories into a new, deconstructive approach to and analysis of the field. Marilyn Strathern's method of category disruption offers one way of approaching this second aim (1988, 16). In the face of contemporary anthropologists' near-ubiquitous NGO dependence, itself a product of standard anthropological fieldsites being saturated by the presence of NGOs, we are faced with the challenge of how to bring this NGO-mediated production of our fields into view *anthropologically*—this is to say: any anthropological fieldwork marked (even without seeming consequence) by the presence of NGOs must account for their influence. We must do this work whether or not we would figure the NGOs in question as our primary object of analysis, simply because their tacit effect can be so great and also so thoroughly invisible.

While none of us can extract ourselves from our own premises or isolate ourselves completely from the premises maintained by the NGOs that grant us entry, we can strive to "make [the] workings [of these premises] visible" (Strathern 1988, 7). And in addition to the strategies discussed in this chapter, more creative and speculative solutions might also exist. As Jean-Klein and Riles have also reminded us, in Strathern's analysis of gender in Melanesia, she does not provide genealogies of the anthropological categories used to frame this fieldsite (2005, 179). Instead, she picks up anthropological categories of analysis and plays with them, positing them as "fictions." Working with these fictions, Strathern is able to simultaneously contest dominant anthropological interpretations and also offer counterinterpretations. Because she constructs these counterinterpretations as fictional, she preempts the possibility that they might be instantiated as dominant categories—replete with the same problems they were designed to challenge. Strathern strives not to "replace exogenous concepts" with their "indigenous counterparts" but to contextualize the complexity of "indigenous concepts" by means of "exposing the contextualized nature of analytical ones" (Strathern 1988, 8). In her case, these analytical concepts are both feminist and anthropological. The two differ from and are sometimes at odds with one another and this is as she intends it to be. In maintaining their difference and the awkwardness of their relationship, the anthropologist is able to produce a different kind of analysis, drawing on the two and putting them into dialogue without risk of their being conflated in the reader's understanding.

In the context of NGO dependence, anthropologists must be prepared to engage such awkward relationships in duplicate, in triplicate. It becomes imperative to approach received categories as "categorical fictions" not only when they are received from disciplines like anthropology (with their colonial accretions) or feminism (with its investment in women's interests) but also when they come to us from NGOs (with their own varied articulations with global and local power relations) as they act in the field more directly. My suggestion here is that bringing the workings of these various frameworks into view, where they can themselves be analyzed, critiqued and evaluated, does not itself require a choice between genealogy and category disruption. Instead, I argue that we might combine the two strategies alongside possible others, by juxtaposing the findings of genealogical analyses such as those performed by Sharma with categorical reframings and destabilizations of the sort performed by Strathern. Both provide valuable pathways for working through, reflecting upon, and reconstituting the way categories provided by NGOs, by anthropologists, and by feminists can and should function. In doing so I do not suggest we can discover a perfect, unflawed frame through which to approach our subjects. On the contrary, such an approach seems most valuable for its ability to overturn received categories suffused with existing power relationships, invisibly functioning to reify and reproduce them without affordances for change and renegotiation.

Conclusion

My effort here has been to shift or expand our frame of analysis beyond NGOs as objects and to NGOs as significant contributors to shaping the field in part because their modes of knowledge production often appear so similar to the anthropologist's. I parse how our questions and our empirical data, our fieldwork, are produced in relation to these modes of knowledge production.

In the case of the mahila panchayats, I have found it necessary to include analyses of Action India, its aims, and its internal debates regarding the need to support women in the communities they engage, and the role they can play in doing so. I have attempted to avoid representations of mahila panchayat proceedings that determine them as successes or failures in relation to the goals set out by Action India. Indeed, I have attempted to avoid providing Action India with a report that might be used by them in determining whether the east Delhi mahila panchayat is a success or failure by their own criteria. But I do try to make it clear that the very project of describing mahila panchayat proceedings demands consideration of just what exactly constitutes women's well-being. The question seems to hinge on how a notion of "empowerment" might be connoted in the surrounding context. There is both an ethics and a politics to such an anthropological process. The aim is to bring out the contradictions, ambivalences, and ambiguities inherent in our own positions, enabling them to propel us to think in ways that unsettle the global power relations within which we work and that in so many ways make our work possible.

Acknowledgments

Thanks to Amanda Lashaw for urging me to write this chapter, to Dace Dzenovska and Matt Goerzen for comments on an earlier draft, and to Jessica Mach for editorial assistance. Thanks also to Catherine Larouche for illuminating discussions about NGOs in her doctoral fieldsite.

Notes

1. The dynamics of the relationships between NGOs and anthropologists and their sites of intervention vary significantly depending on the positions of concerned NGOs, of anthropologists, and of their sites: local NGOs and postcolonial scholars are positioned differently vis-à-vis their sites than are NGO workers and scholars located in the global North, for example. However, the class dynamics of both NGO work and anthropological research in the context of Delhi suggest that the need for access broadly speaking is shared in significant ways by scholars from the global South and the global North (see, for example, Perwez 2008 and Vogler 2007).

2. For an overview of such institutions in India, see Vatuk (2013).

3. In February 2014 the *Times of India* published an article positing that there is one NGO in India for every 600 people, in contrast with 1 police officer for every 945 people. See Mahapatra (2016).

4. This regulation has taken different forms at different times. During the 2010s, there seems to have been a shift to increasing government oversight. In 2014, the new Bharatiya Janata Party (BJP) government issued a notice to more than ten thousand NGOs that had not filed annual returns indicating foreign donations; see New Delhi Television (2014). In June of the same year, the government tightened the restrictions on NGOs receiving any foreign funding on the grounds that such donations undermine the government's development efforts; see Bahree (2014).

5. See Taneja (2013, 143–45) and Zamindar (2007). Zamindar refers to the continuing effects of the 1947 partition of the Indian subcontinent that produced the independent states of India and Pakistan. She argues that structural inequalities in India, and the disproportionate marginalization of Muslims, must be understood in relation to this event. For statistics on Indian Muslim marginality, see Government of India, Industry of Minority Affairs (2016).

6. "Mahila" means "woman," while "panchayat" literally means "five-member council." The institution has a long history in India and currently exists in various forms, some of which typically enforce their decisions using social pressure rather than the coercive apparatuses of the state and others of which are charged with implementing state law at the local level. The modern instantiation of the panchayat form began with Gandhi's efforts to remake historical panchayats organized along caste lines into village-level bodies. The mahila panchayats situate themselves within this Gandhian tradition of dedication to local self-governance and adjudication, understanding the panchayat to be both a promising form of local justice and an institution receptive to reform. All-woman mahila panchayats were established by the NGO Action India in the 1990s to address the caste-based and male-centered character of existing panchayats. See Lemons (2016), Chowdhry (2007), Galanter and Baxi (1979), and Action India (2016).

7. Action India, an NGO founded in 1974 to assist poor women in Delhi and galvanized during the Emergency in 1975, works in the areas of reproductive rights, economic empowerment, and against domestic violence and female infanticide. The organization is not to be confused with Action Aid India, a federal organization affiliated with the international antipoverty organization Action Aid International. Action India receives financial support from the Ford Foundation, Unifem, Oxfam, and the Global Fund for Women.

8. See Englund (2011, 86–87). The difference with Englund's approach, though, is that this incompatibility appears to be somewhat spontaneous in his essay, whereas in my fieldsite, as in Jean-Klein and Riles's work, it is produced through struggle.

9. The passage from the Quran 4:3 reads: "Marry such women / as seem good to you, two, three, four; / but if you fear you will not be equitable, / then only one, or what your right hands own; / so it is likelier you will not be partial."

10

The Anthropologist and the Conservation NGO

Dilemmas of and Opportunities for Engagement

Amanda Woomer

Conservation organizations face some of the world's most critical issues—including climate change, wildlife trafficking, clear-cutting of rainforests, clean water scarcity, and more—issues that have both widespread and long-term impacts. In response to the urgent need for action, conservation scientists and anthropologists alike have called for increased collaboration between the two fields to develop an expanded consideration of the socio-cultural, economic, and political backdrop of conservation, which in turn could contribute to the development of more effective and sustainable solutions (Brosius 2006; Dickman 2010). Yet anthropological engagement with conservation has remained limited (Redford 2011), likely as a result of the dilemmas that anthropologists may face (Sillitoe 2007). This chapter explores these dilemmas and argues for an informed and collaborative commitment by anthropologists to work with conservation organizations.

Conservation NGOs operating internationally—hereafter referred to as conservation INGOs—function in diverse circumstances complete with technical experts, discerning donors, international discourses, local communities of humans and nonhumans, and the physical landscape. Their initiatives are both multicultural and interdisciplinary. As a result of the issues they address, conservation workers operate under a persistent shadow of urgency, all the while accountable to various stakeholders with a multitude of interests. To engage in the conservation process is thus to immerse oneself in a complex environment characterized by a number of dilemmas. These include the dilemma of difference between the discourses and approaches of the natural and social sciences; issues related to the researcher's positionality, commitments, responsibilities, and personal desire for impact in the face of organizational constraints. While many of these dilemmas are common to other forms of engagement, environmental conservation is distinct in that the focus is on target beneficiaries who are generally nonhuman, so conservation workers are often not trained to respond to the social worlds in which they operate (Redford 2011), and conservation solutions at the level of the physical landscape may take decades or longer to manifest themselves.

Given these unique factors, this chapter explores the peculiar ethical and epistemological dilemmas suggested by anthropology's engagement with conservation INGOs as well as options for navigating these dilemmas. It is based on my experience volunteering for a small, American wildlife conservation organization in Tanzania, while simultaneously conducting ethnographic research on expatriate conservation workers. My engagement reflected both my personal desire to support wildlife conservation and my academic ambition to conduct a pilot research project on conservation workers' understandings of culture and its impacts on conservation. I was therefore both conservation worker and anthropologist, challenged by the need to navigate my desire to "do good" while simultaneously trying to "do good research." Nevertheless, these dilemmas can help us reflect on and improve our engagement as anthropologists.

My discussion of the challenge of doing both activism and research is developed predominantly in the context of a specific project in which I was involved while in Tanzania: the redevelopment of an environmental education project. Together with other volunteers, our task was to overhaul the existing curriculum, moving from ad hoc lesson plans to a yearlong, comprehensive curriculum. Upon review of the existing materials, I noted that each relied on the assumption—common among environmental education programs—that human activity leads to environmental degradation and that education can be a tool for changing behavior (Armstrong 2005). My hope in redesigning the education project was to move away from a curriculum dominated by Western conceptualizations of nature and people's relationship to it to one based on culturally relevant lessons. To do so, I believed that we needed local participation and input. Hence, I asked the organization's director if we could invite local community members to participate in drafting the lesson plans or, at the very least, to review the final product's relevancy and usefulness. She responded that time and resources were limited. The education project relied entirely on volunteers, and we needed to move forward as best we could with what resources we had, namely each other, the Internet (when the solar panel was working), and existing lesson plans. As a volunteer, I was required to participate in the curriculum development. However, as an anthropologist conducting research on culture in relation to conservation processes, I was dismayed by our inability to tailor the education curriculum to the community in which we lived. In the end, the practical demands of the work prevailed. We finalized the curriculum and began its implementation before I left Tanzania.

This particular project encompassed many of the broader dilemmas I faced during my time in Tanzania, balancing my identities of researcher and volunteer in an applied setting. Anthropology's use outside of academia has become increasingly accepted since the days of collaboration between anthropologists and colonialists. Today, anthropology often occupies a "middle ground" that combines activism with academic pursuits and theory building (Knauft 2006). In this chapter, I discuss what engaged anthropology means today in relation to environmental conservation. I begin by briefly addressing the history of applied anthropology as well as some key points of the modern debate. In order to provide additional context, I then examine anthropology's evolving relationship with environmental conservation. Using examples from my experience, I describe the dilemmas of anthropological engagement with conservation INGOs, focusing on the key questions of who we work *with*, who and what we work *for*, and *how* we work. I conclude by considering potential ways forward for engagement in spite of the dilemmas, arguing for a reflective, personal, and intelligent engagement directed toward collaborative problem solving in the face of today's conservation challenges.

Engaged Anthropology and Anthropology's Engagement with Conservation

Engaging Anthropology

This chapter eschews the debate about whether or not engaged anthropology is valid. By the 1950s, "gallons of ink" had been spilled on deliberating the merits of pure versus applied science (Mair 1956, 120), and there are a number of sources that provide useful overviews of the history of applied anthropology and the associated debates. It is beneficial to underscore, however, that anthropological engagement over the last century has undergone a process of regular transformation, taking on new forms, expanding and contracting only to expand again. These various forms of engagement—from some degree of collusion with colonial administrations (Bennett 1996; Nolan 2002) to participation in the feminist and civil rights movements in the 1970s (Knauft 2006) to various and often contradictory involvement in US military efforts from World War II to Vietnam to Iraq (Fluehr-Lobban 2008)—have led to continuous reflection over the role of ethics in anthropology, as well as a progressive expansion of the discipline's methods to include collaborative and activist research, social critique, and even advocacy (Kirsch 2010; Low and Merry 2010).

Beginning in the 1970s, anthropology's perceived "detachment from the problems of modern society" (Bennett 1996, S23), combined with a shortage of academic positions and the resulting entry of anthropologists into development and social policy arenas, propelled the discipline to reinvent itself as more engaged (Caplan 2003). Its focus widened to include consideration of issues such as responsibility, objectivity, relevancy, "power relations between the researcher and researched" (12), and positionality vis-à-vis students, colleagues, and other stakeholders. Many anthropologists came to be driven by a desire for "mutually positive relations with the people we study, work with, write about and for, and communicate with more broadly as anthropologists" (Sanjek 2015a, 2). We emphasized our commitment as a profession to the dignity and rights of the communities among whom we work (Low and Merry 2010).

The conviction that anthropology can and should contribute to the amelioration of social ills has subsequently flourished. As a result, engagement exists on a spectrum, ranging from the cursory to the profound. It includes everything from investigating topics useful for policy development (Warren 2006) to making ethnographic information available and accessible to the wider public to attempting to influence policy makers directly (Sanjek 2015b). Sillitoe (2007) explores indigenous knowledge in relation to development agendas. Lobo describes the objective of her work with organizations that serve Native American populations as "answering the needs expressed by the community or organization" with which she engages (2015, 193). For her, anthropologists are not just observers, writers, or analysts, but also "builders" and "technicians" (191). Hastrup and Elsass (1990) grappled with the ethical challenges of supporting an indigenous group's land management project in Colombia.

Engagement, however, precipitates a number of dilemmas. For example, there are ethical questions regarding what topics or areas are appropriate for engagement (such as the case with anthropologists' participation in the US military's Human Terrain project), and these reflect a broader move away from cultural relativism in the face of moral dilemmas. It also suggests a methodological movement from traditional ethnography, by which anthropologists suspend their personal beliefs, to one in which the anthropologists can decide just how to engage (Scheper-Hughes 1995). Indeed, a 2013 American Anthropological Association statement defined engaged anthropology as "committed to supporting social change efforts that arise from the interaction between community goals and anthropological research" (Atalay 2014, 47).

The degree of that support is variable and conditional. In what types of projects or movements can or should anthropologists be involved? To what extent? Under what conditions and motivations? Using what methods? The answers may be in part subjective, a conscious choice of the anthropologist, but they are also contextually situated. For example, in some cases engagement may be considered an ethical obligation for the anthropologist. These issues come to the fore when we examine the dilemmas that anthropologists have faced in their engagement with environmental issues and conservation NGOs.

Anthropology and Environmental Conservation

Institutionalized environmental conservation has evolved substantially over the last two centuries in response to changes in how the natural environment is understood—including the fundamental justifications for conservation, conceptualizations of people's relationships to the environment, and what is considered necessary in order for conservation to be successful—as well as the global growth of civil society. For example, until the late twentieth century, the most prevalent form of institutionalized conservation was the national protected area, which entails creating spaces that exclude humans based on the assumption that people are fundamentally separate from the natural world and necessarily degrade it (Dove and Carpenter 2008; Mulder and Coppolillo 2005). Today, a great deal of conservation work is undertaken by NGOs in the form of community-based projects that incorporate elements of development aid. These approaches, at least theoretically, are based on the assumption that local communities have the most incentive to conserve their natural environment and will do so when provided with sufficient development opportunities.

Despite the increasing incorporation of communities, many conservation strategies still assume a division between the sociocultural world of people and an imagined, objective world of nature, as understood by the natural scientist. To counter this dichotomy, anthropologists have drawn attention to the social aspects of conservation, including the culturally and historically mediated nature of environmental discourse (Brosius 2008), the politics of environmental knowledge (Escobar 1998), and the relevancy of indigenous knowledge (Howard 2015; Mulder and Coppolillo 2005). They have criticized the exclusion of communities in decision-making processes (West and Brockington 2006), calling for more participation and further consideration of how conservation can contribute to sustainable development (Chapin 2004). Anthropology has become more interdisciplinary and reflexive as well (Dove and Carpenter 2008), leading to an expansion of the boundaries of what, how, and whom anthropologists can consider.

Following the growth of civil society, particularly in the global South, since the 1980s (Fisher 1997; Igoe 2003; P. Little 1999), anthropologists discovered that "environmental NGOs have become visible players in the terrain that we once thought we could claim as our own—the rural/remote community" (Brosius 1999, 279). The discipline responded to the opportunity to use our methodological toolbox to "study over" (Markowitz 2001) by providing critical observations on the work of conservation INGOs, particularly on the relationships between organizations and the local communities in which they operate (Kopnina 2012). These critiques center on the importance of and obstacles to community-based, participatory, and socially just conservation strategies (Brosius and Russell 2003), as well as assessments of how these organizations often dictate the kinds of knowledge of and structures that govern the natural world, to the exclusion of local actors (Garland 2008). As a result, anthropologists have called for conservation workers to embrace the social sciences as well as the research and analysis they offer (Waylen et al. 2010). This effort to engage has brought to light a number of dilemmas.

Engaging with Conservation INGOs

Many of the dilemmas of engagement discussed here became apparent to me during my time working with and conducting research on conservation workers in Tanzania. In early 2013, I conducted ethnographic research with expatriate conservation workers to address how this group's understanding of its own cultural background, values, and beliefs related to its conservation work. While there is a wealth of research on the relationships between conservation INGOs and the communities impacted by their activities (e.g., Brosius, Tsing, and Zerner 1998; Chapin 2004; Mulder and Coppolillo 2005; West and Brockington 2006), far less attention has been given to the conservation workers themselves and the way they understand the linkages between their own sociocultural background and the work to which they contribute.

To explore this topic, I took a volunteer position with a small, US-registered organization that seeks to limit human-wildlife conflict for communities living along the border of one of Tanzania's parks by providing environmental education to schoolchildren and tools to local farmers for mitigating human-wildlife conflict and developing alternative livelihoods. The organization also sought to cultivate positive experiences with wildlife through a park visitation program. During my time as a volunteer, the organization's staff employed six Tanzanian workers, two expatriates, and four volunteers from the United States and Europe. Most of the other organizations active in the area were equally small, employing a handful of Western volunteers and employees and some national staff.

As an anthropologist, volunteering afforded me with access to a site at which I could pilot my research. I observed the activities of the INGO for which I worked and conducted semistructured interviews with conservation workers in the area. As a volunteer, I had responsibilities that varied from day to day, depending on the weather and on whether or not we had a functional vehicle. I accompanied my organization's staff on park visits, collected quantitative data on wildlife within the park, interviewed local community members pre- and post-park visit about their perceptions of wildlife, and developed and began implementation of an environmental education curriculum for students in local schools.

In attempting to do good while doing good research in the context of conservation in rural Tanzania, I was exposed to complex and problematic situations that epitomized certain dilemmas. These dilemmas are often interconnected, and they are rooted in issues of positionality, objectivity, responsibility, power relationships, and a desire to contribute, issues that engaged anthropologists have been grappling with for decades. They are worthy of consideration in the context of engaging with conservation organizations not only because they mark a peculiar kind of engagement—"studying over" (Markowitz 2001, 43) rather than up or down, in situations made up of both the human and nonhuman—but also because they have significance for conservation outcomes. I divide the dilemmas among three overarching questions that I believe are essential for the anthropologist doing engaged work to answer: Whom do you work *with*? Whom and what do you work *for*? And *how* do you work?

Whom Do You Work With?

When I was in Tanzania, all of my fellow volunteers and a majority of those that I interviewed for my research were natural scientists. They were trained in biology, ecology, wildlife conservation, and genetics, while I was trained in sociocultural anthropology, ethnographic analysis, and qualitative research methods to critically examine issues of race, gender, class, and culture. As a result, many of our underlying assumptions about conservation—such as the nature of the connections between the physical and social worlds—differed. For them, conservation was exemplified in the protection of a keystone species whose loss would result in ripple effects in the larger ecosystem. For me, conservation also included understanding and addressing socioeconomic conditions that resulted in increased poaching of that species.

These differences in assumptions were evident during the everyday interactions I had with my fellow volunteers, sharing a campsite and stories. Sitting around the fire or a plastic table, sharing our typical dinner of beans, rice, and *pili pili*, we would consider the day's surprises, discomforts, and peculiarities. One night, the conversation turned toward global environmental discourses. We discussed the tensions between different conservation agendas and approaches, the treaties and agreements that govern environmental topics internationally, the presence of volunteers such as us in other, similar situations doing conservation work. I asked the group why they believed we had the right to be there, to be leading (or is it imposing?) conservation action. A fellow volunteer from the United States, Rachel replied, "Because we know better."[1] I was shocked, although I held my tongue for fear of influencing the interviews I would later have with her and the others.

Rachel's response and my shock exemplify the dilemma of difference between those who believe science has objective answers and those who believe even science is rooted in cultural paradigms. Conservation scientists may rely on the "simplistic traditional culture versus modernity dichotomy" (Crewe and Harrison 1998, 46) in which science becomes synonymous with rationality and knowledge, while local communities are associated with tradition and thus backwardness. As a result, conservation scientists may not take local people or the social context seriously (Igoe 2003). Oversimplification of complex sociocultural, economic, and political systems is useful in managing complexity, but it also obscures the fact that conservation workers—like anyone else—base their decisions on cultural constructions that are not necessarily valid.

This lack of awareness of culture's influence on science appeared in my interviews when I asked conservation workers what they had learned about their own culture during their time in Tanzania. Most pointed to "little differences," such as differences in the way time is perceived. Some remarked that they enjoyed the "simplicity" of life in Tanzania. Others noted the disparities in gender roles between Tanzania and their home countries, commenting that Tanzanian culture was very patriarchal and that women did not have many rights. When I subsequently asked respondents more directly how they believed their own cultures impacted the conservation work in which they were involved, almost everyone replied that they had either not considered it or did not think that their cultural backgrounds had any kind of significant impact. These responses indicate a lack of cultural awareness or reflexivity among conservation scientists, which in turn impacts their beliefs about conservation and the approaches that they pursue.

Alternatively, anthropologists dive into cultural complexity, asking questions like, "Who speaks for nature?" (Brosius 2006, 683); How has environmental discourse led to "the production of forms of knowledge and types of power" that in turn support certain conservation strategies? (Escobar 1998, 56); and How does the war on poaching in parts of Africa contribute to a "new moral geography" in relation to shoot-on-sight orders for poachers? (Neumann 2004, 813). We see through the lens of culture, and we seek to understand how sociocultural processes drive action. For conservation scientists, extensive consideration of the political processes, social relationships, and cultural practices of their work is extravagant in the face of "a well-founded sense of urgency. Anthropological critiques are therefore perceived as a luxury that conservationists cannot afford" (Brosius 2006, 684). My request for someone from the local community to review our environmental education curriculum, for example, was judged against the need to start teaching. The director's response was based on the priorities and resource limitations of the organization.

While it is true that conservation workers face urgent issues that require equally urgent responses, successful and sustainable conservation may depend on a better understanding of the broader context in which it occurs (Madden and McQuinn 2014). Anthropologists can contribute to this understanding by going beyond simple critique to suggesting solutions (Brosius 2006). To do so, we should seek not only to share our knowledge but also to better understand the people driving conservation agendas in terms of the assumptions and beliefs that drive them. I sought to do this in my interviews with other volunteers and conservation workers, during which I asked people about why they were involved in conservation, how they defined it, and why they thought it was important. However, that was where the development of understanding ended. In trying to do the "right" thing and maintain the boundaries between professional researcher and personal volunteer, I did not convert the understanding I gained into collaborative problem solving (an issue with *how* I did my work, which I will discuss in a following section).

Whom and What Do You Work For?

While the answer to the question of whom we work *with* when engaging with conservation INGOs may be relatively straightforward, whom and what the anthropologist works *for* is more complicated. Traditionally, anthropology has had a preoccupation with the local, the marginalized, and the other. For example, Hale describes anthropological engagement in terms of working "in dialogue, collaboration, alliance with people who are struggling to better their lives" (2008, 4). Historically, this dialogue and collaboration has implied (if not necessitated) "an explicit ethical orientation to 'the other'" (Scheper-Hughes 1995, 418) and those who are struggling. The environmental realm is no different, and anthropologists have often acted as "advocates and allies of local populations of farmers, indigenous peoples, and other subordinate groups" (Orlove and Brush 1996, 347). However, as anthropology expands into areas in which "studying over" is commonplace, we must consider new questions related to what peoples, causes, and issues we can work for.

When working with conservation INGOs, the community with which we engage are those same, historical outsiders that the indigenous and marginalized have traditionally struggled against, the Americans and Europeans who come to help because "we know better." Because these people were the focus of my ethnography, and in attempting to do good research, I often felt myself to be in the interesting position of colluding with the proverbial "enemy." In the framework of trying to also do good by supporting environmental conservation, the community with which I engaged morphed to include local Tanzanians, the natural landscape, and even the conservation INGO's donors (albeit tangentially).

Attempting to reconcile these different conceptualizations of community resulted in complex dilemmas of responsibility and positionality. As part of engaging, anthropologists must consider whose interests and voices to prioritize. This becomes challenging when we attempt to keep separate our identities as professional researcher and personal activist. For example, if we personally support additional participation for local communities (such as in the case of the development of the education curriculum), but the organization with which we work does not have the resources to support that participation, what do we do? Our choice reflects our beliefs about which community are we working *for*, either the organization or someone else. And once we choose, we have to consider if we are limiting our ability to engage with others (Eldelman 2001).

Responsibility, commitment, and positionality are perhaps more complex when working with NGOs (Low and Merry 2010). These organizations have significant influence in defining and promoting agendas, consequently changing the social, political, and economic landscapes in which they operate. In a comprehensive review of sub-Saharan conservation organizations, Brockington and Scholfield found that the top ten largest organizations—of which only one was headquartered in the global South—account for 80 percent of conservation expenditures (2010, 563). These figures hint at the domination of conservation discourses by Western voices. Tanzania is no exception; with only seventeen registered NGOs in the early 1980s, there were nearly one thousand by the end of the 1990s (Igoe 2004, 11). Although it is difficult to know how many of these were conservation organizations and the peculiarities of their staff, donors, and activities, their large number and pervasive influence led Brockington to remark that the "environmental-conservation complex" in Tanzania plays a significant role in shaping both environmental and national politics (2006, 102).

How do we integrate this knowledge into a decision about whom and what to work for? Lemons (this volume) cautions anthropologists against becoming too entangled in the work and interests of the NGO, which can inhibit our ability to do good anthropology. Indeed, the influence that these conservation organizations have, including on the anthropologist, should not be ignored. Yet engagement in support of an NGO may be necessary as a prerequisite for gaining research access to an organization's staff, project documents, and related stakeholders (Edelman 2001). Reacting to the parachuting anthropologist, one who conducts surveys and interviews and then departs, never to be heard of again (Loode 2011), organizations, communities, and indigenous peoples now insist that the anthropologist gives as well as gets. In the case of conservation INGOs, deeper engagement in the objectives of the organization can also counter conservation scientists' criticism of anthropologists for providing more critiques than potential solutions (Brosius 2006) and for misunderstanding the true nature of conservation work (Redford 2011).

In approaching engagement in this way, however, anthropologists run the risk of being perceived as legitimating certain types of discourses, approaches, or hierarchies (Stoczkowski 2008). This risk was omnipresent during my time in Tanzania. When I, with my colleagues, redeveloped the environmental education curriculum, I wondered if I was unwittingly approving of its content and implementation. Since my focus was on conservation workers, I did not ask local community members about their perceptions of myself or the organization. Our limited interactions meant that it would have been impossible for them to know about my objections to the curriculum. How could they have assumed anything else from my presence there except an explicit support for the organization and its activities?

If we choose to work for an NGO or similar organization, we will undoubtedly face ideological and ethical issues. In order to be well positioned to address the "for *whom*" and "for *what*" of engagement with conservation INGOs, we must remain aware of the context and be prepared to consistently reevaluate that context. Responding to the moral and epistemological dilemmas of positionality, responsibility, and commitment involves reconciling ourselves to our personal and professional goals and responding to the agendas and actions of those around us.

How Do You Work?

When Rachel responded to my questions about why she believed we should be in Tanzania doing conservation work with "we know better," I did not engage in an in-depth conversation. I did not attempt to bridge the gap between her assumptions and mine. Instead, I sought to maintain the line between professional researcher and personal activist. This section addresses *how* we can blur the line between good research and doing good. I start with the assumption that, although "it is traditional for social scientists' attention to NGOs generally to take the form of critique, questioning the difference or viability of alternatives that they offer, or the problems of the images and fund raising they employ" (Brockington and Scholfield 2010, 554), effective engagement with conservation INGOs necessitates going beyond critique to collaborative problem solving.

My engagement with the conservation INGO with which I volunteered was the result of both methodological need (a site for pilot research) and a personal imperative to contribute to environmental conservation. In combining these two objectives, I faced ethical and epistemological dilemmas associated with the process. Ethically, I grappled with the implications of my work for the organization, my fellow volunteers, the people whom I interviewed, and the project beneficiaries (human and nonhuman). For instance, when I think back to the development of the environmental education curriculum, I consider whether I was complicit in the creation of a curriculum that perpetuated Western notions of the environment and people's relationship to it over equally legitimate local ones. In other words, "we [Westerners] know better." I also wondered later that if by taking a stance for cultural relevancy and advocating for community involvement in the redevelopment of the curriculum, I was carelessly, albeit unconsciously, asserting that "we [anthropologists] know better" than conservation scientists and calling into question their value, which did little to support collaborative dialogue and understanding of culture's place in conservation.

The concerns I had are related to a nuanced struggle of who "knows better" between different disciplines and between "experts" and communities. Indeed, the ethics of engagement in postcolonial contexts like Tanzania are complicated by a number of unequal relationships of power such as those between rural and urban, uneducated and educated, local and foreign. If, as Speed (2008) describes it, activist anthropology is about decolonizing the research process, what can anthropologists do to "decolonize" conservation processes as part of our engagement with Western conservationists, a group that both historically and currently occupies a privileged position in determining conservation trajectories throughout the world? One approach is to increase our engagement with conservation workers to collaboratively identify existing sociopolitical structures that either hinder or help conservation and to change them accordingly. For example, adapting education curriculums to the cultural and physical context increases its usefulness for students. And when communities think that projects meet their needs and are involved in their development, there is generally more buy-in and participation.

Ethical considerations may alternatively convince some anthropologists to limit their engagement with conservation NGOs based on their missions or approaches (Chapin 2004; Neumann 2004). Even with the best of intentions, conservation agendas can have detrimental effects on communities as well as the very environments they seek to protect. Like other influential development aid organizations, conservation INGOs are both "enabling and limiting. Defining themselves as filling particular spaces of discourse and praxis, they in effect define (or redefine) the space of action; they privilege some forms of action and limit others; they create spaces for some actors and dissolve spaces for others" (Brosius 2008, 382; see also Brockington and Scholfield 2010).

With so much power, a lack of awareness on the part of conservation INGOs of the broader sociocultural context, as well as their influence on that context, can result in unintended negative consequences. Igoe (2004) provides the example of Maasai in Tanzania who were forced to relocate as a result of the creation of a protected area and were thus alienated from their traditional grazing land. Conservation strategies like this can divorce people from their livelihoods; put them into conflict with other groups as they are forced to find new means of subsistence; and disrupt traditional social structures, leading to increased rates of domestic violence, alcoholism, and depression. With awareness, however, conservation can support economic development, gender equality, and community empowerment.

Conservation INGOs' actions can also be dictated by donor priorities. Seated at a plastic table in a *banda* (hut) on the grounds of her conservation organization's parcel, Carly told me that she had concerns about her organization's relationship to its donors. A young American woman and the only social scientist I interviewed, Carly was troubled by the stipulations that come with donor money. Short funding timelines, she noted, are not compatible with the slower pace of work in the community or the time needed to plan effective projects or build trust. She felt uncomfortable with constantly balancing the competing agendas of the donor and the community, and her discomfort was indicative of the ethical dilemmas anthropologists may feel when asked to comply with organizational and donor mandates as part of their engagement.

While the compromises required to obtain funding are common experiences for all NGOs, they have particular impacts on the work of conservation INGOs as a result of their position at the intersection of diverse human and nonhuman worlds. Donors supporting conservation of a particular wildlife species, for example, may not be aware of the time it takes to build trust within a community or the necessity of doing so. Ignorance of social dynamics can in turn force conservation organizations to alter their objectives or activities or even put INGOs in direct conflict with the needs of the communities most impacted by their work (Igoe 2004; Menon 2013), a situation to which Carly alluded. Donor relationships therefore represent an opportunity for anthropologists to engage with conservation workers to assess the pros and cons of certain approaches and partnerships and to provide information to donors on the social implications of those approaches.

How anthropologists choose to engage can have an impact on what strategies conservation organizations undertake, their relationships to donors and communities, and how conservation workers understand the sociopolitical context in which they operate. It is this potential for impact that may draw us toward engagement initially, as it did for me. But positive results are not guaranteed. Even when seemingly sustainable conservation solutions are identified and natural and social scientists work together effectively, obtaining good results may be limited by external conditions (Charnley and Durham 2013), including natural disasters, civil wars, or a lack of funding. In addition, while human behaviors may change in short order, it can take decades to see the results in the natural environment. Having a direct impact may be difficult if not impossible when the timeframe of our work is too short to effect change (Sillitoe 2007). Although I helped create the environmental education curriculum, I did not stay in Tanzania long enough to see it implemented fully or to see the impacts of that implementation on people's beliefs and behaviors.

Prescriptive methods for engagement are also limited, and I found it difficult during my time in Tanzania to separate my research from my responsibilities as a volunteer. Ethnography in the "field" is considered to be one of the defining (if not the most defining) features of anthropology (Gupta and Ferguson 1997; Knauft 2006). As anthropology becomes more comfortable with engagement, its methods have expanded to include more participatory and collaborative processes, working with communities to influence change (Rylko-Bauer, Singer, and Van Willegen 2006). Participatory processes are not necessarily straightforward, however, and because my research was not designed to be collaborative, I often debated when I should speak up or remain silent and how, if I chose to speak up, my voice would impact my ability to collect valid qualitative data. My presence and actions were likely influencing my fellow volunteers, whom I would later interview and observe, but because I attempted to maintain some degree of separation between anthropologist and volunteer, I lacked the tools to ascertain just how much of an influence my presence had.

Additionally, ethnography is a two-way street, and the anthropologist is changed just as the participant is. When considering how we do our work and what shape our interactions with others will take, we must also consider the danger of the anthropologist being co-opted by the organization and identifying too closely with its mission, purpose, and people (Markowitz 2001). Because the methods of anthropology require personal, face-to-face interaction over long periods of time, it is expected that anthropologists may form close relationships with those they study. Problems arise when we associate so strongly with an organization or its employees that we find it difficult to adhere to our own epistemological and moral standards, particularly when confronted with situations that demand some degree of detachment in order to do the right thing. While I thought that my time in Tanzania was too short for this to be a danger, I recognize the influence that such an association can have on someone, particularly over the long-term.

An anthropologist's engagement in conservation work can also be limited by his or her background and education. In addition to pointing out that the cultural awareness of conservation workers tends to be limited, and that this may hinder their ability to do good conservation work, it is important to recognize that we as anthropologists have deficiencies in skills and knowledge as well. We may lack knowledge about key issues in the fields of biology or ecology for which we chide conservation scientists for their overdependence on. This in turn inhibits our ability to contribute to conservation, a steep learning curve I faced often. While I could advocate for cultural relevancy and local participation, I am not an expert on ecology or biology. My fellow volunteers, while they may have been culturally unaware, had their own scientific contributions to make. We should bear in mind our personal limitations and consider how these can and should influence the ways we choose to engage.

How we engage is thus based on a multitude of considerations. It is complicated by the urgency of the situation, the already uneasy relationships between natural and social scientists, and the multiple levels of obligations and commitments we may confront. We must therefore position ourselves appropriately and purposefully (Markowitz 2001), and this can be challenging. When students in the classroom stared or children on their mothers' laps in the market cried upon seeing me, I felt like a complete outsider. At times I was forced to be a representative for all Americans or all anthropologists, asked to explain why others in my assumedly homogenous group (whatever that might be in the situation) did this or believed that. Still other times I felt compelled to align myself with members of the local community, such as when I attempted to delay the finalization of the education curriculum so that community members could review our work.

These relationships and situational dynamics complicated my ability to keep separate my identities of researcher and volunteer. They also demonstrated to me that separating those identities is both difficult and unnecessary. Even in the face of the dilemmas discussed here and even if we at times have to remain flexible in our choice of methods, rely more or less heavily on our ethics, or simply accept the practical reality of the situation in which we find ourselves, we can find processes for engagement that work. How we choose to work is connected to our personal project, what responsibilities we believe belong to our role as an anthropologist, and the context in which we find ourselves. As a result, our engagement will be personal and particular.

The Way Forward

For some, engagement is an ethical responsibility (Scheper-Hughes 1995). For others, it is "the nature of the mission, rather than any absolutist argument for or against engagement, [that is] key to decision-making when evaluating the goals of the anthropological assignment" (Fluehr-Lobban 2008, 20). Still others consider engagement to be somehow inherent to contemporary anthropology, one component of today's common mélange of activism and academic pursuits (Knauft 2006). If we assume that engagement to some degree is important, if not necessary, then what prevents us from engaging, as is the case of limited anthropological engagement with conservation NGOs? Sillitoe (2007) asks a similar question and concludes that it is the dilemmas that assault the anthropologists that limit their engagement.

Anthropological engagement with conservation INGOs requires a consideration of the ethical and epistemological dilemmas that result from and are simultaneously confounded by the complex, interdisciplinary, multicultural, and urgent nature of environmental conservation. These dilemmas can be found in the differences between anthropologists and conservation scientists as well as in the issues of positionality, commitment, responsibility, and our individual desire for impact. However, if anthropologists are to be increasingly called upon to contribute to the development of environmental initiatives (Charnley and Durham 2013), then we must address these dilemmas by asking ourselves what it means to be engaged and how we can effectively engage in the face of these dilemmas. Based on my experience, I would argue that engagement with conservation INGOs is best conceived as a participatory, deliberate, and personal process geared toward both effective and sustainable conservation solutions and the production of good ethnography.

Engagement inherently leads to contradictions and difficulties, and prescriptive solutions are unavailable or impractical. There are generally more questions than answers. However, with critical reflection we can address those contradictions, "even if the conclusions generated are always partial, contingent, and subject to debate (as they are in all research)" (Speed 2008, 232). Limiting our involvement to cultural critique is no longer advisable for a number of reasons, including the enduring gap between anthropologists and conservation scientists. Understanding is "improved by dialogue across difference" (Tsing 2005, 81), and if our objective is for conservation workers to understand the social world more effectively, we must take part in that dialogue.

Perhaps the most important reason for engagement, however, is a moral one. In the face of such monumental environmental issues, which have the potential for profoundly negative consequences, anthropologists can have an impact. On the African continent and beyond, conservation INGOs are powerful actors, establishing institutions and mechanisms that shape physical, social, and political landscapes (Brockington and Scholfield 2010). They broadcast discourses that often come to dominate the discussion on our natural environment (Garland 2008). Our engagement with conservation INGOs allows us to better understand them as well as the paths to influencing their activities, policies, and goals, and thus conservation outcomes. In Tanzania, I was unable to have a substantial impact, in part because of my approach. Because I was hesitant to believe that I could do good anthropology while doing good, I limited my engagement. While I attempted to solve problems with my fellow volunteers, this was far from the type of collaborative problem solving for which I now argue, an approach that is based on the anthropologist engaging as his or her full self rather than trying to maintain the separation between our identities of researcher and activist.

When considering what engagement looks like, we must remember that the anthropologist is also an individual, with his or her own morals, beliefs, values, proclivities, and experiences. I have come to believe that I should have been more conscious about my engagement, more intentional with how I interacted with those around me. If had engaged in a more collaborative and participatory manner, blurring the lines between volunteer and anthropologists further rather than continually trying to maintain them, I may have been able to have a more positive impact on the organization and conservation generally. Rather than positioning myself as half outsider, half insider, I could have worked more closely with the organization's staff and volunteers and been open about both my personal intentions and professional aspirations. This may have not only reduced delays in the development of the environmental education curriculum or led to better research processes but may have also resulted in a better understanding among my conservation scientist colleagues of the importance of the sociocultural, political, and economic context for conservation. While this would have inevitably altered the data I collected, good ethnography through transparent, reflexive, and documented processes is still possible. I could have also captured different and equally important information based on an iterative dialogue rather than segmented moments of inquiry.

The purpose of this chapter is not to provide a guidebook for engagement with conservation INGOs. Rather, it is to present my experiences, mistakes, and reflections to encourage others to consider deeper forms of engagement based on an intelligent consideration of its relevancy both to anthropology and to conservation. Our choices are deeply professional as well as personal, and the shape our engagement takes will therefore be different. However, perhaps blurring the line between academic and activist is more productive than continually trying to keep them separate. Perhaps blurring the lines positions us both to do better research and to confront significant environmental issues like climate change, wildlife trafficking, and biodiversity loss together with conservation workers.

Note

1. The names used here are pseudonyms to protect the identities and confidentialities of those who participated in this research.

Conclusion

A Second Generation of NGO Anthropology

Christian Vannier and Amanda Lashaw

The scholarship in this book represents a second generation of critical NGO anthropology. Together, contributors to this volume react to and build on a set of conversations that began in the 1990s and examine the symbolic and material power of nongovernmental and nonprofit agencies as institutional actors and distinct social worlds. As Steven Sampson and David Lewis describe in the introduction and chapter 1, respectively, first-generation research grew from diverse anthropology subfields. Critical analyses converged around processes that seemed to capture some distinctive effects of the nearly global "NGO Boom" (Alvarez 1999): the technicalization of political conflicts, the professionalization of social movements, the privatization of state power and resources, the discursive production of "target populations" as needing intervention, the depoliticization of feminist activism, and the proliferation of standardized knowledge practices through which transnational development institutions governed local populations. Whereas some scholars conceptualized NGO worlds as particularly agile, fluid, and innovative social fields that are unusually capable of transcending or breaking down geographical, political, economic, and ethnic barriers, critical scholars saw a vanguard of neoliberal governmentality.

In the second wave of critically theorized research, we are seeing more reflection on the somewhat distinctive methodological dilemmas of NGO ethnography, such as how to contend with the bewildering heterogeneity of collectivities organized under the "NGO" sign; how to manage multiple roles when researchers are engaged in NGO missions as volunteers, consultants, participants, and fellow travelers; how to represent the power and subjectivity of NGO experts who both care for and govern aid recipients; and how to position one's moral commitments in the study of morally charged worlds. We also see in new work more detailed and contextualized accounts of NGOs as vectors of colonialism and capitalism. Whereas first-generation studies drew heavily on theories of neoliberalism and governmentality, recent work attends to some new phenomena that require new explanatory concepts. For instance, current work reflects the stratifications of labor (always racialized and gendered) that structure work in nonprofit sectors. Whereas earlier NGO ethnography emphasized the life-worlds of cosmopolitan professionals serving as experts in the massive aid system, now we are seeing documentation of the moral lives of volunteers, contingent workers, and indigenous professionals. The prevailing contrast between aid workers from the global North and aid recipients from the global South is being complicated as NGOs create career trajectories for locally based activists, academics, and other professionals. Moreover, studies are tracing social networks that distinguish elite NGO workers from their vulnerable and exploited counterparts. Many chapters in this volume capture middle-class actors struggling with what it means to "do good" in bad worlds. As anthropologists innovate ways to focus directly on middle-class NGO workers (rather than on their so-called target populations), ethnographies are telling us more about political economies based on both professional and volunteer labor, about the ethnic (and not just technical) basis of problem-posing authority, and about counterhegemonic activist strategies for creatively exploiting neoliberal systems.

A second thread of new inquiry reflects the fact that, across the globe, NGOs have saturated fields of "doing good" for some time now. Whether already established in a locale or new to a locale, NGOs operate through thickened layers of NGO history, identity, and reputation that are creatively deployed by diverse groups of actors. Many people and many anthropologists view this history, identity, and reputation not through an aura of virtue, but through a sober analysis of failed projects, broken promises, resources extracted, cultures stolen, and even, as Bernal remarks (this volume), research fatigue. A third line of new research intersects with the rise of moral anthropology and examines ethical culture in NGOs, moral economies of suffering, and transformations of religious notions of care. Chapters in this volume highlight the overlapping moral and political economies that structure NGO fields of practice. Prominent in the work presented here, we see that academic and activist critiques are particularly effective against organizations that claim a moral legitimacy based on representation of particular communities and particularly evident in faith-based or religious organizations.

Despite the diversity of research contexts, contributors to this volume are united in a critical awareness of their position and how this affects field relationships, data collection, and writing. All contributors contend with situatedness in their research, some more explicitly, some more implicitly.

Across all contributions and the reflexivity demanded of them, we detect four strategies of analysis that reflect distinctly anthropological perspectives on the value of studying NGO practices.

NGO Anthropology: Four Strategies of Analysis

1. Unsettling Received Moral Categories

Lemons's chapter on the pitfalls of "NGO-dependent" ethnography force-fully argues that the virtue of anthropological inquiry is its capacity to interrogate and disrupt received categories that obscure power relations. She urges scholars in the field to highlight NGOs as knowledge producers and to negotiate epistemological and methodological dilemmas (which we discuss later) so as to maintain a space for critique and avoid mimicking paradigms of success or failure. Through her description of legal proceedings in a women's arbitration organization in India, she strives to contextualize the organization's particular conception of women's "empowerment" by tying it to processes of population management. The aim of such work is not to expose NGOs as agents of neocolonial power; rather, to enable a reconsideration of just what, exactly, constitutes women's well-being. The challenge to such reflection is that the global power relations in question also make the work of anthropologists possible. The task, then, is "to bring out the contradictions, ambivalences, and ambiguities inherent in our own positions." Her insight into the dangers of mimesis is critical for subfields such as institutional ethnography, where anthropologists often share the epistemological frameworks of their informants.

With a similar eye to problems of ethnographic mimesis, Mouftah challenges anthropologists of religion to question the taken-for-granted category of "faith-based organization," which opposes secular and religious modes of "doing good." Her chapter shows the socially and politically constructed character of the very meaning of religious-based charity, as participants de-emphasize their claim to Islamic virtue to avoid the critical gaze of a non-Islamist government regime. In this same vein, Kapusta-Pofahl's chapter unsettles the category of "gender equality," Sinervo's disrupts "poor Peruvian children," and Kornfeld challenges the construct of "politically neutral aid." The motivations cutting across these works are to unveil the processes and power relations behind naming social categories and to show the contingency of social practices in NGO fields.

2. Highlighting the Production of Progressive Power Formations

Some of the chapters represent the potential for anthropology to highlight distinctively progressive modes of power. To step beyond the first generation of studies, they push back on the tendency to reduce NGO effects to the installation of neoliberalism. Vetta, for example, argues that NGOs are "key symbolic operators of a distinct ideological field" and demonstrates that enactment of values surrounding "democracy" and "freedom" takes place in existing nationalistic contexts that absorb and assimilate these enactments. Kornfeld's aim is to show that New Orleans Jews who are united by their commitment to helping black victims of Hurricane Katrina are also ideologically divided by the degree of "political" action that they find acceptable. He aims not only to denaturalize the apparently universal good of humanitarian assistance, but also to show, through a historical account of Jewish philanthropy in the city, how a dominant progressive institution maintains power and a certain moral identity by marginalizing more critical Jewish activists. For several contributors to this volume, activists play central roles in political negotiations over representation, service delivery, and advocacy. These analyses lay bare the view of NGO worlds as spaces of struggle among left-of-center radicals and moderates, locals and foreigners. Whereas Kapusta-Pofahl describes the ideological ambivalence of postsocialist Czech activists in their engagement of academics as activists and the use of scholarship to negotiate meanings of gender equality, Synková details how Czech NGOs avoid activities that are overtly activist or radical since they are too often tied to distinct ideologies and threaten fragile relationships with authorities. Altogether, analyses presented here upset any perception of homogeneity within or between advocacy NGOs. Rather, they illuminate the messiness and contradictions inherent to the strategies, motivations, and commitments of multiple actors engaging one another in often competitive fields of "doing good."

3. Examining How the NGO Identity Stabilizes Power Formations

A third strategy for NGO anthropology lies in examining how power formations hold together despite fundamental contradictions and tensions. Many contributors find that the NGO narratives of civic action, democratization, human rights, and the like play a prominent role in stabilizing contentious fields. The "NGO" identity itself also masks the legal and social contradictions that enable the form. As Bernal remarks in her chapter in this book, the identity articulates otherwise opposite categories: "NGOs are at once nongovernmental and governmental, deeply local and inherently foreign, an expression of the global South and an instrument of the global North, grassroots and elitist, expanding possibilities for women's activism, and yet also limiting those possibilities." Her approach is to shift focus from technical rationalities as stabilizers, which has dominated previous literature on NGOs, toward the ambiguous social relations, intense energy, and ambitious imaginaries that made the NGO form popular at a particular time in Tanzania. She posits that understanding "NGO fever" is critical to understanding the sturdiness of neoliberal hegemony. Relatedly, Vetta's chapter historicizes the so-called democratization of political culture in Serbia by showing that narratives of building an independent civil society flourish alongside—not in place of—old power networks. Here, the contradictions of an antinationalist nationalism are held together by the continuities of authoritarian and neoliberal statecraft.

Sinervo's chapter shows participants commenting directly on how the label "NGO" shapes the political economy of children's services in Peru. The director of Children for Change creatively makes use of the organizational form while fiercely rejecting the implied and material dependence on foreign aid. As such, we see a grounded critique of "NGOism." At the same time, though, the director reinforces the structuring effects of volunteer tourism by extracting social and cultural capital from the encounters between local children and foreign volunteers. This third strategy of analysis emphasizes that the virtue of ethnography is not to illuminate the secret workings of power, rather to understanding the production of its self-justification.

4. Reflecting on Possibilities for Doing Good

A number of contributors see NGO anthropology as an opportunity to reflect on possibilities for building movements, for improving social and economic advancement projects, and for otherwise trying to do good in the world. Woomer's chapter implores NGO ethnographers to get involved with the action. She reflects on the dilemmas of working with an environmental conservation organization in Tanzania in order to demonstrate that anthropologists can help NGO workers see past the practical limitations that block their work. She argues that critique aimed merely at anthropological knowledge production is a luxury in postcolonial, multicultural, interdisciplinary, and demanding contexts in which rapid action is imperative. That said, she argues that anthropologists do not have to be squeamish about confronting dilemmas they see in organizational life.

Although Woomer's commitment to applied NGO anthropology is more overt, Kapusta-Pofahl's chapter shares an interest in improving the efforts under study. She describes the detailed, historical collaboration between participants in academic gender studies and women's activist NGOs in the Czech Republic to show that, in the absence of a mass movement, women's advocacy networks must contend with governance by state and supranational bodies. Having laid out the complex of players struggling to define gender equality, her purpose is to explore the benefits and pitfalls of academic-NGO collaboration under such conditions. Synková, for her part, develops a triangular comparison of groups purporting to represent the interests of Roma facing housing evictions in the Czech Republic and engenders a rich portrait of political perspectives for readers. She amplifies the critique of left-wing activists to highlight the assimilationist politics that unite two apparently different NGO groups. She ultimately argues that the hybrid network formed by all three groups can strengthen both the reformist and revolutionary tendencies of advocacy. In her study, the smaller activist organizations and other "revolutionists" were most active during the critical moments of public protests, while the "reformist" NGOs were more interested in negotiating technicalities of the housing policy and implementing them. She notes that keeping the political network together, however, requires effective mechanisms of communication and not losing sight of making real change. This fourth value to anthropology represents an open recognition that many anthropologists seek to do good when doing ethnography—from participant observation through writing up research. Many contributors to this volume discuss the hazards of such overt engagements, no matter the motivations that lie behind them.

The Value of NGO Anthropology

Altogether, the current trends in NGO anthropology offer the discipline an intense microscopic view of the power dimensions inherent to all anthropological research and representation. The lessons in epistemology and methodology offered in this volume speak to these dimensions and the role of the anthropologist in creating them, purposefully or not. Groups engaged in NGOs or outside authorities (e.g., the state, donors) may use or deploy anthropological representations in ways unintended by the anthropologist who produced them. Though anthropologists encounter this dilemma in many different research contexts, the shared epistemological frameworks, a shared sense of mission, and the frequent academic backgrounds of NGO employees all heighten this hazard for anthropologists conducting research in or alongside NGOs. As such, ethnographic participation in the social fields of NGOs, as well as the ethnographic works produced by the anthropologist, often hold direct and immediate consequences for vulnerable populations under study and for the NGO and its employees or volunteers. For these reasons, NGO anthropology is in a position to force us to confront the consequences of our work that are inherent to our participation in the social worlds of others.

This participation, even if indirect, is political and impactful. A value that NGO anthropology holds for the discipline of anthropology is a deep recognition of this aspect of our work. Indeed, the hallmark of ethnographic engagement with NGOs is the extent of reflexivity it requires of anthropologists to understand and contend with their own roles. Anthropologists always create representations that are influenced by personal dispositions and political situation; however, the moral charge and social stakes of NGO work exacerbate common quandaries surrounding trust, access, accountability, and representation, as Erica Bornstein's introduction to part III in this volume makes plain. Ethnographers must create clear boundaries around their multifaceted roles as employee, volunteer, and researcher, adopting an insider stance in some contexts, an outsider stance in others. NGO anthropology forces anthropologists to build the terms of their engagement into their research design through a reflexivity that must be constantly and consistently reassessed. Anthropologists engaged with NGOs recognize that conditions surrounding their engagement will impact their research study from field introductions, through data collection and analysis, and into write-up. Moreover, because NGOs contribute to shifting landscapes of power and, simultaneously, to anthropologists' perceptions and analyses of them, anthropologists must interrogate and disrupt the categories and frames constructed by NGOs that obscure the shaping of these landscapes. This must be done in a way that avoids the dangers inherent to identifying with the mission, purpose, and people of the organizations, even when researchers and informants share a moral point of view. Ethnographers must situate themselves and their research in such a way that enables the production of critiques that do not entirely reject or accept the premises under which the NGO operates and create anthropological representations in a collaborative manner that is neither wholly harmonized with how groups represent themselves nor wholly separated.

Other anthropologists have faced similar challenges and questions for quite some time. What seems new are the proliferation of NGOs in almost every corner of the world and the subsequent changes in the social and political landscapes this proliferation often heralds. There is no doubt that engagements between NGOs and anthropologists have multiplied and intensified. This intensification, coupled with the diversity of NGO forms that anthropologists encounter, requires equally diverse methodologies and steadfast commitments to our ethics and mission. Moving forward, the issues and lines of inquiry raised in this volume will demand greater and greater recognition. Contributors to this volume have issued challenges and offered answers that pertain not only to the anthropological study of NGOs, but to anthropologists engaged in the contemporary, globalized field more generally.

References Cited

Abdelrahman, Maha. 2004. *Civil Society Exposed: The Politics of NGOs in Egypt*. New York: I. B. Taurus.

Abramson, David. 1999. "A Critical Look at NGOs and Civil Society as Means to an End in Uzbekistan." *Human Organization* 58 (3): 240–50.

Abu-Lughod, Lila. 1999. *Veiled Sentiments: Honor and Poetry in a Bedouin Society*. Berkeley: University of California Press.

Acosta, Raúl. 2004. "The Halfhearted Politics of NGOs." Paper presented at NGO Study Group Seminar, Ethnography of NGOs: Understanding Organizational Processes, Oxford, UK, April 28.

———. 2012. "Scaling Claims of Common Good: Transnational and Intercultural Advocacy in the Brazilian Amazon." MMG Working Paper 12-03. Göttingen: Max Planck Institute for the Study of Religious and Ethnic Diversity.

Action Aid India. 2016. Accessed February 12, 2017. www.actionaid.org/india.

Action India. 2016. Accessed February 12, 2017. www.action-india.org/.

Adams, Vincanne. 2013. *Markets of Sorrow, Labors of Faith*. Durham, NC: Duke University Press.

Agrama, Hussein Ali. 2012. *Questioning Secularism: Islam, Sovereignty, and the Rule of Law in Modern Egypt*. Chicago: University of Chicago Press.

Ahmed, Sara. 2004. *The Cultural Politics of Emotion*. New York: Routledge.

Alexander-Block, Benjamin. 2013. "Department of Justice and St. Bernard Settle in Post-Hurricane Katrina Housing Discrimination Case." *Times Picayune*. May 10. Accessed January 10, 2013. www.nola.com/crime/index.ssf/2013/05/-department_of_justice_and_st_b.html.

Allahyari, Rebecca Anne. 2000. *Visions of Charity: Volunteer Workers and Moral Community*. Berkeley: University of California Press.

Alvaré, Bretton. 2010. "Babylon Makes the Rules: Compliance, Fear, and Self-Discipline in the Quest for Official NGO Status." *PoLAR: Political and Legal Anthropology Review* 33 (2): 178–200.

Alvarez, Sonia. 1999. "Advocating Feminism: The Latin American Feminist NGO 'Boom.'" *International Feminist Journal of Politics* 1 (2): 181–209.

American Anthropological Association. "AAA Statements on Ethics." Accessed March 23, 2017. http://www.americananthro.org/ParticipateAndAdvocate/Content.aspx?ItemNumber=1656.

Anderson, Benedict. 1991 [1983]. *Imagined Communities*. London: Verso.

Appadurai, Arjun. 2002. "Deep Democracy: Urban Governmentality and the Horizon of Politics." *Public Culture* 14 (1): 21–47.

Apthorpe, Raymond. 1997. "Writing Development Policy." In *Anthropology and Policy*, edited by Cris Shore and Susan Wright, 42–58. London: Routledge.

Armstrong, Hyacinth G. 2005. "Environmental Education in Tobago's Primary Schools: A Case Study of Coral Reef Education." *International Journal of Tropical Biology* 53 (1): 229–38.

Arnove, Robert F., and Harvey J. Graff, eds. 1987. *National Literacy Campaigns: Historical and Comparative Perspectives*. New York: Plenum Press.

Asad, Talal. 1975. Introduction to *Anthropology and the Colonial Encounter*, edited by Talal Asad, 9–19. New York: Humanities Press.

———. 1993. *Genealogies of Religion*. Baltimore: Johns Hopkins University Press.

———. 2002. "Reading a Modern Classic: W. C. Smith's 'The Meaning and End of Religion.'" In *Religion and Media*, edited by Hent de Vries and Samuel Weber, 131–47. Stanford: Stanford University Press.

———. 2012. "Thinking about Religion, Belief, and Politics." In *The Cambridge Companion to Religious Studies*, edited by Robert Orsi, 36–57. Cambridge: Cambridge University Press.

Asad, Talal, Wendy Brown, Judith Butler, and Saba Mahmood. 2009. *Is Critique Secular? Blasphemy, Injury, and Free Speech*. Berkeley: Townsend Center for the Humanities.

Aswat Masraya. 2015. "Egypt Shuts Down 50 NGOs for Brotherhood Ties." Accessed May 26, 2015. http://en.aswatmasriya.com/news/view.aspx?id=a7e57a0a-2abc-4fab-b5d3-a048c8cff1ae&mc_cid=7e771854f6&mc_eid=a813c0ff6e.

Atalay, Sonya. 2014. "Engaging Archaeology: Positivism, Objectivity, and Rigor in Activist Archaeology." In *Transforming Archaeology: Activist Practices and Prospects*, edited by Sonya Atalay, Lee Rains Clauss, Randall H. McGuire, and John R. Welch, 47. New York: Routledge.

Atia, Mona. 2007. "In Whose Interest? Financial Surveillance and the Circuits of Exception in the War on Terror." *Environment and Planning D: Society and Space* 25(3): 447–75.

———. 2012. "'A Way to Paradise': Pious Neoliberalism, Islam, and Faith-Based Development." *Annals of the Association of American Geographers* 102 (4): 808.

———. 2013. *Building a House in Heaven: Pious Neoliberalism and Islamic Charity in Egypt*. Minneapolis: University of Minnesota Press.

Aufseeser, Dena. 2014. "Control, Protection and Rights: A Critical Review of Peru's Begging Bill." *International Journal of Children's Rights*. 22: 241–67.

Baaz, Maria Eriksson. 2005. *The Paternalism of Partnership: A Postcolonial Reading of Identity in Development Aid*. London: Zed Books.

Bahree, Megha. 2014. "Modi Government's Message to the NGOs in India: Big Brother Is Watching You." *Forbes*, June 16. Accessed March 31, 2016. www.forbes

.com/sites/meghabahree/2014/06/16/modi-governments-message-to-ngos-in
-india-big-brother-is-watching-you.

Bakić-Hayden, Milica. 1995. "Nesting Orientalisms: The Case of Former Yugoslavia." *Slavic Review* 54 (4): 917–31.

Ballon, Eduardo. 2011. "Decentralization." In *Fractured Politics: Peruvian Democracy Past and Present*, edited by J. Crabtree, 187–216. London: University of London Press.

Banks, Sarah. 2006. *Ethics and Values in Social Work*. Basingstoke, UK: Palgrave.

Basu, Srimati. 2015. *The Trouble with Marriage: Feminists Confront Law and Violence in India*. Berkeley: University of California Press.

Bebbington, Anthony. 2005. "Donor-NGO Relations and Representations of Livelihood in Nongovernmental Aid Chains." *World Development* 33 (6): 937–50.

Bender, Courtney, and Ann Taves. 2012. *What Matters?: Ethnographies of Value in a Not So Secular Age*. New York: Columbia University Press.

Bennett, John W. 1996. "Applied and Action Anthropology: Ideological and Conceptual Aspects." *Current Anthropology* 36: S23–S53.

Benthall, Jonathan. 2007. "The Overreaction against Islamic Charities." *Islam Review* 20: 2.

Benthall, Jonathan, and Jérôme Bellion-Jourdan. 2009. *The Charitable Crescent: Politics of Aid in the Muslim World*. New York: I. B. Tauris.

Berger, Julia. 2003. "Religious Nongovernmental Organizations: An Exploratory Analysis." *Voluntas: International Journal of Voluntary and Nonprofit Organizations* 14 (1): 15–39.

Berlant, Lauren. 2011. *Cruel Optimism*. Durham, NC: Duke University Press.

Berman, Lila C. 2015. "Donor Advised Funds in Historical Perspective." *Boston College Law Forum on Philanthropy and the Public Good* 1: 5–27.

Bernal, Victoria, and Inderpal Grewal. 2014a. "The NGO Form: Feminist Struggles, States, and Neoliberalism." In *Theorizing NGOs: States, Feminisms, and Neoliberalism*, edited by Bernal, Victoria and Inderpal Grewal, 1–18. Durham, NC: Duke University Press.

———, eds. 2014b. *Theorizing NGOs: States, Feminisms, and Neoliberalism*. Durham, NC: Duke University Press.

Bierschenk, Thomas, and Jean-Pierre Olivier de Sardan. 1993. "Les Courtiers Locaux du Développement." *Bulletin de l´APAD* 5: 71–76.

Billis, David. 2010. *Hybrid Organizations and the Third Sector. Challenges for Practice, Theory and Policy*. New York: Palgrave Macmillan.

Blundo, Giorgio. 1995. "Les Courtiers Du Développement En Milieu Rural Sénégalais." *Cahiers d'Études Africaines* 35 (137): 73–99.

Boissevain, Jeremy. 1974. *Friends of Friends: Networks, Manipulators and Coalitions*. Oxford: Basil Blackwell.

Bonner, Michael David, Mine Ener, and Amy Singer, eds. 2003. *Poverty and Charity in Middle Eastern Contexts*. Albany: State University of New York Press.

Bornstein, Erica. 2003. *The Spirit of Development: Protestant NGOs, Morality, and Economics in Zimbabwe*. New York: Routledge.

———. 2005. *The Spirit of Development: Protestant NGOs, Morality, and Economics in Zimbabwe.* Stanford CA: Stanford University Press.

———. 2012a. *Disquieting Gifts: Humanitarianism in New Delhi.* Stanford, CA: Stanford University Press.

———. 2012b. "Volunteer Experience." In *What Matters?: Ethnographies of Value in a Not So Secular Age,* edited by Courtney Bender and Ann Taves, 119–43. New York: Columbia University Press.

Bornstein, Erica, and Aradhana Sharma. 2016. "The Righteous and the Rightful: The Technomoral Politics of Nonstate and State Actors in Contemporary India." *American Ethnologist* 43 (1): 76–90.

Bourdieu, Pierre. 1994. "Stratégies de Reproduction et Modes de Domination." *Actes de la Recherche en Sciences Sociales* 105 (4): 3–12.

Bouvard, Marguerite Guzman. 1996. *Gertrude Mongella.* In *Women Reshaping Human, Rights: How Extraordinary Activists Are Changing the World,* edited by Marguerite Guzman Bouvard, 221–34. Wilmington, DE: SR Books.

Brockington, Dan. 2006. "The Politics and Ethnography of Environmentalisms in Tanzania." *African Affairs* 105 (418): 97–116.

Brockington, Dan, and Katherine Scholfield. 2010. "The Conservationist Mode of Production and Conservation NGOs in Sub-Saharan Africa." *Antipode* 42 (3): 551–75.

Bromley, Rosemary D. F., and Peter K. Mackie. 2008. "Identifying the Role of Children in Informal Trade: Evidence for Urban Policy." *International Development Planning Review* 30 (2): 113–31.

Brosius, J. Peter. 1999. "Analyses and Interventions: Anthropological Engagement with Environmentalism." *Current Anthropology* 40 (3): 277–309.

———. 2006. "Common Ground between Anthropology and Conservation Biology." *Conservation Biology* 20 (3): 683–85.

———. 2008. "Green Dots, Pink Hearts: Displacing Politics from the Malaysian Rainforest." In *Environmental Anthropology: A Historical Reader,* edited by Michael R. Dove and Carol Carpenter, 363–92. Malden, MA: Blackwell Publishing.

Brosius, J. Peter, and Diane Russell. 2003. "Conservation from Above: An Anthropological Perspective on Transboundary Protected Areas and Ecoregional Planning." *Journal of Sustainable Forestry* 17 (1/2): 39–65.

Brosius, J. Peter, Anna Lowenhaupt Tsing, and Charles Zerner. 1998. "Representing Communities: Histories and Politics of Community-Based Natural Resource Management." *Society and Natural Resources* 11: 157–68.

Brown, Keith. 2006. *Transacting Transition: The Micropolitics of Democracy Assistance in the Former Yugoslavia.* Bloomfield, CT: Kumarian Press.

Brož, Miroslav. 2012. "Otevřený dopis organizaci Člověk v tísni k situaci v Předlickém ghettu" (Open letter to the organization people in need concerning the situation of the ghetto in Předlice). Deník Referendum, November 6. Accessed December 15, 2014. http://denikreferendum.cz/clanek/14289-otevreny-dopis-organizaci-clovek-v-tisni-k-situaci-v-predlickem-ghettu.

Butcher, Jim, and Peter Smith. 2010. "'Making a Difference': Volunteer Tourism and Development." *Tourism Recreation Research* 35 (1): 27–36.

Butler, Judith. 2009. *Undoing Gender*. New York: Routledge.

Čada, Karel, and Kateřina Ptáčková. 2014. "Between Clients and Bureaucrats: An Ambivalent Position of NGOs in the Social Inclusion Agenda in Czech Statutory Cities." *Policy and Society* 33: 129–39.

Campanella, Thomas J. 2006. "Urban Resilience and the Recovery of New Orleans." *Journal of the American Planning Association* 72 (2): 141–46.

Campoamor, Leigh M. 2012. "Public Childhoods: Street Labor, Family, and the Politics of Progress in Peru." PhD diss., Duke University.

Caplan, Pat. 2003. "Anthropology and Ethics." In *The Ethics of Anthropology: Debates and Dilemmas*, edited by Pat Caplan, 1–33. New York: Routledge.

Castelli, Elizabeth A. 2007. "Theologizing Human Rights: Christian Activism and the Limits of Religious Freedom." In *Nongovernmental Politics*, edited by Michel Feher, 673–87. Cambridge, MA: Zone Books.

Černý, Jan. 2013. "Nejsme politická organizace. S Janem Černým nejen o sociální práci" (We are not a political organization. With Jan Černý about social work). *A2* (7): 20.

Chapin, Mac. 2004. "A Challenge to Conservationists." *World Watch* November/December, 17–31.

Charnley, Susan, and William H. Durham. 2013. "Anthropology and Environmental Policy: Joint Solutions for Conservation and Sustainable Livelihoods." In *Environmental Anthropology: Future Directions*, edited by Helena Kopnin and Eleanor Shoreman-Ouimet, 266–97. New York: Routledge.

Choudry, Aziz, and Dip Kapoor. 2013. *NGOization: Complicity, Contradictions, and Prospects*. London: Zed Books.

Chowdhry, Prem. 2007. *Contentious Marriages, Eloping Couples: Gender, Caste, and Patriarchy in Northern India*. New Delhi: Oxford University Press.

Clark, Janine A. 2004. *Islam, Charity, and Activism Middle-Class Networks and Social Welfare in Egypt, Jordan, and Yemen*. Bloomington: Indiana University Press.

Clarke, Gerard, and Michael Jennings, eds. 2008. *Development, Civil Society and Faith-Based Organizations: Bridging the Sacred and the Secular*. New York: Palgrave Macmillan.

Clarke, John. 2008. "Living with/in and without Neo-Liberalism." *Focaal Journal of Global and Historical Anthropology* 51: 135–47.

Člověk v tísni. 2013. "Přes ideologické brýle. Ke kritice Člověka v tísni" (Through the ideological lenses. To the critique of people in need). *A2* (8): 28.

Cohen, Steven M. 1980. "Trends in Jewish Philanthropy." *American Jewish Year Book* 80: 31.

———. 2011. "From Jewish People to Jewish Purpose: Establishment Leaders and Their Nonestablishment Successors." In *The New Jewish Leaders*, edited by Jack Wertheimer, 45–83. Waltham, MA: Brandeis University Press.

Comaroff, Jean, and John Comaroff. 1999. *Civil Society and the Political Imagination in Africa: Critical Perspectives*. Chicago: University of Chicago.

Cook, Thomas J., and Ivo Spalatin. 2002. *Final Evaluation of OTI's program in Serbia-Montenegro*. Arlington, VA: Development Associates.

Costa, LeeRay. 2014. "Power and Difference in Thai Women's NGO Activism." In

Theorizing NGOs: States, Feminisms, and Neoliberalism, edited by Victoria Bernal and Inderpal Grewal, 166 92. Durham, NC: Duke University Press.

Crewe, Emma, and Elizabeth Harrison. 1998. *Whose Development? An Ethnography of Aid*. New York: Zed Books.

Czech Academy of Sciences. 2016. "Gender and Sociology." Accessed August 13, 2016. www.soc.cas.cz/en/department/gender-sociology.

Daily News (Tanzania). 1999. Accessed February 24.

Dave, Naisargi. 2012. *Queer Activism in India: A Story in the Anthropology of Ethics*. Durham, NC: Duke University Press.

Davis, Coralynn. 2003. "Feminist Tigers and Patriarchal Lions: Rhetorical Strategies and Instrumental Effects in the Struggle for Definition and Control over Development in Nepal." *Meridians: Feminism, Race, Transnationalism* 3 (2): 204–49.

Deeb, Hadi Nicholas, and George Marcus. 2011. "In the Green Room: An Experiment in Ethnographic Method at the WTO." *PoLAR: Political and Legal Anthropology Review* 34 (1): 51–76.

Delcore, Henry D. 2003. "Nongovernmental Organizations and the Work of Memory in Northern Thailand." *American Ethnologist* 30 (1): 61–84.

DeTemple, Jill. 2005. *Building Faith: Christianity, Development Organizations and Community in Highland Ecuador*. Chapel Hill: University of North Carolina Press.

———. 2006. "'Haiti Appeared at My Church': Faith-Based Organizations, Transnational Activism, and Tourism in Sustainable Development." *Urban Anthropology and Studies of Cultural Systems and World Economic Development* 35 (2/3): 155–81.

Dickman, A. J. 2010. "Complexities of Conflict: The Importance of Considering Social Factors for Effectively Resolving Human-Wildlife Conflict." *Animal Conservation* 13: 458–66.

DIRCETUR. 2007. *Boletín Estadístico de Turismo 2007*. Cusco, Peru: Dirección Regional de Comercio Exterior y Turismo-Cusco.

Dove, Michael R., and Carol Carpenter. 2008. "Major Historical Currents in Environmental Anthropology." In *Environmental Anthropology: A Historical Reader*, edited by Michael R. Dove and Carol Carpenter, 1–88. Malden, MA: Blackwell Publishing.

Dzenovska, Dace. 2015. "'Know Your Diaspora!' Knowledge Production and Governing Capacity in the Context of Latvian Diaspora Politics." In *Diasporas Reimagined: Spaces, Practices and Belonging*, edited by Nando Sigona Alan Gamlen, Giulia Liberatore, and Helen Neveu Kringelbach, 190–93. Oxford: Oxford University Press.

Eaton, Kent. 2010. "Subnational Economic Nationalism? The Contradictory Effects of Decentralization in Peru." *Third World Quarterly* 31 (7): 1205–22.

———. 2015. "Disciplining Regions: Subnational Contention in Neoliberal Peru." *Territory, Politics, Governance* 3 (2): 124–46.

Edelman, Marc. 2001. "Social Movements: Changing Paradigms and Forms of Politics." *Annual Review of Anthropology* 30: 285–317.

———. 2005. "When Networks Don't Work: The Rise and Fall of Civil Society Initiatives in Central America." In *Social Movements: An Anthropological Reader*, edited by June Nash, 29–45. London: Blackwell.

Einhorn, Barbara. 2010 [2006]. *Citizenship in an Enlarging Europe: From Dream to Awakening*. London: Palgrave Macmillan.

Elazar, Daniel. 1995 [1976]. *Community and Polity: The Organizational Dynamics of American Jewry*. Philadelphia: Jewish Publications Society of America.

Elisha, Omri. 2011. *Moral Ambition: Mobilization and Social Outreach in Evangelical Megachurches*. Berkeley: University of California Press.

Elyachar, Julia. 2005. *Markets of Dispossession: NGOs, Economic Development, and the State in Cairo*. Durham, NC: Duke University Press.

Ener, Mine 2003. *Managing Egypt's Poor and the Politics of Benevolence, 1800–1952*. Princeton, NJ: Princeton University Press.

Engel-Di Mauro, Salvatore, ed. 2006. *The European's Burden: Global Imperialism in EU Expansion*. New York: Peter Lang Publishers.

Englund, Harri. 2011. "The Anthropologist and His Poor." In *Humanitarianisms between Ethics and Politics*, edited by Erica Bornstein and Peter Redfield, 71–93. Santa Fe: SAR Press.

Equal Opportunity for All Trust Fund (EOTF). 2016. Accessed August 13, 2016. www.envaya.org/eotf.

Erdely, Jennifer L. 2011. "When the Saints Go Marching In: An Ethnography of Volunteer Tourism in Post-Katrina New Orleans." PhD diss., Louisiana State University.

Escobar, Arturo. 1995. *Encountering Development: The Making and Unmaking of the Third World*. Princeton, NJ: Princeton University Press.

———. 1998. "Whose Knowledge, Whose Nature? Biodiversity, Conservation, and the Political Ecology of Social Movements." *Journal of Political Ecology* 5: 53–82.

Fassin, Didier. 2011. "Noli Me Tangere: The Moral Untouchability of Humanitarianism." In *Forces of Compassion: Humanitarianism between Ethics and Politics*, edited by Erica Bornstein and Peter Redfield, 35–52. Santa Fe: School for Advanced Research Press.

———. 2012. *Humanitarian Reason: A Moral History of the Present*. Berkeley: University of California Press.

Fassin, Didier, and Mariella Pandolfi, eds. 2010. *Contemporary States of Emergency: The Politics of Military and Humanitarian Interventions*. New York: Zone Books.

———. 2013. *Contemporary States of Emergency: The Politics of Military and Humanitarian Interventions*. New York: Zone Books.

Fechter, Anne-Meike, and Hindman, Heather, eds. 2011. *Inside the Everyday Lives of Aidworkers: The Challenges and Futures of Aidland*. Sterling, VA: Kumarian Press.

Feldman, Ilana, and Miriam Iris Ticktin, eds. 2010. *In the Names of Humanity: The Government of Threat and Care*. Durham, NC: Duke University Press.

Ferguson, James. 1994. *The Anti-Politics Machine: "Development," Depoliticization, and Bureaucratic Power in Lesotho*. Minneapolis: University of Minnesota Press.

———. 2005. "Anthropology and Its Evil Twin: "Development" in the Constitution of a Discipline." In *The Anthropology of Development and Globalization: From Classical Political Economy to Contemporary Neoliberalism*, edited by Marc Edelman and Angelique Haugerud, 140–53. Malden, MA: Blackwell Publishing.

Ferguson, James, and Akhil Gupta. 2002. "Spatializing States: Toward an Ethnography of Neoliberal Governmentality." *American Ethnologist* 29 (4): 981–1002.

Finger, Davida. 2008. "Stranded and Squandered: Lost on the Road Home." *Seattle Journal for Social Justice* 7 (1): 59–100.

Fisher, William F. 1997. "Doing Good? The Politics and Antipolitics of NGO Practices." *Annual Review of Anthropology* 26: 439–64.

———. 2010. "Civil Society and Its Fragments." In *Varieties of Activist Experience: Civil Society in South Asia*, edited by David N. Gellner, 250–68. London: Sage.

Flaherty, Jordan. 2010. *Floodlines: Community and Resistance from Katrina to the Jena Six*. Chicago: Haymarket Books.

Fluehr-Lobban, Carolyn. 2008. "Anthropology and Ethics in America's Declining Imperial Age." *Anthropology Today* 24 (4): 18–22.

Foucault, Michel. 1997. *The Politics of Truth*. Cambridge, MA: MIT Press

Fountain, Philip. 2011. "Orienting Guesthood in the Mennonite Central Committee, Indonesia." In *Inside the Lives of Everyday Development Workers: The Challenges and Futures of Aidland*, edited by Anne Meike-Fechter and Heather Hindman, 83–106. Sterling, VA: Kumarian Press.

Freidus, Andrea. 2010. "'Saving' Malawi: Faithful Responses to Orphans and Vulnerable Children." *NAPA Bulletin* 33 (1): 50–67.

Freund, Michael. 1931. "The Community Chest and Its Influence on the Jewish Community." *Jewish Social Service Quarterly*, June.

Friedman, Jonathan. 2008. "Indigeneity: Anthropological Notes on a Historical 'Variable.'" In *Indigenous Peoples: Self-Determination, Knowledge, Indigeneity*, edited by Henry Minde, 29–48. Delft, Netherlands: Eburon.

Gagné, Natasha. 2009. "The Political Dimensions of Coexistence." *Anthropological Theory* 9 (2): 33–58.

Gal, Susan, and Gail Kligman. 2000. *The Politics of Gender after Socialism*. Princeton, NJ: Princeton University Press.

Galanter, Marc, and Upendra Baxi. 1979. "Panchayat Justice: An Indian Experiment in Legal Access." In *Access to Justice*. Vol. 3, *Emerging Issues and Perspectives*, edited by M. Cappelletti and B. Garth, 341–86. Milan: Guiffre; Alphen aan den Rijn: Sijthoff and Noordhoff.

Gardet, Louis. 2012. "Īmān." In *Encyclopaedia of Islam*, edited by P. Bearman, Th. Bianquis, C. E. Bosworth, E. van Donzel, and W. P. Heinrichs. Brill Online. Accessed March 7, 2017. http://referenceworks.brillonline.com.myaccess.library .utoronto.ca/entries/encyclopaedia-of-islam-2/iman-COM_0370.

Gardner, Katy, and David Lewis. 2015. *Anthropology and Development: Challenges for the Twenty-First Century*. London: Pluto.

Garland, Elizabeth. 2008. "The Elephant in the Room: Confronting the Colonial Character of Wildlife Conservation in Africa." *African Studies Review* 51 (3): 51–74.

Gasper, Des. 1997. "'Logical Frameworks': A Critical Assessment Managerial Theory, Pluralistic Practice." Working Paper Series No. 264. The Hague: Institute of Social Studies.

Gay y Blasco, Paloma. 2002. "Gypsy/Roma Diasporas. A Comparative Perspective." *Social Anthropology* 10 (2): 173–88.

Gellner, David N. 2010. "Introduction: Making Civil Society in South Asia." In *Varieties of Activist Experience: Civil Society in South Asia*, edited by David N. Gellner, 1–16. London: Sage.

Gender Studies. 2016. "History of Gender Studies." Accessed August 13, 2016. www.genderstudies.cz/gender-studies/historie.shtml.

Gilbert, Neil. 2005. "The 'Enabling State'? From Public to Private Responsibility for Social Protection, Pathways and Pitfalls." *OECD-Social, Employment and Migration Working Papers 26*. Paris: OECD.

Goldberg, J. J. 1996. *Jewish Power: Inside the American Jewish Establishment*. Reading, MA: Addison Wesley.

Goodenough, Ward H. 1963. *Cooperation in Change: An Anthropological Approach to Community Development*. New York: Russell Sage Foundation.

Government of India. 2011. "Census." Accessed April 11, 2016. www.censusindia.gov.in/2011census/C-01.html.

———. 2016. "NGO Partnership System." Accessed March 31, 2016. http://ngo.india.gov.in/ngo_stateschemes_ngo.php.

Government of India, Industry of Minority Affairs. 2016. "Sachar Committee Report." Accessed April 11 2016. www.minorityaffairs.gov.in/sachar.

Government of India, Ministry of Home Affairs Foreigners Division. 2015a. Cancellation Order, April 6, 2015. Accessed March 7, 2017. http://mha1.nic.in/pdfs/FCRACAncellationOrder_270415.pdf.

———. 2015b. "Contribution (Regulation) Amendment Rules, 2015." Accessed June 17, 2015. http://mha1.nic.in/pdfs/draftamendment_170615.pdf.

———. 2015c. "Making All FCRA Services Online–Regarding," Accessed July 28, 2015. http://mha1.nic.in/pdfs/FCRAOnlineServicesCircular_280715.PDF.

Grewal, Inderpal. 2016. "The Masculinities of Post-Colonial Governance: Bureaucratic Memoirs of the Indian Civil Service." *Modern Asian Studies* 50 (2): 602–35.

Griffin, Gabriele, ed. 2005. *Doing Women's Studies: Employment Opportunities, Personal Impacts and Social Consequences*. London: Zed Books.

Grover, Shalini. 2011. *Marriage, Love, Caste and Kinship Support*. Delhi: Social Science Press.

Guardian (Tanzania). 1999. "Canada to Provide 7.2 m for Human Rights Training." May, 27.

Guilhot, Nicolas. 2005. *The Democracy Makers: Human Rights and the Politics of Global Order*. New York: Columbia University Press.

Gupta, Akhil, and James Ferguson, eds. 1997. *Anthropological Locations: Boundaries and Grounds of a Field Science*. Berkeley: University of California Press.

Gusterson, Hugh. 1997. "Studying Up Revisited." *PoLAR: Political and Legal Anthropology Review* 20 (1): 114–19.

Haas, Ernst B. 1991. "Collective Learning: Some Theoretical Speculations." In *Learning in U.S. and Soviet Foreign Policy*, edited by George W. Breslauer and Philip Tetlock, 62–99. Boulder: Westview Press.

Haenni, Patrick. 2005. *L'Islam de Marché: L'autre Révolution Conservatrice*. Paris: Seuil.

Hafez, Sherine. 2011a. *An Islam of Her Own: Reconsidering Religion and Secularism in Women's Islamic Movements*. New York: New York University Press.

———. 2011b. "Women Developing Women: Islamic Approaches for Poverty Alleviation in Rural Egypt." *Feminist Review* 97 (1): 56–73.

Hale, Charles R. 2006. "Activist Research vs. Cultural Critique: Indigenous Land Rights and the Contradictions of Politically Engaged Anthropology." *Cultural Anthropology* 21 (1): 96–120.

———. 2008. Introduction to *Engaging Contradictions: Theory, Politics, and Methods of Activist Scholarship*, edited by Charles R. Hale, 1–28. Berkeley: University of California Press.

Halkin, Hillel. 2008. "How Not to Repair the World." *Commentary Magazine*, October.

Hamdy, Sherine. 2012. *Our Bodies Belong to God: Organ Transplants, Islam, and the Struggle for Human Dignity in Egypt*. Berkeley: University of California Press.

Haney, Lynne. 2002. *Inventing the Needy: Gender and the Politics of Welfare in Hungary*. Berkeley: University of California Press.

Hann, Chris, ed. 2001. *Postsocialism: Ideals, Ideologies and Practices in Eurasia*. London: Routledge.

Hann, Chris, and Elisabeth Dunn, eds. 1996. *Civil Society: Challenging Western Models*. London: Routledge.

Haraway, Donna. 1991. *Simians, Cyborgs, and Women: The Reinvention of Nature*. New York: Routledge.

Harrigan, Jane, and Hamed El-Said. 2009. *Economic Liberalisation, Social Capital and Islamic Welfare Provision*. New York: Palgrave MacMillan.

Hastrup, Kristen, and Peter Elsass. 1990. "Anthropological Advocacy: A Contradiction in Terms?" *Current Anthropology* 31 (3): 301–11.

Havelková, Hana, and Libora Oates-Indruchová. 2014. *The Politics of Gender Culture under State Socialism: An Expropriated Voice*. London: Routledge.

Hearn, Julie Hewitt. 2007. "African NGOs: The New Compradors?" *Development and Change* 38 (6): 1095–110.

Heemeryck, Antoine. 2010. *L'importation Démocratique En Roumanie*. Paris: L'Harmattan.

Hefferan, Tara. 2007. *Twining Faith and Development: Catholic Parish Partnering in the US and Haiti*. Bloomfield, CT: Kumarian Press.

Hefferan, Tara, Julie Adkins, and Laurie A. Occhipinti, eds. 2009. *Bridging the Gaps: Faith-Based Organizations, Neoliberalism, and Development in Latin America and the Caribbean*. Lanham, MD: Lexington Books.

Helms, Elissa. 2003. "The 'Nation-ing' of Gender? Donor Policies, Islam and Women's NGOs in Post-War Bosnia-Herzegovina." *Anthropology of East Europe Review* 21 (2): 85–92.

Hemment, Julie. 2007. *Empowering Women in Russia: Activism, Aid and NGOs.* Bloomington: Indiana University Press.

Hesse-Biber, Sharlene, and Michelle Yaiser, eds. 2004. *Feminist Perspectives in Social Research.* New York: Oxford University Press.

Hickey, Samuel, and Giles Mohan. 2004. *Participation: From Tyranny to Transformation? Exploring New Approaches to Participation in Development.* London: Zed Books.

Hilhorst, Dorothea. 2003. *The Real World of NGOs: Discourses, Diversity and Development.* London: Zed Books.

Hindle, Charlotte. 2013. *Volunteer: A Traveller's Guide to Making a Difference around the World.* Footscray, Victoria: Lonely Planet.

Hirschkind, Charles. 2006. *The Ethical Soundscape: Cassette Sermons and Islamic Counterpublics.* New York: Columbia University Press.

Ho, Karen. 2009. *Liquidated: An Ethnography of Wall Street.* Durham, NC: Duke University Press.

Hodžić, Saida. 2014. "Feminist Bastards: Toward a Posthumanist Critique of NGO-ization." In *Theorizing NGOs: States, Feminisms, and Neoliberalism*, edited by Victoria Bernal and Inderpal Grewal, 221–47. Durham, NC: Duke University Press.

Howard, Patricia L. 2015. "Women and Plants: Gender Relations in Biodiversity Management and Conservation." In *The Routledge Handbook of Gender and Development*, edited by Anne Coles, Leslie Gray, and Janet Momsen, 117–28. New York: Routledge.

Huberman, Jenny. 2012. *Ambivalent Encounters: Childhood, Tourism, and Social Change in Banaras, India.* New Brunswick, NJ: Rutgers University Press.

Huebler, Friedrich, and Weixin Lu. 2012. "Adult and Youth Literacy, 1990–2015: Analysis of Data for 41 Selected Countries." Montreal: UNESCO Institute for Statistics.

Ibrahim, Barbara, and Dina Sherif. 2008. *From Charity to Social Change: Trends in Arab Philanthropy.* Cairo: American University in Cairo Press.

Igoe, Jim. 2003. "Scaling up Civil Society: Donor Money, NGOs and the Pastoralist Land Rights Movement in Tanzania." *Development and Change* 34 (5): 863–85.

———. 2004. *Conservation and Globalization: A Study of the National Parks and Indigenous Communities from East Africa to South Dakota.* Belmont, CA: Wadsworth/Thomson Learning.

INCITE! Women of Color against Violence, ed. 2007. *The Revolution Will Not Be Funded: Beyond the Non-Profit Industrial Complex.* Cambridge, MA: South End Press.

INEI. 2008. *Perú: Crecimiento y Distribución de la Población, 2007.* Lima: Instituto Nacional de Estadística e Informática.

International Center for Not-for-Profit Law (ICNL). 2013. "The Legal and Regulatory Framework for Civil Society: Global Trends in 2012–2013." *Global Trends in NGO Law: A Quarterly Review of NGO Law around the World* 4 (2). Accessed August 8, 2014. www.icnl.org/research/trends/Global%20Trends%20in%20NGO%20Law%20Final%20October%2016.pdf.

Ishkanian, Armine. 2008. *Democracy Building and Civil Society in Post-Soviet Armenia*. London: Routledge.

Jakimow, Tanya. 2012. *Peddlers of Information: Indian Nongovernmental Organizations in the Information Age*. Sterling, VA: Kumarian Press.

Jakoubek, Marek. 2006. Přemyšlení (rethinking) "Romů" (Rethinking [rethinking] of "Roma"). In *Romové" v osidlech sociálního vyloučení* ("Roma" in the Toils of Social Exclusion), edited by Tomáš Hirt and Marek Jakoubek, 322–400. Plzeň, Czech Rep.: Vydavatelství anakladatelství Aleš Čeněk.

Janoušková, Klára, and Dana Nedělníková, eds. 2008. *Profesní dovednosti terénních pracovníků. Sborník studijních textů pro terénní pracovníky* (Professional skills of field social workers. Collection of study texts for field social workers). Ostrava, Czech Rep.: Ostravskáuniverzita v Ostravě Zdravotně sociální fakulta–Katedra sociální práce.

Jansen, Stef. 2009. "Hope and the State in the Anthropology of Home: Preliminary Notes." *Ethnologica Europaea* 39 (1): 54–60.

Jean-Klein, Iris E. F., and Annelise Riles. 2005. "Introducing Discipline: Anthropology and Human Rights Administration." *PoLAR: Political and Legal Anthropology Review* 28 (2): 173–202.

Jewish Federation of Greater New Orleans. 1941. Minutes of Meeting of Committee on Community Council. Box 111: folder 13. Howard Tilton Memorial Library Special Collections, Tulane University, New Orleans.

———. 2009. "Statement on Housing Discrimination." Accessed February 3, 2014. www.jewishnola.com/page.aspx?id=210255 (page no longer available).

Johnson, Cedric, ed. 2011. *The Neoliberal Deluge: Hurricane Katrina, Late Capitalism, and the Remaking of New Orleans*. Minneapolis: Minnesota University Press.

Joseph, Miranda. 2002. *Against the Romance of Community*. Minneapolis: University of Minnesota Press.

Jung, Dietrich, Marie J. Petersen, and Sara Lei Sparre. 2014. *Politics of Modern Muslim Subjectivities: Islam, Youth, and Social Activism in the Middle East*. New York: Palgrave-MacMillan.

Kamat, Sangeeta. 2002. *Development Hegemony: NGOs and the State in India*. New Delhi, India: Oxford University Press.

Kanarek, Jane. 2009. "What Does *Tikkun Olam* Actually Mean." In *Righteous Indignation: A Jewish Call for Justice*, edited by Or N. Rose, Jo Ellen Green Kaiser, and Margie Klein, 15–22. Woodstock, VT: Jewish Lights Publishing.

Kapusta-Pofahl, Karen. 2002. "Who Would Create a Czech Feminism? Challenging Assumptions in the Process of Creating Relevant Feminisms in the Czech Republic." *Anthropology of East Europe Review* 20 (2): 61–68.

———. 2008. "Legitimating Czech Gender Studies: Articulating Transnational Feminist Expertise in the 'New' Europe." PhD diss., University of Minnesota.

Karim, Lamia. 2011. *Microfinance and Its Discontents: Women in Debt in Bangladesh*. Minneapolis: University of Minnesota Press.

Keck, Margaret, and Kathryn Sikkink. 1998. *Activists beyond Borders: Advocacy Networks in International Politics*. Ithaca, NY: Cornell University Press.

Kelner, Shaul. 2013. "Religious Ambivalence in Jewish American Philanthropy." In *Religion in Philanthropic Organizations: Family, Friend, Foe*, edited by Thomas J. Davis, 28–49. Bloomington: Indiana University Press.

Kelsey, Nola Lee. 2010. *700 Places to Volunteer before You Die: A Traveler's Guide*. Hot Springs, SD: Dogs Eye View Media.

Kenny, Sally. 2002. "Breaking the Silence: Gender Mainstreaming and the Composition of the European Court of Justice." *Feminist Legal Studies* 10 (3): 257–70.

Kerri, James N. 1976. "Studying Voluntary Associations as Adaptive Mechanisms: A Review of Anthropological Perspectives." *Current Anthropology* 17: 23–47.

Kilivata, Vedastus. 1999. *Guardian*, May 3, p. 2.

Kirsch, Stuart. 2010. "Experiments in Engaged Anthropology." *Collaborative Anthropologies* 3: 69–80.

Kitururu, Moses. 1999. "Dar Vows to Cut Down Dependence." Dar es Salaam *Daily News*. February 23, p. 1.

Klein, Naomi. 2007. *The Shock Doctrine: The Rise of Disaster Capitalism*. New York: Palgrave Macmillan.

Knauft, Bruce M. 2006. "Anthropology in the Middle." *Anthropological Theory* 6 (4): 407–30.

Konrad, Monica. 2002. "Pre-symptomatic Networks: Tracking Experts across Medical Science and the New Genetics." In *Elite Cultures: Anthropological Perspectives*, edited by Cris Shore and Stephen Nugent, 227–48. London: Routledge.

Kopnina, Helen. 2012. "Toward Conservation Anthropology: Addressing Anthropocentric Bias in Anthropology." *Dialectical Anthropology* 36: 127–46.

Kranser, Jonathan. 2013. "The Place of Tikkun Olam in American Jewish Life." *Jewish Political Studies Review* 25 (3/4): 59–98.

Krištof, Roman. 2006. "Nezamýšlené důsledky podpory romské 'integrace': aneb Systém 'trvale udržitelného vyloučení'" (Unintended consequences of the support of Romani "integration": or a system of "sustainable exclusion). In *"Romové" v osidlech sociálního vyloučení* ("Roma" in the toils of social exclusion), edited by Tomáš Hirt and Marek Jakoubek, 165–80. Plzeň, Czech Rep.: Aleš Čeněk.

Lacey, Robert, and Jonathan Benthall, eds. 2014. *Gulf Charities and Islamic Philanthropy in the "Age of Terror" and Beyond*. Berlin: Gerlach.

Lakshmi, Rama. 2015. "India Cracks down on Foreign Funding of NGOs." *Guardian*, June 11, 2015, sec. World News. Accessed September 13, 2015. www.theguardian.com/world/2013/jun/11/india-crackdown-foreign-funded-ngos.

Lang, Sabine. 1997. "The NGOization of Feminism." In *Transitions, Environments, Translations: Feminisms in International Politics*, edited by D. Keates, 101–20. New York: Routledge.

———. 2014. *NGOs, Civil Society, and the Public Sphere*. Reprint ed. Cambridge: Cambridge University Press.

Lashaw, Amanda. 2013. "How Progressive Culture Resists Critique: The Impasse of NGO Studies." *Ethnography* 14 (4): 501–22.

Latour, Bruno. 2005. *Reassembling the Social: An Introduction to Actor-Network Theory*. Oxford: Oxford University Press.

Lauper, Cyndi. 1984. "Money Changes Everything" (vocal performance). By Tom Gray. Recorded June 1983. On *She's So Unusual*, Portrait Records, Vinyl (7", 12").

Lemons, Katherine. 2016. "The Politics of Livability: Tutoring 'Kinwork' in a New Delhi Women's Arbitration Center." *PoLAR: Political and Legal Anthropology Review* 9 (2): 244–60.

Lewis, David. 1998. "Partnership as Process: Building an Institutional Ethnography of an Inter-Agency Aquaculture Project in Bangladesh." In *Development as Process: Concepts and Methods for Working with Complexity*, edited by David Mosse, J. Farrington, and A. Rew, 99–114. London: Routledge.

———. 1999. "Revealing, Widening, Deepening?: A Review of the Existing and the Potential Contribution of Anthropological Approaches to 'Third Sector' Research." *Human Organization* 58 (1): 73–81.

———. 2005. "Individuals, Organizations and Public Action: Trajectories of the 'Non-Governmental' in Development Studies." In *A Radical History of Development Studies*, edited by Uma Kothari, 200–221. London: Zed Books.

———. 2011. "Exchanges of Professionals between the Public and Non-Governmental Sectors: Life-Work Histories from Bangladesh." *Modern Asian Studies* 45 (3): 735–57.

Lewis, David, and Nazneen Kanji. 2009. *Non-Governmental Organizations and Development*. New York: Routledge.

Lewis, David, and David Mosse, eds. 2006. *Development Brokers and Translators: The Ethnography of Aid and Agencies*. Bloomfield, CT: Kumarian Press.

Lewis, Oscar. 1959. *Five Families; Mexican Case Studies in the Culture of Poverty*. New York: Basic Books.

Liganga, Lucas. 1999. "Swedish Aid Helps Tanzanians Combat Poverty, Improve Lives." *Guardian* (Tanzania), August 18.

Lister, Sarah. 2003. "NGO Legitimacy: Technical Issue or Social Construct?" *Critique of Anthropology* 23 (2): 175–92.

Little, Kenneth. 1965. *West African Urbanization: A Study of Voluntary Associations in Cultural Change*. Cambridge: Cambridge University Press.

Little, Paul E. 1999. "Environments and Environmentalisms in Anthropological Research: Facing a New Millennium." *Annual Review of Anthropology* 28: 253–84.

Lobo, Susan. 2015. "Why? And How? An Essay on Doing Anthropology and Life." In *Mutuality: Anthropology's Changing Terms of Engagement*, edited by Roger Sanjek, 191–202. Philadelphia: University of Pennsylvania Press.

Loode, Serge. 2011. "Navigating the Uncharted Waters of Cross-Cultural Conflict Resolution Education." *Conflict Resolution Quarterly* 29 (1): 65–84.

Lorenz-Meyer, Dagmar. 2013. "Timescapes of Activism: Trajectories, Encounters and Timings of Czech Women's NGOs." *European Journal of Women's Studies* 20 (4): 408–24.

Louisiana Justice Institute Blog. 2009. "Pledge in Support of a Just Rebuilding of St. Bernard Parish, Louisiana and the U.S. Gulf Coast." Accessed July 12, 2015. http://louisianajusticeinstitute.blogspot.com/2009/09/pledge-in-support-of-just-rebuilding-of.html.

Low, Setha M., and Sally Engle Merry. 2010. "Engaged Anthropology: Diversity and Dilemmas." *Current Anthropology* 51 (2): S203–26.

Lutz, Catherine, and Lila Abu-Lughod, eds. 1990. *Language and the Politics of Emotion*. Paris: Editions de la maison des sciences de l'homme.

Lyimo, Henry. 1999. No title. *Guardian* (Tanzania), May 7, p. 3.

Lyons, Kevin D., and Stephen Wearing, eds. 2008. *Journeys of Discovery in Volunteer Tourism: International Case Study Perspectives*. Wallingford, UK: CAB International.

Madden, Francine, and Brian McQuinn. 2014. "Conservation's Blind Spot: The Case for Conflict Transformation in Wildlife Conservation." *Biological Conservation* 178: 97–106.

Mahapatra, Dhananjay. 2016. "India Witnessing NGO Boom, There Is 1 for Every 600 People." *Times of India*, February 23, 2014. Accessed March 31, 2016. http:// timesofindia.indiatimes.com/india/India-witnessing-NGO-boom-there-is-1-for -every-600-people/articleshow/30871406.cms.

Mahmood, Saba. 2005. *Politics of Piety: The Islamic Revival and the Feminist Subject*. Princeton, NJ: Princeton University Press.

Mair, Lucy P. 1956. "Applied Anthropology and Development Policies." *The British Journal of Sociology* 7 (2): 120–33.

Malkki Liisa. 1996. "Speechless Emissaries: Refugees, Humanitarianism, and Dehistoricization." *Cultural Anthropology* 11 (3): 377–404.

Marcus, George. 1995. "Ethnography In/Of the World System." *Annual Review of Anthropology* 24: 95–117.

Markowitz, Lisa. 2001. "Finding the Field: Notes on the Ethnography of NGOs." *Human Organization* 60 (1): 40–46.

Mazey, Sonia. 2002. "Gender Mainstreaming Strategies in the E.U.: Delivering on an Agenda?" *Feminist Legal Studies* 10 (3): 227–40.

McAdam, Doug, Sidney Tarrow, and Charles Tilly. 2001. *Dynamics of Contention*. Cambridge: Cambridge University Press.

McAlister, Melani. 2008. "What Is Your Heart For? Affect and Internationalism in the Evangelical Public Sphere." *American Literary History* 20 (4): 870–95.

McMillon, Bill, Doug Cutchins, and Anne Geissinger. 2012. *Volunteer Vacations: Short-Term Adventures That Will Benefit You and Others*. Chicago: Chicago Review Press.

McNulty, Stephanie. 2011. *Voice and Vote: Decentralization and Participation in Post-Fujimori Peru*. Stanford, CA: Stanford University Press.

Menon, Vivek. 2013. "A Triangular Playing Field: The Social, Economic, and Ethical Context of Conserving India's Natural Heritage." In *Ignoring Nature No More: The Case for Compassionate Conservation*, edited by Marc Bekoff, 331–41. Chicago: University of Chicago Press.

Mercer, Claire, and Maia Green. 2013. "Making Civil Society Work: Contracting, Cosmopolitanism and Community Development in Tanzania." *Geoforum* 45: 106–15.

Messer-Davidow, Ellen. 2002. *Disciplining Feminism: From Social Activism to Academic Discourse*. Durham, NC: Duke University Press.

Milivojević, Zdenka. 2006. "Civil Society in Serbia: Suppressed during the 1990s—Gaining Legitimacy and Recognition after 2000." *Civicus, Civil Society Index Report for Serbia*. Belgrade: Argument and Centre for Development of the Nonprofit Sector.

Mitchell, Timothy. 2002. *Rule of Experts: Egypt, Techno-Politics, Modernity*. Berkeley: University of California Press.

Mittermaier, Amira. 2014. "Beyond Compassion: Islamic Voluntarism in Egypt." *American Ethnologist* 41 (3): 518–31.

Miyazaki, Hirokazu. 2003. "Temporalities of the Market." *American Anthropologist* 105 (2): 255–65.

Moll, Yasmin. 2010. "Islamic Televangelism: Religion, Media and Visuality in Contemporary Egypt." *Arab Media and Society* 10. Accessed September 5, 2015. www.arabmediasociety.com/?article=732.

Moodie, Megan. 2013. "Microfinance and the Gender of Risk: The Case of Kiva.org." *Signs* 38 (2): 279–302.

Moravec, Štěpán. 2006. "Nástin problému sociálního vyloučení romských populací" (Outline of a problem of social exclusion of Romani populations). In *"Romové" v osidlech sociálního vyloučení* ("Roma" in the toils of social exclusion), edited by Tomáš Hirt and Marek Jakoubek, 11–69. Plzeň, Czech Rep.: Vydavatelství a nakladatelství Aleš Čeněk.

Mosse, David. 2001. "People's Knowledge, Participation and Patronage: Operations and Representations in Rural Development." In *Participation: The New Tyranny?*, edited by B. Cooke and Uma Kothari, 16–35. London: Zed Books.

———. 2005. *Cultivating Development: An Ethnography of Aid Policy and Practice*. Ann Arbor, MI: Pluto Press.

———. 2006a. "Anti-social Anthropology? Objectivity, Objection, and the Ethnography of Public Policy and Professional Communities." *Journal of the Royal Anthropological Institute* 12 (4): 935–56.

———. 2006b. "Collective Action, Common Property, and Social Capital in South India: An Anthropological Commentary." *Economic Development and Cultural Change* 54 (3): 695–724.

———. 2007. "Notes on the Ethnography of Expertise and Professionals in International Development." Paper presented at Ethnografeast III: Ethnography and the Public Sphere, Lisbon, June 20–23.

———, ed. 2011. *Adventures in Aidland: The Anthropology of Professionals in International Development*. Oxford: Berghahn Books.

———. 2013. "The Anthropology of International Development." *Annual Review of Anthropology* 42 (1): 227–46.

Mostafanezhad, Mary. 2014. *Volunteer Tourism: Popular Humanitarianism in Neoliberal Times*. Burington, VT: Ashgate.

Mostafanezhad, Mary, and Kevin Hannam, eds. 2014. *Moral Encounters in Tourism*. Burlington, VT: Ashgate.

Mtema, Nelly. 1999. "Sida to Give Women NGO 25m." Dar es Salaam *Daily News*, April 23.

Mulder, Monique Borgerhoff, and Peter Coppolillo. 2005. *Conservation: Linking Ecology, Economics, and Culture.* Princeton: Princeton University Press.

Nader, Laura. 1972. "Up the Anthropologist: Perspectives Gained from Studying Up." In *Reinventing Anthropology*, edited by Dell H. Hymes, 284–311. New York: Pantheon Books.

National Contact Center for Gender and Science. 2016. "Who We Are." Accessed August 13, 2016. http://en.zenyaveda.cz/about-the-project/2380-who-we-are/.

Nešpor, Zdeněk R., and Marek Jakoubek. 2004. "Co je a co není kulturní/sociální antropologie?" ("What is and what is not social anthropology?"). *Český lid. Etnologický časopis* 1: 53–79.

Neumann, Roderick P. 2004. "Moral and Discursive Geographies in the War for Biodiversity in Africa." *Political Geography* 23: 813–37.

Newberry, Jan. 2010. "The Global Child and Non-governmental Governance of the Family in Post-Suharto Indonesia." *Economy and Society* 39 (3): 403–26.

New Delhi Television. 2014. "Home Ministry Issues Notices to 10,000 NGO's for Not Filing Tax Returns." October 1, 2014. Accessed March 31, 2016. www.ndtv.com/india-news/home-ministry-issues-notices-to-10-000-ngos-for-not-filing-tax-returns-673682.

NGO Law Monitor: Egypt. International Center for Not-For-Profit Law. 2016. Last updated March 23, 2016. Accessed May 10, 2016. wwvw.icnl.org/research/monitor/egypt.html#glance.

NGO Policy Group. 2001. *The Third Sector in Serbia: Status and Prospects.* Belgrade: Center for the Development of the Nonprofit Sector.

Nolan, Riall. 2002. *Development Anthropology: Encounters in the Real World.* Boulder: Westview Press.

Novák, Karel A. 2003. "Romská osada—tradice versus regres" (Romani settlement—Tradition versus regress). In *Romské osady v kulturologické perspective* (Romani settlements in culturological perspective), edited by Marek Jakoubek and Ondřej Poduška, 31–40. Brno, Czech Rep.: Doplněk.

Occhipinti, Laurie A. 2005. *Acting on Faith : Religious Development Organizations in Northwestern Argentina.* Lanham, MD: Lexington Books.

———. 2015. "Faith-Based Organizations and Development." In *The Routledge Handbook of Religions and Global Development*, edited by Emma Tomalin, 183–99. New York: Routledge.

Ong, Aihwa, and Stephen J. Collier, eds. 2005. *Global Assemblages: Technology, Politics, and Ethics as Anthropological Problems.* Malden, MA: Blackwell Publishing.

Orlove, Benjamin S., and Stephen B. Brush. 1996. "Anthropology and the Conservation of Biodiversity." *Annual Review of Anthropology* 25: 329–52.

Ottaway, Marina, and Thomas Carothers. 2000. *Funding Virtue: Civil Society Aid and Democracy Promotion.* Washington, DC: Carnegie Endowment for International Peace.

Outlook India. 2015. "Teesta Setalvad's NGO's License Suspended for Six Months." Accessed September 13, 2015. www.outlookindia.com/news/article/teesta-setalvads-ngos-license-suspended-for-six-months/912484.

Parpart, Jane. 1999. "Rethinking Participation, Empowerment, and Development from a Gender Perspective." In *Transforming Development: Foreign Aid for a Changing World*, edited by Jim Freedman, 250–67. Toronto: University of Toronto Press.

Pavlík, Petr, ed. 2004. *Shadow Report on the Equal Treatment and Equal Opportunities for Women and Men*. Prague: Gender Studies.

Peck, Jamie, and Adam Tickell. 2002. "Neoliberalizing Space." *Antipode* 34 (3): 380–404.

PEDRC. 2008. *Plan Estratégico de Desarrollo Regional Concertado Cusco al 2021*. Cusco, Peru: Gobierno Regional Del Cusco.

Pelkmans, Mathijs. 2009. *Conversion after Socialism: Disruptions, Modernisms, and Technologies of Faith in the Former Soviet Union*. New York: Berghahn Books.

Perwez, Shahid. 2008. "Towards an Understanding of the Field within the Field: Researching Female Infanticide by Researching NGOs in Tamil Nadu." In *Anthropologists inside Organizations: South Asian Case Studies*, edited by Devi Sridhar, 72–88. New Delhi: SAGE Publications India.

Pieterse, Jan Nederveen. 2000. "After Post-Development." *Third World Quarterly* 21 (2): 175–91.

Poppendieck, Janet. 1998. *Sweet Charity? Emergency Food and the End of Entitlement*. New York: Viking.

Poradna pro občanství. 2013. "Poradna pro občanství: Naši pracovníci vyjednali v Krásném Březně přidělení nájemních smluv všem dosavadním obyvatelům ubytovny" ("Counseling Center for Citizenship: Our workers negotiated the allocation of lease agreements to all existing inhabitants of the dormitory"). ROMEA, February 2. Accessed December 7, 2014. www.romea.cz/cz/zpravodajstvi/domaci/poradna-pro-obcanstvi-nasi-pracovnici-vyjednali-prideleni-najemnich-smluv-vsem-dosavadnim-obyvatelum-ubytovny.

Prell, Riv-Ellen. 1989. *Prayer and Community: The Havurah in American Judaism*. Detroit: Wayne State University Press.

Rabinow, Paul. 1977. *Reflections on Fieldwork in Morocco*. Berkeley: University of California Press.

Rajak, Dinah. 2011. *In Good Company: An Anatomy of Corporate Social Responsibility*. Stanford, CA: Stanford University Press.

Ramakrishnan, S. Karthic, and Irene Bloemraad. 2008. *Civic Hopes and Political Realities: Immigrants, Community Organizations, and Political Engagement*. New York: Russell Sage Foundation.

Redfield, Peter. 2011. "The Impossible Problem of Neutrality." In *Forces of Compassion: Humanitarianism between Ethics and Politics*, edited by Peter Redfield and Erica Bornstein, 53–70. Santa Fe: School for Advanced Research Press.

———. 2013. *Life in Crisis: The Ethical Journey of Doctors without Borders*. Berkeley: University of California Press.

Redford, Kent H. 2011. "Misreading the Conservation Landscape." *Oryx* 45 (3): 324–30.

Richard, Analiese. 2009. "Mediating Dilemmas: Local NGOs and Rural Development in Neoliberal Mexico." *PoLAR: Political and Legal Anthropology Review* 32 (2): 166–94.

Richard, Analiese, and Daromir Rudnyckyj. 2009. "Economies of Affect." *Journal of the Royal Anthropological Institute* 15 (1): 57–77.

Riddell, Roger C. 2007. *Does Foreign Aid Really Work?* New York: Oxford University Press.

Riles, Annelise. 2001. *The Networks Inside Out.* Ann Arbor: University of Michigan Press.

———. 2004. "Real Time: Unwinding Technocratic and Anthropological Knowledge." *American Ethnologist* 31 (3): 392–405.

———. 2006a. "[Deadlines]: Removing the Brackets on Politics in Bureaucratic and Anthropological Analysis." In *Documents: Artifacts of Modern Knowledge*, edited by Annelise Riles, 71–94. Ann Arbor: University of Michigan Press.

———, ed. 2006b. *Documents: Artifacts of Modern Knowledge.* Ann Arbor: University of Michigan Press.

Riles, Annelise, and Iris E. F. Jean-Klein. 2005. "Introducing Discipline: Anthropology and Human Rights Administration." *PoLAR: Political and Legal Anthropology Review* 28 (2): 173–202.

Rist, Gilbert. 1996. *Le Développement: Histoire D'une Croyance Occidentale.* Paris: Presses de la Fondation nationale des sciences politiques.

Rosenthal, Gilbert S. 2005. "*Tikkun ha-Olam*: The Metamorphosis of a Concept." *Journal of Religion* 85: 214–24.

Rosga, AnnJanette. 2005. "The Traffic in Children: The Funding of Translation and the Translation of Funding." *PoLAR: Political and Legal Anthropology Review* 28 (2): 258–81.

Rutzen, Douglas. 2015. "Aid Barriers and the Rise of Philanthropic Protectionism." *International Journal of Not-for-Profit Law* 17 (1): 5–44. Accessed July 9, 2015. www.icnl.org/research/journal/vol17ss1/Rutzen.pdf.

Rylko-Bauer, Barbara, Merrill Singer, and John Van Willegen. 2006. "Reclaiming Applied Anthropology: Its Past, Present and Future." *American Anthropologist* 108 (1): 178–90.

Sabra, Adam. 2000. *Poverty and Charity in Medieval Islam: Mamluk Egypt, 1250–1517.* Cambridge: Cambridge University Press.

Said, Edward. 1983. *The World, the Text, and the Critic.* Cambridge, MA: Harvard University Press.

Sampson, Steven. 1996. "The Social Life of Projects: Importing Civil Society to Albania." In *Civil Society: Challenging Western Models*, edited by Chris Hann and Elizabeth Dunn, 121–42. London: Routledge.

———. 2003. "'Trouble Spots': Projects, Bandits and State Fragmentation." In *Globalization, the State and Violence*, edited by Jonathan Friedman, 309–42. Walnut Creek, CA: AltaMira Press.

Sangtin Writers and Richa Nagar. 2006. *Playing with Fire: Feminist Thought and Activism through Seven Lives in India.* Minneapolis: University of Minnesota Press.

Sanjek, Roger. 2015a. "Deep Grooves: Anthropology and Mutuality." In *Mutuality:*

Anthropology's Changing Terms of Engagement, edited by Roger Sanjek, 1–7. Philadelphia: University of Pennsylvania Press.

———. 2015b. "Mutuality in Anthropology: Terms and Modes of Engagement." In *Mutuality: Anthropology's Changing Terms of Engagement*, edited by Roger Sanjek, 285–310. Philadelphia: University of Pennsylvania Press.

Schatzki, Theodore R. 2002. *The Site of the Social: A Philosophical Account of the Constitution of Social Life and Change*. University Park: Pennsylvania State University Press.

Scheper-Hughes, Nancy. 1995. "The Primacy of the Ethical: Propositions for a Militant Anthropology." *Current Anthropology* 36 (3): 409–40.

Schmidt, Verena. 2005. *Gender Mainstreaming—An Innovation in Europe?: The Institutionalization of Gender Mainstreaming in the European Commission*. Opladen, Germany: Barbara Budrich Publishers.

Schuller, Mark. 2007. "Seeing Like a 'Failed' NGO: Globalization's Impacts on State and Civil Society in Haiti." *PoLAR: Political and Legal Anthropology Review* 30 (1): 67–89.

———. 2009. "Gluing Globalization: NGOs as Intermediaries in Haiti." *PoLAR: Political and Legal Anthropology Review* 32 (1): 84–104.

———. 2012. *Killing with Kindness: Haiti, International Aid, and NGOs*. New Brunswick, NJ: Rutgers University Press.

Scott, David. 1992. "Anthropology and Colonial Discourse: Aspects of the Demonological Construction of Sinhala Cultural Practice." *Cultural Anthropology* 7 (3): 301–26.

Seeley, John R. 1989 [1957]. *Community Chest: A Case Study in Philanthropy*. With Buford R. Junker and R. Wallace Jones Jr. New Brunswick, NJ: Transaction Publishers.

Sharma, Aradhana. 2008. *Logics of Empowerment: Development, Gender, and Governance in Neoliberal India*. Minneapolis: University of Minnesota Press.

———. 2014. "The State and Women's Empowerment in India: Paradoxes and Politics." In *Theorizing NGOs: States, Feminisms, and Neoliberalism*, edited by Victoria Bernal and Inderpal Grewal, 93–114. Durham, NC: Duke University Press.

Shivji, Issa G. 2007. *Silences in NGO Discourse: The Role and Future of NGOs in Africa*. Oxford, UK: Fahamu.

Shore, Cris. 2000. *Building Europe: The Cultural Politics of European Integration*. New York: Routledge.

Shore, Cris, and Susan Wright, eds. 1997. *Anthropology of Policy: Critical Perspectives on Governance and Power*. London: Routledge.

———. 2000. "Coercive Accountability: The Rise of Audit Culture in Higher Education." In *Audit Cultures: Anthropological Studies in Accountability: Ethics and the Academy*, edited by Marilyn Strathern, 57–89. London: Routledge.

Shore, Cris, Susan Wright, and Davide Però. 2011. *Policy Worlds: Anthropology and the Analysis of Contemporary Power*. New York: Berghahn Books.

Sillitoe, Paul. 2007. "Anthropologists Only Need Apply: Challenges of Applied Anthropology." *Journal of the Royal Anthropological Institute* 13: 147–65.

Simmie, J. M., and D. J. Hale. 1978. "Urban Self-management in Yugoslavia." *Regional Studies: The Journal of the Regional Studies Association* 12 (6): 701–12.

Simpson, Kate. 2004. "'Doing Development': The Gap Year, Volunteer-Tourists and a Popular Practice of Development." *Journal of International Development* 16: 681–92.

Sinervo, Aviva. 2011. "Connection and Disillusion: The Moral Economy of Volunteer Tourism in Cusco, Peru." *Childhoods Today* 5 (2): 1–23.

———. 2013. "'No Somos los Pobrecitos': Negotiating Stigma, Identity, and Need in Constructions of Childhood Poverty in Cusco, Peru." *Childhood* 20 (3): 398–413.

———. 2015. "Brokering Aid through Tourism: The Contradictory Roles of Volunteer Coordinators in Cusco, Peru." *Tourist Studies* 15 (2): 156–74.

Singer, Amy. 2008. *Charity in Islamic Societies.* Cambridge: Cambridge University Press.

Slačálek, Ondřej, and Lukáš Rychetský. 2013. "Strážci postkomunistického dobra" ("Guardians of the Postcommunist Good"). *A2* (7): 18–19.

Šmejkalová, Jiřina. 2004. "Feminist Sociology in the Czech Republic after 1989: A Brief Report." *European Societies* 6 (2): 169–80.

Smith, Daniel Jordan. 2010. "Corruption, NGOs and Development in Nigeria." *Third World Quarterly* 31 (2): 243–58.

Sobhy, Hania. 2011. "Amr Khaled and Young Muslim Elites: Islamism and the Consolidation of Mainstream Muslim Piety in Egypt." In *Cairo Contested: Governance, Urban Space and Global Modernity*, edited by Diane Singerman, 415–54. Cairo: American University Press.

Speed, Shannon. 2008. "Forged Dialogue: Toward a Critically Engaged Activist Research." In *Engaging Contradictions: Theory, Politics, and Methods of Activist Scholarship*, edited by Charles R. Hale, 213–36. Berkeley: University of California Press.

Stapp, Darby C., ed. 2012. *Action Anthropology and Sol Tax in 2012: The Final Word?* Richland, WA: Northwest Anthropology LLC.

Starrett, Gregory. 2010. "The Varieties of Secular Experience." *Comparative Studies in Society and History* 52 (3): 626–51.

Steel, Griet. 2008. *Vulnerable Careers: Tourism and Livelihood Dynamics among Street Vendors in Cusco, Peru.* Amsterdam: Rozenberg Publishers.

Stein, Janice Gross. 2008. "Humanitarian Organizations: Accountable—Why, to Whom, for What and How?" In *Humanitarianism in Question: Politics, Power, Ethics*, edited by Michael Barnett and Thomas G. Weiss, 124–42. Ithaca, NY: Cornell University Press.

Stephens, Sharon, ed. 1995. *Children and the Politics of Culture.* Princeton, NJ: Princeton University Press.

Stern, Steve J., ed. 1998. *Shining and Other Paths: War and Society in Peru, 1980–1995.* Durham, NC: Duke University Press.

Stewart, Michael. 1997. *The Time of the Gypsies.* Boulder, CO: Westview Press.

Stirrat, R. L., and Heiko Henkel. 1997. "The Development Gift: The Problem of Reciprocity and the NGO World." *The Annals of the American Academy of Political and Social Science* 554: 66–80.

Stoczkowski, Wiktor. 2008. "The 'Fourth Aim' of Anthropology: Between Knowledge and Ethics." *Anthropological Theory* 8 (4): 345–56.

Strathern, Marilyn. 1988. *The Gender of the Gift*. Berkeley: University of California Press.

———, ed. 2000. *Audit Cultures: Anthropological Studies in Accountability, Ethics, and the Academy*. London: Routledge.

Stubbs, Paul. 2001. "New Times?: Towards a Political Economy of 'Civil Society' in Contemporary Croatia." *Narodna Umjetnost* 38 (1): 89–103.

Sukarieh, Mayssoun. 2012. "The Hope Crusades: Culturalism and Reform in the Arab World." *PoLAR: Political and Legal Anthropology Review* 35 (1): 115–34.

Sukarieh, Mayssoun, and Stuart Tannock. 2011. "The Positivity Imperative: A Critical Look at the 'New' Youth Development Movement." *Journal of Youth Studies* 14 (6): 675–91.

Sunder Rajan, Rajeswari. 2003. *The Scandal of the State*. Durham, NC: Duke University Press.

Svadbová, Blanka. 1998. *Zpráva o Nadaci Gender Studies v Praze 1991–1997* (Report on the Prague Gender Studies Foundation 1991–1997). Prague: Nadace Gender Studies.

Synková, Hana. 2010. "Claiming Legitimacy in/of a Romani NGO." In *Multi-disciplinary Approaches to Romany Studies*, edited by Michael Stewart and Márton Rövid, 280–91. Budapest: Central European University Press.

———. 2011. "Legitimation and Professionalization of a Romani NGO in the Czech Republic." PhD diss., Prague, Czech Republic: Charles University.

Taneja, Anand. 2013. "Jinnealogy: Everyday Life and Islamic Theology in Postpartition Delhi." *Hau: Journal of Ethnographic Theory* 3 (3): 139–65.

Taylor, Marilyn. 2010. "Community Participation." In *The Human Economy*, edited by Keith Hart, Jean-Louis Laville, and Antonio David Cattani, 236–47. Cambridge, UK: Polity.

Temple, Dominique. 1997. "NGOs: A Trojan Horse." In *The Post-Development Reader*, edited by Majid Rahnema and Victoria Bawtree, 202–3. London: Zed Books.

Terry, Fiona. 2002. *Condemned to Repeat: The Paradox of Humanitarian Action*. Ithaca, NY: Cornell University Press.

Thayer, Millie. 2010. *Making Transnational Feminism: Rural Women, NGO Activists, and Northern Donors in Brazil*. New York: Routledge.

———. n.d. "Movements, Markets, and International Aid: Brazilian Feminist NGOs on the Shadow Commodity Chain." Paper presented at the Mini-Conference on NGOs, States, and Feminisms, University of California, Irvine, California, March 7, 2014.

Ticktin, Miriam. 2011. *Casualties of Care: Immigration and the Politics of Humanitarianism in France*. Berkeley: University of California Press.

Tsing, Anna L. 2005. *Friction: An Ethnography of Global Connection*. Princeton, NJ: Princeton University Press.

Tvedt, Terje. 1998. *Angels of Mercy or Development Diplomats? NGOs and Foreign Aid*. Trenton, NJ: Africa World Press.

UNICEF. 2008. *Estado de la Niñez en el Perú: Resumen Ejecutivo*. Lima: Fondo de las Naciones Unidas para la Infancia (UNICEF) y Instituto Nacional de Estadística e Informática.

United Jewish Communities. 2007. *Hurricane Katrina Fund. Final Report*. New York: Jewish Federations of North America.

USAID. 1994. "Democracy Promotion Programs Funded by the US Government. A Report to the Senate Foreign Relations Committee and the House Foreign Affairs Committee of the US Congress." Accessed May 14, 2016. http://pdf.usaid .gov/pdf_docs/Pcaaa756.pdf.

———. 2005. "Mid-term Evaluation Junior Achievement/Youth Enterprise Serbia." Accessed August 22, 2016. www.oecd.org/countries/serbiaandmontenegropre -june2006/36013557.pdf.

———. 2007. "Community Revitalization through Democratic Action—Economy Program." Accessed August 21, 2016. http://pdf.usaid.gov/pdf_docs/Pdack679.pdf.

USAID, Beata Czajkowska, Judith Dunbar, Mike Keshishian, Caroline Sahley, and Kelley Strickland. 2005. "Assessment of the Serbian Community Revitalization through Democratic Action Activity (CRDA)." USAID/Serbia and Montenegro. Accessed February 12, 2017. http://pdf.usaid.gov/pdf_docs/PDACF026.pdf.

US Census Bureau. 1995. "Historical Population Counts, 1900 to 1990, for all Counties in Louisiana." Accessed September 30, 2015. www.census.gov/population/ cencounts/la190090.txt.

Valentine, Charles A. 1968. *Culture and Poverty. Critique and Counter-proposals*. Chicago: University of Chicago Press.

Vannier, Christian. 2010. "Audit Culture and Grassroots Participation in Rural Haitian Development." *PoLAR: Political and Legal Anthropology Review* 33 (2): 282–305.

Vatuk, Sylvia. 2013. "The 'Women's Court' in India: An Alternative Dispute Resolution Body for Women in Distress." *Journal of Legal Pluralism and Unofficial Law* 45 (1): 76–103.

Velloso Santistiban, Agustin. 2005. "The Poor Will Always Be with Us—And So Will NGOs." *Development in Practice* 15 (2): 200–209.

Vermeersch, Peter. 2005. "Marginality, Advocacy, and the Ambiguities of Multiculturalism: Notes on Romani Activism in Central Europe." *Identities: Global Studies in Culture and Power* 12: 451–78.

Vetta, Theodora. 2011. "Nationalism Is Back! *Radikali* and Privatization Processes in Serbia." In *Headlines of Nation, Subtext of Class*, edited by Don Kalb and Gabor Halmai, 37–56. EASA Book Series. New York: Berghahn Books.

———. 2012. "NGOs and the State: Clash or Class?" In *Democracy at Large: NGOs, Political Foundations, Think Tanks and International Organizations*, edited by Boris Petric, 169–90. Series in International Relations and Political Economy. New York: Palgrave Macmillan.

———. 2017. *"Let's Get Up": NGOs, Class and Culture in Serbia: An Anthropology of Democracy Aid.* New York: Berghahn Books.

Vogler, Pia. 2007. "Into the Jungle of Bureaucracy: Negotiating Access to Camps at the Thai-Burma Border." *Refugee Survey Quarterly* 26 (3): 51–60.

Vrasti, Wanda. 2013. *Volunteer Tourism in the Global South: Giving Back in Neoliberal Times.* New York: Routledge.

Wacquant, Loic. 2010. "Crafting the Neoliberal State: Workfare, Prisonfare, and Social Insecurity." *Sociological Forum* 25 (2): 197–230.

———. 2012. "Three Steps to a Historical Anthropology of Actually Existing Neoliberalism." *Social Anthropology/Anthropologie Sociale* 20 (1): 66–79.

Warren, Kay B. 2006. "Perils and Promises of Engaged Anthropology: Historical Transitions and Ethnographic Dilemmas." In *Engaged Observer: Anthropology, Advocacy, and Activism*, edited by Victoria Sanford and Asale Angel-Ajani, 213–27. New Brunswick, NJ: Rutgers University Press.

Waylen, Kerry A., Anke Fischer, Philip J. K. McGowan, Simon J. Thirgood, and E. J. Milner-Gulland. 2010. "Effect of Local Cultural Context on the Success of Community-Based Conservation Interventions." *Conservation Biology* 24 (4):1119–29.

Wearing, Stephen, Matthew McDonald, and Jess Ponting. 2005. "Building a Decommodified Research Paradigm in Tourism: The Contribution of NGOs." *Journal of Sustainable Tourism* 13 (5): 424–39.

Wearing, Stephen, and Nancy Gard McGehee. 2013. "Volunteer Tourism: A Review." *Tourism Management* 38: 120–30.

Wedel, Janine. 2001. *Collision and Collusion: The Strange Case of Western Aid to Eastern Europe.* New York: Palgrave Macmillan.

———. 2009. *Shadow Elite: How the World's New Power Brokers Undermine Democracy, Government, and the Free Market.* New York: Basic Books.

Weiner, Elaine. 2010. "Morality, Biology, and the Free Market: (De)Naturalizing the EU's Gender Equality Agenda in the Czech Republic." *Women's Studies International Forum* 33: 13–20.

West, Paige, and Dan Brockington. 2006. "An Anthropological Perspective on Some Unexpected Consequences of Protected Areas." *Conservation Biology* 20 (3): 609–16.

Wickham, Carrie Rosefsky. 2002. *Mobilizing Islam: Religion, Activism and Political Change in Egypt.* New York: Columbia University Press.

Wilson, William J. 1987. *The Truly Disadvantaged.* Chicago: University of Chicago Press.

Winegar, Jessica. 2014. "Civilizing Muslim Youth: Egyptian State Culture Programmes and Islamic Television Preachers." *Journal of the Royal Anthropological Institute* 20 (3): 445–65.

Woocher, Jonathan S. 1986. *Sacred Survival: The Civil Religion of American Jews.* Bloomington: University of Indiana Press.

World Bank. 2015. World Bank Open Data: Peru. World Bank Group. Accessed February 1, 2015. http://data.worldbank.org/country/peru.

Yarrow, Thomas. 2008. "Life/history: Personal Narratives of Development amongst Workers and Activists in Ghana." *Africa* 78 (3): 334–58.

Zamindar, Vazira Fazila Yacoobali. 2007. *The Long Partition and the Making of Modern South Asia: Refugees, Boundaries, Histories.* New York: Columbia University Press.

Zeitz, Joshua. 2007. *White Ethnic New York: Jews, Catholics, and the Shaping of Postwar Politics.* Chapel Hill: University of North Carolina Press.

Contributors

Victoria Bernal is a professor of anthropology at the University of California, Irvine. She is the author of *Nation as Network: Diaspora, Cyberspace, and Citizenship* and *Cultivating Workers: Peasants and Capitalism in a Sudanese Village* and the coeditor with Inderpal Grewal of the anthology *Theorizing NGOs: States, Feminisms, and Neoliberalism.*

Erica Bornstein is an associate professor of anthropology at University of Wisconsin–Milwaukee. She is the author of *The Spirit of Development: Protestant NGOs, Morality and Economics in Zimbabwe*, and *Disquieting Gifts: Humanitarianism in New Delhi* and the coeditor of *Forces of Compassion: Humanitarianism between Ethics and Politics.*

Inderpal Grewal is a professor in the Women's, Gender, and Sexuality Studies Program, a professor in the Ethnicity, Race, and Migration Studies Program, a faculty member in the South Asia Council, and an affiliate faculty member in the American Studies Department at Yale University. She is the author of *Home and Harem: Nation, Gender, Empire, and the Cultures of Travel*, *Transnational America: Feminisms, Diasporas, Neoliberalisms*, and *Saving the Security State: Exceptional Citizens in Twenty-First-Century America*. She is the coeditor of *Scattered Hegemonies: Postmodernity and Transnational Feminist Practices, An Introduction to Women's Studies: Gender in a Transnational World*, and *Theorizing NGOs: States, Feminisms, and Neoliberalism.*

Karen Kapusta-Pofahl is a lecturer in the Department of Sociology and Anthropology at Washburn University in Topeka, Kansas. Her research areas include feminism, knowledge production, ethnicity, and politics in European societies.

Moshe Kornfeld is a postdoctoral research associate at the John C. Danforth Center on Religion and Politics at Washington University in St. Louis.

His current book project examines Jewish philanthropy, service, and activism in post-Katrina New Orleans.

Amanda Lashaw is a visiting assistant professor in the Education Department at the University of California, Santa Cruz. Her research interests include education politics, anthropology of NGOs and nonprofits, and progressive political culture. She is working on a book that examines optimism and moral identity among US education reformers.

Katherine Lemons is an assistant professor of anthropology at McGill University. Her research areas are anthropology of Islam, religion, law, and gender in contemporary north India.

David Lewis is a professor of social policy and development at the London School of Economics and Political Science. He is the author of *Bangladesh: Politics, Economy and Civil Society* and coauthor of *Anthropology and Development: Challenges for the Twenty-First Century*.

Nermeen Mouftah is a postdoctoral fellow at the Buffett Institute for Global Studies at Northwestern University.

Steven Sampson is a professor emeritus of social anthropology at Lund University. He has been an NGO consultant in southeast Europe and carried out research on socialism and postsocialism, democracy export, anticorruption, and business ethics.

Mark Schuller is an associate professor of anthropology and NGO leadership and development at Northern Illinois University and an affiliate at the Faculté d'Ethnologie, Université d'État d'Haïti. He is the author of *Humanitarian Aftershocks in Haiti* and *Killing with Kindness: Haiti, International Aid, and NGOs* and a coeditor of five volumes, including *Contextualizing Disaster*.

Aviva Sinervo is a lecturer in anthropology at San Francisco State University. She has published in the *Journal of Latin American and Caribbean Anthropology*, *Childhood*, and *Tourist Studies*.

Hana Synková is an assistant professor of anthropology at the University of Pardubice, Czech Republic. She researches the anthropology of politics and cooperates on applied projects with public and private institutions.

Christian Vannier is a lecturer in the Departments of Anthropology and Africana Studies at the University of Michigan, Flint. He is the coauthor of *An Ethnography of a Vodu Shrine in Southern Togo: Of Spirit, Slave, and Sea*.

Theodora Vetta is a European Research Council postdoctoral fellow at the University of Barcelona. She is the author of "NGOs and the State: Clash or Class?" and "Nationalism Is Back! Radikali and Privatization Processes in Serbia" and the coauthor of *Moral Economy: Rethinking a Radical Concept*. Her current research focuses on private/public debt, class fragmentation, and energy production in crisis-ridden Greece.

Amanda Woomer is a doctoral candidate in international conflict management at Kennesaw State University. Her research interests include the relationship between environmental conservation and conflict, cultural competency, and context sensitivity among NGOs and the use of evaluation for developing adaptive NGO interventions.

Index

academics, 2, 13, 14, 52, 75, 82, 84, 88, 91, 94, 97, 101–5, 106–7, 108, 119, 185, 188, 213, 214, 231, 234; and activism, 4, 52, 88, 90, 100, 105–6, 109, 188, 227, 229, 233; employed by NGOs, 22, 45, 52, 81, 87, 235; as expert, 101–2; and NGO collaboration, 95, 103, 108, 235; as researcher, 5, 10, 32, 34, 91, 115

accountability, 50, 54, 55, 94, 95, 97, 119, 159, 185, 212, 236; "fuzzy," 16, 73; to NGO constituents/clients 63, 92, 135; of NGOs to donors 23, 47, 48–49

accountability politics, 16, 73, 94, 97, 99, 108

activism, 15–16, 32, 49, 54, 85, 90, 92, 110n9, 189, 231; ethnic, 18, 81–83, 173, 174; feminist, 13, 18, 25, 106, 108, 230; by NGOs, 13, 22, 24, 27, 35, 56, 61, 81, 90, 92; political, 57, 106, 165, 184; professionalization of, 15, 24, 39, 50–52; religious, 127, 130; women's, 33, 37, 39, 40–41, 55, 233. *See also* academics: and activism

activists, 14–15, 26, 37, 44, 50, 55, 75, 83–84, 87, 104, 117–18, 164, 198; against NGOs, 85–87, 89–91, 163, 172–78; networks, 7, 15, 47, 51, 54, 91–92; movements, 13; in NGOs, 2, 3, 6, 9, 24–25, 33, 40, 45–47, 188, 231, 234; religious, 168–69, 171–73, 180n7, 233; research on, 34, 192; women's rights, 44, 46, 234

adjudication, 196, 198, 199, 205, 211

advocacy, 4, 32, 61, 99, 169, 233; by academics, 6, 106–7, 214; by NGOs, 5, 9, 22, 103, 105, 108, 110n10, 114, 178, 190

advocacy networks, 75, 87–88, 90–93, 95, 108, 234, 235

affect, 16, 115, 119, 120, 123–24, 136–37, 140, 141n2, 142, 148, 152–53, 158

agency, 29, 134, 135, 152, 176

aidnography, 30

American Anthropological Association, 7, 8, 193n1, 215

anthropology: applied, 28–29, 34–35, 81, 214, 234; engaged, 10, 23, 28, 36, 214–15, 218

antipolitics, 163, 177, 178, 179

Asad, Talal, 123, 127, 128, 141n4, 207, 208

assemblage, 6–8

Associational Revolution, 21, 56

associations, 79, 129; of NGOs, 45, 54, 61; voluntary, 6, 27, 28, 59

audit, 9, 65, 80, 89

audit culture, 23, 48

Bernal, Victoria, 3, 6, 13, 16, 17, 18, 21, 23, 24, 25, 37–55, 231, 233; and Grewal, Inderpal, 7, 16, 21, 34, 37, 42, 50, 94, 114, 115, 144, 189, 194, 196

Bornstein, Erica, 17, 18, 28, 38, 117, 127, 135, 183–93, 197, 236

Catholicism, 145, 150, 152, 169, 180n5

children, 2, 205, 217, 226; aid for, 13, 15, 76,

85, 119, 142, 146–47, 149–60; as target
group, 14, 143–44, 145, 148, 232
Christianity, 91, 119, 126, 127, 135, 169;
NGOs, 126–27, 185–86. *See also* World
Vision
citizens, 15, 28, 42, 44, 47, 50, 55, 60–62, 68,
71, 116, 159; citizenship, 58, 119, 121,
153; movements, 64
civil society, 15–16, 31, 37–38, 51, 57, 71,
127, 129, 140, 149, 184, 215, 234; as opposed to state, 54–55, 72–73, 95; represented by NGOs, 58, 61, 68, 125–26,
185; as theoretical concept, 6–7, 24, 26,
29–30, 35, 48, 56, 59
clientelistic networks, 63, 69
clients, 32, 60, 64, 75–78, 80, 85–86, 88–92,
93n7, 113, 117, 119, 144, 156, 158–59,
161n6, 198
Cold War, 24, 26, 114
colonialism, 29, 207, 231
commodification of poverty, 159
competition, 63, 65, 83; between NGOs, 23,
41, 52, 79, 81, 85, 88, 114, 191
conflict, 13, 16, 24, 57, 63–64, 66, 70–71,
201, 217, 230; between activists and others, 85; between anthropologists and
others, 35; between NGOs and others,
13, 103, 123, 224; domestic, 196–97,
199; as war, 32, 58–59, 62, 224
conservatism: political, 177; religious, 180n2
cooperation, 27, 82, 86, 133; through networks, 81, 87, 90–91
corruption, 47, 150, 156, 159
cosmopolitanism, 3, 5, 56, 83, 153, 190, 231
critique, 10, 17, 18, 74nn2–3, 123–24, 130–
32, 134–40, 171–74, 188, 207, 214; by
anthropologists, 14, 17, 29–30, 82–83,
97, 177, 184–85, 188, 191, 200, 232,
234–36; cultural, 35, 227; of NGOs, 25,
35, 79, 84–85, 88, 91, 104, 113, 115, 118,
121, 123, 152, 159, 164, 217, 220, 222–
23; self-critique, 67
cultural capital, 115, 143, 234
culture of poverty. *See* poverty: culture of
poverty
Czech Republic, 10, 12, 13, 14, 15, 18, 75,
80–87, 93n3, 94–103, 105–9, 109nn1–2,
233, 234, 235

de-ethnicization, 78, 84
democracy, 44, 50–51, 54, 56–63, 65, 67, 68,
70–73, 74n4, 191, 233; as goal of NGO
work, 21, 26, 29, 38, 50, 56–59, 59, 62,
67–68; represented by NGOs, 24, 58, 95;
in Serbia, 10, 14, 234; Western, 6
depoliticization, 24, 50, 74n3, 177, 200, 230
development, 5, 22, 33, 51, 61, 114, 127–28,
140, 142, 230; as aid project, 2, 43, 57,
58–59, 67, 73, 74n2, 160, 216; anthropological study of, 6, 28–30, 32, 50, 124,
177–78; critiques of, 22, 24, 84; as expertise, 7, 44, 60, 66, 203; and government, 132, 144, 197, 211n4; as international industry, 66, 140, 145–46; and
NGOs, 7, 12, 17, 27, 35, 93n9, 116–18,
125–26, 132, 177, 224; sustainable, 216;
and tourism, 149, 160, 161n8. *See also*
Ferguson, James; postdevelopment
discrimination, 90, 98, 106; ethnic, 78–79,
82–84, 86, 90; gender, 98, 106; housing,
172, 173, 174; racial, 171–174
dissent, 89, 115, 167, 184, 185
document, 23, 33, 52, 64, 77, 144, 199; as
anthropological data, 5, 97, 104, 222;
and anthropological methods, 22, 192–
93; and policy, 96
documentation, 43, 49, 80, 231
domestic violence, 196, 198, 199–201, 205,
211n7, 224. *See also* conflict: domestic
donations, 13, 117, 119, 123, 133, 144–46,
155–61, 170; foreign, 115, 148–49, 153–
54, 184, 211n4
donor fatigue, 3, 40
donors, 2–3, 6–7, 9, 38–55, 92; conflicts
with NGOs, 13–15, 66; as funding
agents, 22–24, 31–32, 79, 115, 119, 121,
159, 184, 187; relationships with NGOs,
39, 62, 113, 185, 188, 190, 224–25; as
tourists, 143–44, 148, 156. *See also* international donor regime

elites: NGO, 2–5, 38, 84, 89, 92, 160, 190,
231; indigenous, 76, 83, 87–88, 131; political, 58, 72, 125
entrepreneurialism, 96, 143, 158; of NGOs,
3, 9, 31
environment, 220–29; destruction of, 29; and

NGOs, 149, 165, 187, 216, 234; and the state, 1, 31, 197; projects, 213–14, 217–18; social, 82, 133, 147, 185, 190, 212

environmentalism, 188

Escobar, Arturo, 29, 59, 216, 219

essentialism, 72, 79, 81, 82–83, 98

ethics (ethical), 162n11; in anthropology, 35, 164, 193n1, 200, 210, 213, 214, 215–16, 220, 236; and NGO practice, 88, 122, 134–35, 142, 148, 151, 231; professional, 78; religious, 123, 127, 137, 163; in social work, 78; in the study of NGOs, 18, 22, 30, 161n8, 164, 185–93, 196, 200, 210, 213, 215, 222–27

ethnicity: and discrimination, 174; as segmentation, 4; as strategy, 78, 86

ethnography, 5, 17, 31, 83, 96–97, 225, 227–28; engaged, 23, 215; in NGOs, 34–35, 118–19, 121, 183, 187–93, 207, 230–35

European: as donor, 40, 46, 48, 79; as citizen, 119, 121, 221; as consciousness, 96; embassy, 45; integration into, 56, 71, 96

Europeanization, 96, 109n1

European Union, 1, 78, 93n8, 110n4; and Eastern Europe, 3, 6, 94, 95–99, 109n1; and feminism, 95–96, 101–2, 109n2; and NGOs, 21. See also gender mainstreaming

expertise, 13, 75; academic, 102, 203; and gender, 99; of NGO personnel, 40, 45, 75, 77, 82, 96, 104

Facebook, 87, 136

faith, 114, 118, 124–28, 132–40, 141n4; and development, 117, 122–23, 140

faith-based NGO, 18, 36n1, 116, 126–27, 231–32

Fassin, Didier, 32, 79, 113, 114, 117, 164, 184, 188

feminism, 37, 55, 79, 97, 101, 106, 176, 201, 203, 209; academic, 100, 104, 109, 110n9; activist, 13, 18, 44, 47, 95, 214, 230; NGOs, 194, 196; scholarship, 24, 34, 102, 107–8, 200. See also gender experts

Ferguson, James, 22, 24, 29, 31, 50, 74n3, 114, 225

field(site), 21–22, 28, 39–40, 47, 93n5, 183, 193, 195–96, 198, 202, 204, 206–10

fieldwork, 41, 46–47, 100, 108, 110n6, 171, 207, 210; ethnographic, 1, 4–5, 225; and NGOs, 8, 11, 14, 27, 33–36, 189, 194, 196, 201; in NGOs, 7, 125, 135, 148, 161n9, 162n11, 184, 188

Fisher, William, 10, 21, 31–33, 79, 177, 184, 216

Foucault, Michel, 29, 30, 31, 123, 189, 193

gender experts, 94–96, 101–2. See also feminism: academic; feminism: scholarship

gender mainstreaming, 2, 44, 96, 98, 100–102, 109n2, 110n4

gift, 152–53; humanitarian/development, 119, 166, 197; theory, 30–32

good works, 188; Islamic, 122–23, 127, 132–36, 139–40; organizations, 124, 126, 130

government, 26, 38, 47–48, 54, 117, 161n5, 177, 183, 190, 208; agency/ministry, 1, 13, 87–89, 93n3, 94; of Czech Republic, 79, 82–83, 88–89, 95–102, 108–9; as donor, 21, 29, 49, 119, 152, 170, 200; of Egypt, 119, 126–32, 232; of India, 115, 197–98; and NGO oversight, 3, 9, 41, 52, 55, 106, 145, 184–85, 211n4; partnerships with NGOs, 2, 34, 42–43, 91; of Peru, 142–54, 160, 160n4; programs, 58, 82, 143–44, 149, 154; of Serbia, 69–70; of the United States, 58, 116

governmentality, 31, 54, 230–31

Gramsci, Antonio, 26, 31

grassroots, 75, 86, 88, 180n7, 200; feminism, 55; and NGOs, 17, 37, 39, 58, 61, 194, 233; organizing, 130; political, 57, 71

Grewal, Inderpal, 18, 113–21; and Bernal, Victoria, 7, 16, 21, 34, 37, 42, 50, 94, 114, 115, 144, 189, 194, 196

Hilhorst, Dorothea, 3, 8, 12, 29, 32, 38, 57, 79, 149

humanitarianism, 32, 113–14, 116, 117, 118–19, 121, 233; aid, 6, 22, 62, 146, 177–78, 197; and anthropology, 163–64; organizations, 79, 184–85, 192; religious, 117, 168–69, 171; tourism, 120. See also projects: humanitarian

human rights, 6, 55, 192, 233; anthropology of, 203; campaigns, 7, 90; discourses of, 44, 54, 116; organizations, 22, 81, 129; training 42
Human Terrain project, 215
hybridity, 24, 128, 235; of NGOs, 91

identity: collective, 62, 74n4, 159, 179; ethnic, 75, 79, 87, 163–65, 168; of NGOs, 55, 106, 115, 231, 233; of NGO workers, 32, 117
ideology, 85, 91, 120, 122, 130; ethnic, 86; Marxist, 83; neoliberal 26; political, 84
INCITE!, 24, 79, 184, 193n2
India, 115, 117, 135, 184, 186, 188, 194, 196–206, 210, 210–11nn1–7, 232. *See also* government: of India
indigenous: conceptualization of, 209; economies, 29; elites, 83; knowledge, 215–16; feminism, 55; peoples, 6, 220, 221; professionals, 231
international donor regime, 21, 39, 47–48. *See also* donors
Islam, 13, 122–41, 186, 197, 198, 205–6, 211n5, 211n9, 232; charities, 116–18, 125, 127; duty, 13, 15; law, 196, 206; women, 12, 79, 205, 206, 209; youth, 14, 141n6. *See also* good works: Islamic
Islamic reform, 124, 127, 132, 137

Judaism: denominations, 170, 180n2; humanitarianism, 117, 118; NGOs, 163, 164, 165, 168, 173, 174, 177–78, 179, 233; philanthropy, 10, 13, 14, 16, 18, 118, 163–80, 233

Kamat, Sangeeta, 23, 57, 114, 196
knowledge, 4, 47, 79, 85, 97, 103, 107, 117, 121, 190–91, 208, 219, 225–26, 230; local, 28–29, 33, 215–17
knowledge production, 22, 39–40, 95, 106, 109, 189, 191, 193, 203–4, 210, 232, 234
knowledge workers, 102

labor, 177; child, 143; NGO, 30, 54, 231; volunteer, 134–35, 142–45, 151, 158, 161n6, 231
labor market, 3, 82, 95, 100

labor union, 176
Lang, Sabine, 7, 95, 96, 106
language, 98, 120, 124, 141n2, 147; of business, 151; of democracy, 44; expert, 22, 77–78, 80, 96, 103–4, 169, 202; good works, 134; human rights, 116; of NGOs, 6, 10, 13, 21, 23; of optimism, 138; training, 33, 142, 144, 146, 153, 155
Lashaw, Amanda, 21, 30, 34, 38, 164
Latin America 6, 26, 127, 147, 151
legitimacy, 63, 72, 83, 96–97, 205; moral, 9, 11, 231; of NGOs, 83, 113, 149, 188; scientific, 108
leverage politics, 99–100
Lewis, David, 5, 6, 8, 18, 26–36, 56, 142, 183, 189, 230
local knowledge. *See* knowledge: local
loyalty, 14, 96, 183–84, 185, 187, 188

managerial, 66, 78, 80
micropolitics, 193
microprojects, 57
middle-class, 30, 34, 84, 144, 147, 197, 231; values, 82
missionary: anthropology, 36n1; organizations, 9, 28; work, 114, 119
moral economy, 32, 114, 135
morality, 30, 113–14
moral legitimacy, 9, 11, 231
Mosse, David, 30, 56, 73, 159, 177, 183, 187, 189
Muslim. *See* good works: Islamic; Islam
Muslim Brotherhood, 125, 128–30

nationalism, 56, 74n4, 114–15, 234
neoliberalism, 18, 26, 57, 116, 170, 180n3, 231, 233
neutrality, 16–17, 75, 79, 177–79
new public management, 32
NGO: as political actor, 31, 35, 56, 58, 75, 85, 91, 184, 221; dependence, 196, 200, 207–9; embedded in political contexts, 32, 91–92, 114, 149, 187, 228; industry, 144; staff, 2, 34, 117, 144, 185, 190
NGO activists, 2, 3, 6, 9, 16, 17, 23, 34, 35, 63, 188. *See also* activism; activists
"NGO fever," 3, 6, 16, 17–18, 21, 37–40, 43, 45–49, 234

NGO field, 39–41, 48–50, 57, 88, 193, 231–32, 235
NGO form, 7, 10–11, 15, 17–18, 21, 24–25, 37–38, 57, 95, 108, 116–17, 149, 158, 234, 236
NGO-ization, 7–8, 16, 118, 177, 200
NGO-ography, 11
NGO-speak, 23, 79. *See also* language: of NGOs
NGO studies, 3, 10, 27, 121, 126, 140

optimism, 98, 123–24, 130, 136–40

participant observation, 5, 39–40, 235
participatory: groups, 87; processes, 217, 225, 227–28 ; research, 192
participatory research, 192, 225
partnership: anthropologist-NGO, 225; company-NGO, 32; government-government, 42; government-NGO, 2, 12, 34, 197; language, 13; NGO-NGO, 163–64, 169–74, 177; public-private, 3, 65
police, 86, 143, 154–58, 210n3
politics, 16, 34, 72, 94, 117–18, 164; and anthropology, 35, 185–86, 188–92, 196, 200, 235; and economy, 7, 96, 190, 231, 234; and the environment, 216, 219; formal, 50, 54, 56, 70, 83, 99–100, 129, 145, 161n4, 191, 221; and gender, 95, 97, 108; and Islam, 128, 130, 139–40; and Judaism, 163–68, 176, 178–79; marginalization, 79; movements, 115; and NGOs, 8, 12, 24, 27, 31, 37, 55, 113–21, 125, 130, 139–40, 142, 177, 185, 236; between NGOs, 11; parties, 9, 12, 62, 64, 69–70, 87, 128; politicization, 66, 68, 70, 92; and religion, 123–26, 130–31; resources, 10, 63, 89; science, 24, 26, 59, 84, 87, 95; theoretical, 29, 32, 57–60, 97, 106, 113, 177–78. *See also* accountability politics; leverage politics; neoliberalism; NGO
postdevelopment, 29, 34
postmodernism, 29, 83
postsocialism, 1, 21, 57, 81, 233
poverty, 6, 32, 42, 50, 123, 142–43, 145, 146, 147, 152, 161n7, 185, 211n7; child, 142–

46, 159–60, 161n7; culture of poverty, 82, 159
privatization, 26, 60, 74n4, 86, 115, 124, 170, 230
projects, 2–17, 24–25, 45, 50, 61–73, 83, 89, 103–5, 110n8, 116–20, 124, 128, 132–34, 136, 146–47, 154–59, 161n6, 162n13, 196, 215; anthropological, 4, 14, 190, 192, 203, 213, 215, 227; community-based, 85, 123, 216, 223–24; democracy promotion, 6, 56–59; development, 2, 43, 129, 197; environmental education, 213; evaluation, 38, 74n2; failure, 29, 231; humanitarian, 118, 169, 171; management, 3, 77, 81; moral, 9–11, 113–14; and the NGO Form, 37; political, 10, 16, 57, 59, 96, 184; religious, 117, 119, 138; women's, 42, 46, 100, 106–7; writing, 6, 61, 80. *See also* microprojects; social projects
project beneficiaries, 223
projectization, 24, 80
project regime, 91–92
professionalization, 13, 48, 75, 79, 81, 90–93, 230
progressivism, 29, 34–35, 50, 81–82, 92, 114–15, 117–18, 165, 168–69, 171–72, 176, 214, 232–33
protest, 84, 86–88, 129, 172, 174, 235; movement, 91, 92
Protestant, 126
public-private partnerships, 3, 63–64, 65
public relations, 22, 105, 137, 174

Redfield, Peter, 164, 177, 178–79, 184
reform, 75, 85, 90, 93, 126, 164, 190, 211, 235; democratic 57; experts, 60; free-market, 116; land tenure laws, 53, 54; market, 84, 116; municipal, 68; and NGOs, 21, 30, 88, 92, 118; political, 3, 53, 56–57, 73, 77, 81, 90; religious, 116, 118, 127–28, 131, 132, 135, 137, 140, 141n6; restructuring, 3; school, 164; "self-reform," 88; state, 65, 68, 73, 81. *See also* Islamic reform
representation: anthropological, 189, 203, 210, 235–36; crises of, 15; political, 62, 72; power of, 29; regimes of, 59; reli-

gious, 168, 179; of target groups, 32, 231, 233
revolving door, 22, 45
Riles, Annaliese, 23, 34, 95, 97, 104, 196, 201, 203, 204, 208, 211n8
Roma, 10, 12, 13, 15, 16, 18, 22, 75–93, 235

Sampson, Steven, 1–18, 24, 32, 34, 57, 160, 230
Schuller, Mark, 8, 18, 21–25, 38, 42, 57, 144
Shadow Report on the Equal Treatment and Equal Opportunities for Women and Men, 22, 94–95, 97–104, 108–9, 110n8
Sharma, Aradhana, 23, 38, 114, 183–85, 196–97, 209
social entrepreneurship, 3
social projects, 116, 143, 147, 149–54
social services, 3, 77–78, 85–86, 160n4, 166; provided by NGOs, 6, 12, 13, 27, 81, 87–89, 91, 92, 133, 144–47
social work, 15, 75–84, 93nn5–7; organizations, 75, 88–90, 91
standardization, 59, 60, 71, 76–79, 230
supranational governance, 95–96, 102, 234

tourism, 60, 116, 118–21, 142, 144, 145, 161n8; donors, 13, 152; volunteer, 15, 18, 116, 119–21, 142–49, 150, 151–52, 153–54, 155–60, 161nn6–8, 234

transparency, 49, 55, 72, 76, 102, 146, 191

UNESCO, 46
UNICEF, 49, 142, 146
United Nations, 26, 42, 49, 52, 104, 128, 141n3, 145, 194
United States, 30, 34, 41, 84, 116–17, 119, 127, 163, 165, 167, 169, 191, 217, 219
university, 1, 45, 80, 82, 86, 138, 193; anthropology department, 29; employees, 52, 77, 81. *See also* academic; academics
USAID, 13, 22, 42, 46, 49–52, 56, 58–59, 61–68, 70–71

volunteerism, 116. *See also* tourism: volunteer

welfare, 72, 91, 95, 113–14, 116–17, 119, 121, 128, 130, 159–60, 162n12, 175, 184, 194, 197, 198
welfarism, 149, 154, 158, 162n12
women. *See* activism: feminist; activism: women's; activists: women's rights; conflict: domestic; European Union: and feminism; expertise: and gender; feminism; gender experts; gender mainstreaming; Islam: women; projects: women's
World Bank, 26, 142
World Vision, 185–86